The Great Masters
of Italian Art

The Great Masters of Italian Art

Introduction by *Cristina Acidini Luchinat*
Texts by *Elena Capretti*

BARNES & NOBLE BOOKS

NEW YORK

This edition published by Barnes & Noble, Inc.,
by arrangement with SCALA Group S.p.A.

2005 Barnes & Noble Books

Copyright © 2000 SCALA Group S.p.A., Florence

M 10 9 8 7 6 5 4 3 2 1
ISBN 0-7607-7146-4

Translation: Huw Evans

Photographic acknowledgments: SCALA Picture
Library (Falsini, Sarri, Lampredi) except for p. 70
(Museo di Castelvecchio, Verona); pp. 82 a, 109 a,
189, 198 a (National Gallery, London); pp. 134-7
(Soprintendenza per i Beni A.A.A.S. di Arezzo;
photographs by Alessandro Benci); pp. 192-3, 263,
366-7 (Kunsthistorisches Museum, Vienna); cover,
pp. 232-3, 242-3 (Archivio Fotografico Musei
Vaticani); pp. 386-7 (Museum of Fine Arts, Boston)

The images in the SCALA ARCHIVES that reproduce
cultural assets owned by the Italian State are
published by kind permission of the Ministry for the
Cultural Heritage and Activities

Printed in China

Introduction

This book offers a highly condensed overview, if that is the right choice of words, of the art that flourished in Italy between the end of the thirteenth century and the beginning of the nineteenth: five centuries during which, in the various states into which the peninsula was divided prior to its unification (1861, followed by the taking of Rome in 1870), great master followed after great master, producing masterpiece upon masterpiece.

It is true that it is Italy's privilege and pride to be able to offer an unparalleled "dispersed museum." Archeological sites, churches and monasteries, civic monuments of architecture and statuary, museums, public and private art collections, historic gardens, landscapes shaped by centuries of human labor: all these and more form a network of high-quality art that covers not only the great urban centers but the whole of the territory. A network that, despite the destruction wrought by thousands of agonizing events, from pillage by armies to natural disasters, has held and still holds magnificently, thanks to the strength of its historical structure, made up of institutional and human relationships. Admiring a work of art in an Italian museum or church, where the work itself still holds a dialogue, beyond the walls that enclose it, with the urban or rural environment of which it is an expression and reflection, is always a quite different thing from looking at it in the often impeccable but inevitably aseptic surroundings of a great museum in Europe, America or any other part of the world.

But if, taking up the challenge presented by our peculiar and impatient times, an attempt is made to compress the output of the five centuries in which Italy held undisputed sway in the world of art, then it becomes necessary to abandon contemplation of that artistic and historical tissue in all its variegated and fascinating complexity and to aim our sights high, at the galaxy of great masters, and pick out their finest and most expressive works. It is rather like shifting our gaze from a densely populated and intensively cultivated valley bottom and staring up at the mountain peaks instead. Here the panorama is no longer complex and detailed, but simple and majestic. In making this choice, which has entailed leaving out a great deal, an effort has been made to stick to a number of basic, though flexible and multifaceted guidelines. The focus has been placed on the authors and the works without which the history of art – and to a degree the very history – of Western civilization would have been different; in other words, on artists whose names are widely or universally known and on works of art that have acquired a strong identity over the course of time and whose aesthetic value is generally recognized. Works that we would like to save, if we were ever threatened by planetwide catastrophe, by sending them into space as evidence of human creativity…

The result is a succinct and powerful vision of Italian art, emphasizing certain specific values. Prominent among these is the individual and collective aptitude for innovation and change, while remaining within the bounds of tradition, until well into the nineteenth century. This is something which marks a profound difference with respect to the art forms of various Asian civilizations, exquisitely beautiful but inclined to the repetition of established models. Another aspect that emerges is the fact that many, indeed the vast majority of the most celebrated works are paintings, while statues and reliefs are represented in much smaller numbers. The reason for this may be, as was said and written on the occasion of a famous "debate" over the superiority of the arts that involved the greatest intellectuals and artists of the sixteenth century in Florence, painting with its colors has a greater narrative and evocative capacity and therefore has a firmer grip on the feelings and memories of the observer.

Italian art is held to have begun in Tuscany, and the claim is an entirely justifiable one. The credit for having taken up and reinterpreted the example of ancient Roman sculpture, giving substance to a form of expression that was then to come under the influence of the Gothic style coming from the other side of the Alps, goes to two great sculptors working in various cities under Ghibelline rule, Nicola Pisano and his son Giovanni. In Florence and Rome, Arnolfo di Cambio embodied the transition from the Romanesque tradition (enriched by the legacy of the Cosmati) to that of Gothic architecture and sculpture. With the great Florentine Cimabue, Italian painting, dominated by the Byzantine style of the "Greek masters" up until the 1270s, took a different direction and evolved toward a naturalism that was henceforth to remain a constant feature, notwithstanding the variety and diversity of interpretations. All it takes to be persuaded of this is a glance at the great *Crucifix* in Santa Croce, which is not a symbolic icon, but the image of a body whose stylized form does not conceal its human suffering. Duccio, his Sienese and much younger contemporary, accentuated the elements of preciosity and linearity in his sacred compositions. It was at this point that the gulf in art (and not just in art) opened up between the West and the countries where the Orthodox faith held sway, like Greece and Russia. There Byzantine art became an expressive canon in which for centuries variations and inventions were admitted only on the rarest occasions, until Western art was suddenly and forcibly introduced into Tsarist Russia in the eighteenth century by Peter the Great (with the traumatic effects of which we are well aware). But to go back to medieval Italy, it was in Tuscany again that new impetus was given to the development of Western painting, around the time of the great Jubilee proclaimed by Boniface VIII for the year 1300: an acceleration, it could almost be said, that was to be repeated at the beginning of the next three centuries, for as long as faith served as a stimulus to patrons and artists. The fourteenth century got under way under the sign of Giotto, who legend has it was "discovered," as a talented child, by Cimabue. The succession of one master by the other, symbolizing the emergence of a new and different artistic current out of the previous one, was clearly perceived by their contemporaries. Dante Alighieri put it wonderfully in a celebrated passage from the *Divine Comedy*: "In painting Cimabue thought that he / Should hold the field, now Giotto has the cry, / So that the other's fame is growing dim." In Siena, Simone Martini and the Lorenzetti brothers trained under Duccio before emerging as masters in their own right.

By the fourteenth century it was already clear which cities were going to become the principal hubs of art in Central Italy: Florence, Siena, Orvieto, Rome and Assisi, with its basilica of San Francesco, decorated with frescoes by the greatest artists of the time. But the renewal of Italian art, largely as a consequence of the industry and mobility of the Tuscan workshops, was soon to reach the South and the North, spreading to places like Naples, Rimini and Padua. Nor should it be forgotten that the transfer of the papal curia to Avignon, drawing to it such figures as Simone Martini, made the city the crucible of the refined International Gothic style.

The art of the thirteenth and fourteenth century was predominantly, though not exclusively, dedicated to religious subjects: a strong descriptive and narrative tendency was developed in the great cycles that were covering the walls of churches and chapels, whether ordered by the clergy with the aim of instructing their illiterate congregations (painting as the "Poor Man's Bible"), or commissioned by wealthy patrons to redeem their sins and to acquire merit in this world and the next. Out of this came the perfecting of the magnificent technique of mural painting known as *buon fresco* and its best applications. Yet the life of the inhabitants of the free communes, with its multitude of figurative suggestions, had a powerful impact on the sacred stories – it suffices to think of the many crowded city scenes, of the many images of the brightly colored towers of Jerusalem – and triumphed in civil contexts like the Palazzo Pubblico of Siena, where Simone Martini's *Guidoriccio* was painted not far away from Lorenzetti's extraordinary fresco of *Good and Bad Government*. Moving on to the art of the Italian cities and courts in the fifteenth century, after examining the works of such exquisite exponents of courtly Gothic as Gentile da Fabriano and, in his own way, Pisanello, means – metaphorically – turning the lens on a galaxy of such density and luminosity that we are likely to be dazzled. The splendid trajectory of Renaissance art commenced in Florence, where in 1401 a secular public body, the Arte della Seta or Silk Guild, held a competition that can be taken as its symbolic launch pad: the design of a bronze panel representing the *Sacrifice of Isaac*, the winner to be assigned the execution of the North Door of the baptistery. We know that Jacopo della Quercia, Filippo Brunelleschi and Lorenzo Ghiberti took part in the competition, and that the latter won, going on over the

next half century to create not just that door but also his masterpiece, the East Door, known as the Porta d'Oro or Porta del Paradiso. What is most amazing, however, is that the small city state was already assembling a group of artists, each in his own way an innovator within the tradition, whose names can be linked to form the supporting scaffold of the Renaissance art of Humanism: Masolino and Masaccio (portrayed along with Brunelleschi and the great theoretician of art Leon Battista Alberti in the Brancacci Chapel of the church of Santa Maria del Carmine), Donatello, Luca della Robbia, Paolo Uccello, Fra Giovanni Angelico, Benozzo Gozzoli and Filippo Lippi. The systematization of perspective on the basis of rules of a scientific nature – demonstrated by Brunelleschi, given a theoretical basis by Alberti, applied with enthusiasm by Masaccio and obsessively pursued by Paolo Uccello – was part of the cultural process of affirmation of human and earthly values, which found powerful expression in philosophy and literature as well. The use of a gold ground, widespread in fourteenth-century religious art as an allusion to the undifferentiated luminosity of the kingdom of heaven, gave way to naturalistic representations of the city and the countryside. Art gave visible form to the political and social concept of the "citizen," a person who had a right to self-determination within a system of civil government.

There was no less a concentration of artistic genius in the Florence of the second half of the fifteenth century, dominated by the large and versatile workshops of the Pollaiolo brothers and Verrocchio: the latter was the crucible from which emerged no lesser figures than Sandro Botticelli, creator of magical mythological "fables" (including the venerated *Primavera*) and Leonardo da Vinci, inventor and scientist. The presence of so many artists of the first rank over the course of the century was already viewed with wonder and admiration by their contemporaries and by the generations that followed immediately afterward. Giorgio Vasari, the first great historian of Italian art with his *Lives* of artists published in two editions (1550 and 1568), attempted to come up with more or less convincing explanations, such as the salubrious "fineness" of the city's air or, more credibly, the natural competitiveness of the Florentines. Part of the reason was undoubtedly the political and economic conditions favorable to lively patronage, whether public or private, religious or secular, aristocratic or mercantile, that were created in a system of republican government in which the power of the Medici, from Cosimo *Pater Patriae* to Lorenzo the Magnificent, was being discreetly but firmly established.

Other great figures, scattered over the peninsula's cities and courts, were creating masterpieces that would come to represent some of the highest peaks in the history of Italian art. Piero della Francesca at Urbino and Arezzo, Mantegna at Padua, Giovanni Bellini and Carpaccio in Venice, Antonello da Messina in the South and the North, and Perugino and Pintoricchio, natives of Umbria, in Central Italy.

Different artistic styles came into contact with one another and new ones sprung from the encounter. Italian painting opened up to a variety of influences, from classical antiquity to the rich and diverse range of Flemish art. A number of extremely important technical innovations were introduced, of which the most significant were the use of oil and tempera as mediums. Finally, this period saw the emergence of those local groupings of artists which came to be known as "schools" in eighteenth-century historiography (a term that we have inherited).

But we cannot begin to discuss the sixteenth century without first mentioning three great artistic personalities whose contemporary presence in Florence marked an extraordinary and unique moment not just for the city itself, but for the entire course of Western art. In 1504, in fact, Leonardo and Michelangelo were working opposite one another in Palazzo Vecchio, while Raphael was putting the finishing touches to his artistic apprenticeship. They were soon to head in different directions: Leonardo went to work for the king of France, the other two to Rome. Raphael shone at the court of Leo X before meeting a premature death in 1520, while Michelangelo worked unflaggingly in solitude until extreme old age. The first few decades of the century saw the creation of the *Mona Lisa*, the *David*, the *Medici Tombs*, the ceiling of the Sistine Chapel, the *Stanze* in the Vatican and then the *Last Judgment*, again in the Sistine Chapel: works for which it is not even necessary to name their respective authors, given the worldwide fame they have acquired and the vast numbers of tourists who now flock to see them.

With the change in the political map of Europe, as strong rulers and powerful states established themselves over the course of the century, the balance of power among the small states of the peninsula also shifted and this was to have repercussions on the life and work of artists. The sack of Rome in 1527 scattered Raphael's collaborators, driving some as far as the north of Italy, where the brief career of the sublime Giorgione had already come to an end and Titian was emerging as a force to be reckoned with in Venice, and where the painting of Correggio had bloomed like a solitary and surprising flower in Parma and Mantua. Parmigianino was to imitate the softness of his style and take its elegance to extremes. The eccentric Rosso Fiorentino and Benvenuto Cellini found it worth their while to move to France, where they worked in the refined royal palace of Fontainebleau (which had also attracted, though just for a short time, the "flawless" Florentine painter Andrea del Sarto). In the Florence dominated by Cosimo I de' Medici the cerebral ardor of Pontormo's manner burned itself out, while artistic undertakings on behalf of the ruling family provided work for Agnolo Bronzino, Giorgio Vasari and Francesco Salviati. Sculpture regained its political role with Cellini's *Perseus* and the publicly displayed statues of Ammannati, Danti and Giambologna.

In Venice, a republic relatively immune from the new austerity imposed on the arts by the Church (following the reforms decided on at the Council of Trent), a century dominated by Titian came to an end with the visionary and vibrant painting of Tintoretto and the luminous and striking pictures of Veronese. But it was the Lombard hinterland that was to produce the artist destined to revolutionize easel painting, shaping the future of seventeenth-century art: the unmistakable handling of light in the memorable pictures painted by Michelangelo da Caravaggio in Rome was to give rise to a genuine international movement, Caravaggism.

Throughout the seventeenth century Rome was the peninsula's main center of art, attracting not only the great Bolognese artists, Guercino, Domenichino and the Carracci, but also great foreign painters like Poussin. As a consequence diverse artistic currents flourished, making the city a melting pot of "genres." From 1630 onward it is possible to speak of the baroque, the last Italian artistic current of high originality and international significance. Its chief exponents were the painter Pietro da Cortona and above all the sculptor and architect Gian Lorenzo Bernini, the main interpreter of the artistic intentions of the Church, which now saw itself as triumphant and was filled with missionary zeal, and of the magnificence of Louis XIV's absolute monarchy. In Bernini's statues – *Apollo and Daphne*, *Costanza Bonarelli*, *The Ecstasy of Saint Teresa* and a hundred others – the marble conveys a sense of movement and instability, of natural beauty and supernatural splendor, of the softness of flesh and the roughness of rock or bark, in an endless series of stunning inventions.

During the long period over which the baroque held sway, spanning the seventeenth and eighteenth centuries, only a few other strong personalities emerged, such as Andrea Pozzo and Luca Giordano, before the appearance of the exquisite painting of Tiepolo, the last star in the glittering galaxy of great Venetian artists, and the masterly *vedutismo* of Canaletto and Guardi, charged with exporting the image of Venice through the channels of international collecting that were nurtured by the Grand Tour.

Italy's contribution to neoclassicism, an artistic and stylistic current that spread throughout Europe from France, was made by Antonio Canova. It seems fitting to conclude by considering his marble sculpture of *Cupid and Psyche* as the figurative emblem of a harmonious embrace between art and Humanistic learning. An embrace which has made and still makes a visit to Italy, or at least to the Italian sections of the world's great museums, such a desirable and unique experience.

Cristina Acidini Luchinat

Contents

14TH CENTURY

Nicola and Giovanni Pisano

Nicola (1215/20?-1278/1284?) was probably born in the region now known as Puglia, as can be deduced from documents in which he is referred to as "Nicolas de Apulia." The artist may have received his training in Southern Italy, among the cultural circles of Frederick II of Hohenstaufen, who had promoted the rediscovery of classical art. After this, Nicola must have moved to Tuscany, going to cities that were affiliated with Hohenstaufen and therefore Ghibelline policy, such as Pisa and Siena. An architect and sculptor, he carved the pulpit of Pisa Baptistery in 1260 and that of Siena Cathedral between 1266 and 1268: on the latter he was assisted by – among others – his son Giovanni and his pupil, the Florentine Arnolfo di Cambio. In 1273 Nicola was active in Pistoia, at the same time as he was working on Pisa Baptistery. In 1277-78, Nicola and his collaborators built the Fontana Maggiore in Perugia. Nicola Pisano's son Giovanni (Pisa *c.* 1248-Siena after 1314) was to become, along with Arnolfo di Cambio (Colle Val d'Elsa *c.* 1245-Florence 1302), one of the leading sculptors of the period between the end of the thirteenth century and the beginning of the fourteenth. After his father's death, Giovanni went to live in Siena, where he was master builder of the cathedral from 1284 to 1296, carving a number of figures of *Prophets* and *Sibyls* for the façade. The psychological insight, dramatic poses and great expressiveness of these statues make them some of the most significant Gothic works of sculpture in Europe. Moving to Pisa, he served as master builder of the cathedral from 1297 onward. He carved two important pulpits, that of Sant'Andrea at Pistoia in 1301 and the one in Pisa Cathedral from 1302 to 1310, depicting scenes from the Gospels with great emotional force. A series of sculptures representing the *Madonna and Child* testify to Giovanni's interest in the direct and affectionate exchange between Mother and Son, offering a new key to interpretation of the sacred group. The artist executed these sculptural groups for Pisa Cathedral and Baptistery (*c.* 1284 and *c.* 1304; now in

the museum), the Scrovegni Chapel in Padua (1305-06), Prato Cathedral (*c.* 1312). Sometime after 1311, Giovanni made the tomb of Margaret of Brabant, wife of Henry VII of Luxembourg (fragments of which are now in the Palazzo Bianco in Genoa): the scheme of the monument is a highly original one, with the deceased raised up by two angels toward the light shining on her beautiful face.

Nicola Pisano
Pulpit
marble, ht. 465 cm
Baptistery, Pisa

In the pulpit of Pisa Baptistery, carved between 1255 and 1260, Nicola produced a work that was innovative in its structure,

conception and style. It showed the decisive influence of classical models and marked the beginning of the Italian Gothic. Instead of the quadrangular form typical of Romanesque pulpits, Nicola adopted a hexagonal layout supported by six columns, the outer ones standing on

lions and the central one decorated with representations of human beings and animals on the base. Along the parapet are set five panels with scenes depicting the *Nativity*, *Adoration of the Magi*, *Presentation in the Temple*, *Crucifixion* and *Last Judgment*.

The *Nativity* is a fine example of Nicola's stately and courtly style. Its main source of inspiration lies in the reliefs on Roman sarcophagi, whose motifs are reinterpreted in Christian terms. The scene is carved in full relief and given a solemn tone. The Madonna, immobile and on a larger scale than the rest of the composition, is reclining in the manner of a Roman matron. The idealized faces with their broad and regular profiles, curly hair and well-trimmed beards are also a reference to Roman art, as are the veils covering the women's heads.

Giovanni Pisano
Pulpit
marble, ht. 460 cm
Sant'Andrea, Pistoia

According to the Latin inscription carved on the band underneath the parapet, the pulpit was completed by Giovanni Pisano in 1301 to a commission from the parish priest Arnoldo degli Arnoldi. It is one of the most important sculptural complexes of the Middle Ages.

The pulpit in Pistoia echoes the hexagonal scheme used by Nicola for the baptistery in Pisa, but displays a greater tension and dynamism. The columns are more slender and graceful, as are the arches, which are pointed this time. The narrative scenes on the parapet are separated by statues instead of columns, creating an impression of greater continuity. While Nicola had given the pulpit in Pisa a powerful and solid architectural structure, his son Giovanni made the architecture subordinate to the sculpture and the representation of the scenes. The *Crucifixion* includes the two thieves executed alongside Christ, left out of the corresponding relief on Nicola's pulpit. In the middle, Christ's suffering is conveyed through the painful tension in his body, with the arms spread upward and outward so that the bones of his chest are clearly outlined against the skin. The upward tension of the arms is in line with the centrifugal movement of the composition, dividing the two groups of figures symmetrically: on one side the followers of Christ and the Madonna and on the other his persecutors, who are thrusting in the opposite direction toward the edge of the panel, displaying powerful emotions. Allegorical figures are set on each side of the cross: on the left a woman supported by an angel symbolizes the Church, while the old woman driven away by another angel on the right represents the Synagogue.

Cimabue

The earliest reference to Cenni di Pepo, called Cimabue (recorded from 1272-1302), dates from June 18, 1272, when the artist's presence in Rome was recorded in a deed under the seal of a notary. We know very little about Cimabue's life, owing on the one hand to the absence of any documentary records and on the other to the contradictory information to be found in the literary sources of the fourteenth and fifteenth centuries. Yet he was an artist of great standing among his contemporaries, to the point where he was even mentioned by Dante in the *Divine Comedy* (*Purgatorio* XI, 94-96), who speaks of the painter's great fame and how he was eventually overshadowed by Giotto.

It is possible to trace the painter's development through two themes that he tackled on many occasions: *Christ Crucified* and the *Maestà*. From the *Crucifix* in San Domenico at Arezzo (*c.* 1265) to that of Santa Croce in Florence (*c.* 1272) and the *Crucifixion* frescoes in the upper basilica of San Francesco at Assisi (*c.* 1290), we can see how the painter's style gradually freed itself from Byzantine schematism, taking on a new intensity of expression and sense of volume. The same thing is apparent from a comparison of his three *Maestà*, in the Louvre (originally in San Francesco at Pisa), Santa Maria dei Servi in Bologna and the Uffizi (formerly in Santa Trinita in Florence), works that cover the period from around 1280-85 to 1300.

Over the course of the century's ninth decade, Cimabue set about frescoing the apse and transept of the upper basilica of San Francesco in Assisi with a large cycle of scenes from the Gospels and Revelation. It has also been suggested that Cimabue's collaborators here included Duccio da Buoninsegna and the young Giotto. Another important joint enterprise in which Cimabue took part was that of the mosaics in Florence Baptistery: the artist provided the designs for several of the *Scenes from the Life of Joseph the Patriarch* and the *Scenes from the Life of Saint John the Baptist*.

The date of Cimabue's death is not known, but it must have been after 1302, the year when the artist received the last payment for the mosaic in the apse of Pisa Cathedral.

Maestà
panel, 425x243 cm
Galleria degli Uffizi, Florence

Cimabue painted the solemn *Maestà* now in the Uffizi for the Florentine church of Santa Trinita, which belonged to the Vallombrosian Order. The date of the work is uncertain but it must have been executed sometime in the last two decades of the thirteenth century. The Madonna, represented as the *Regina Coeli* in the act of showing her son the Redeemer to the faithful, is seated on a monumental throne of inlaid wood. It has a solid architectural structure that opens up like a fan before the observer. The angels that frame the sacred group are arranged symmetrically at the sides, while at the bottom, between the columns at the base of the throne, we find Abraham and David in the middle and the prophets Jeremiah and Isaiah at the sides: the latter are turned to face the Mother of God. In addition to the subject of the work, the gold ground, the gold highlights of the folds in the clothing, the marked profiles of the faces and the bright colors, especially in the drapery and the wings of the angels, all derive from the Byzantine tradition. The size of the figures is governed by a proportion of the "hierarchical" type, so that Mary and the Child are much bigger than the other figures.

The Four Evangelists
fresco
Upper Basilica, Assisi

The pictorial decoration of the basilica of
San Francesco in Assisi was carried out at
the behest of the Franciscan popes
Nicholas III Orsini (1277-80) and
Nicholas IV Masci (1288-90), who
brought in the best artists in Florence and
Rome to do the job. Cimabue frescoed the
transept and presbytery of the upper
church with a cycle of scenes from the
lives of Mary and the evangelists and from
Revelation. Unfortunately, however, these
deteriorated rapidly and are now beyond
repair.
On the cross vault where the transept
intersects the nave, Cimabue painted the
Four Evangelists (badly damaged in the
recent earthquake). Each figure is

accompanied by his symbol and seated on a wooden chair while an angel reaches down to inspire him from on high. Each evangelist is represented in front of the city where he wrote his Gospel: thus Matthew is seated before Jerusalem in Judea, Mark before Rome in Italy, Luke in front of Corinth in Greece (*Ypnacchaia*, in the inscription) and John before Ephesus in Asia Minor.

The image of Rome (see page on the left) is particularly interesting, consisting of a few representative buildings hemmed in by the city walls, most of them easily recognizable: from the right, we see Castel Sant'Angelo, the pyramid of Gaius Cestius and the ancient Vatican basilica with the mosaic on its façade; on the left stand the Pantheon with the Torre delle Milizie alongside and the Palazzo Senatorio above, decorated with the Orsini coats of arms.

Crucifix
panel, 448x390 cm
Museo di Santa Croce, Florence

The *Crucifix*, painted by Cimabue for the Franciscan church of Santa Croce perhaps around 1285, was irretrievably damaged by the flood in 1966 (reproduced on left; the work prior to the flood can be seen on facing page). Following this tragic event the painting was subjected to a complex restoration, designed to make the work legible again and providing an opportunity to perfect modern methods of intervention. The large areas where the paint is missing have been filled in a manner that is distinguishable from the original, using materials that can be removed.

In comparison with earlier crosses, here Cimabue has softened the forms, showing a preference for pale shades of color and ennobling Christ's features. Instead of the incisive and schematic lines of the Byzantine tradition, the body has rounded shapes and mellow tones. Between the outstretched arms, the abandoned torso is twisted to the side, producing a gentle and sinuous curve. Any hint of opulence has been dropped in favor of a more human interpretation that is conveyed even through such external details as the transparent loincloth, with its soft folds. The same is true for Mary and John, represented at half length and weeping at the end of the cross's arms: their drapery is soft and shaded, without the lines of gilt that ran along folds and edges in the late Byzantine tradition.

Duccio
di Buoninsegna

Recorded for the first time in 1278, Duccio di Buoninsegna (Siena *c.* 1260-1318) was probably born on Sienese territory sometime between 1255 and 1260. Little is known about the artist's training, although it is supposed that between the end of the seventies and the beginning of the following decade he was one of Cimabue's collaborators in Assisi.

Shortly afterward, in 1285, Duccio received his first major commission: the *Maestà* for the Laudesi Chapel in the Florentine church of Santa Maria Novella (now in the Uffizi). His versatile talents and the constantly high quality of his work allowed him to try his hand at commissions of various kinds and attain results that met with general approval. As well as painting panel pictures, in fact, he was an illuminator, illustrated the covers of books produced by the municipal administration (*Biccherne*) and made designs for stained-glass windows. One of these was the circular window of Siena Cathedral with the *Coronation of the Virgin* (1288), the oldest example of a work of Italian stained glass that can be attributed to a great artist. In the meantime Siena was growing increasingly receptive to cultural influences of various sources, from the refined Gothic of Northern Europe to the rediscovery of classical art promoted by Frederick II's court in Palermo. In a period so fervid with experimentation and innovation, Duccio became an artistic personality of great prestige, so that in 1295 he was the only painter to be called on to serve on the commission set up to decide the location of the new city gate, the Porta d'Ovile. The sculptor Giovanni Pisano was also a member of the commission.

The peak of Duccio's artistic career was marked by the commission for the *Maestà* to be placed on the high altar of the cathedral (1308-11), a monumental work whose conception and significance represents a fundamental stage in the development of the altarpiece in Western art.

Before his death in 1318, Duccio exercised a decisive influence on the training and early activity of the Sienese artists who frequented his workshop, including Simone Martini and Pietro Lorenzetti.

Maestà
panel, 450x290 cm
Galleria degli Uffizi, Florence

In 1285 Duccio was commissioned to paint a *Maestà* for the confraternity of the Laudesi, which had its seat at Santa Maria Novella in Florence. Set up around 1244 under the auspices of the Dominican Order, the sodality was devoted in particular to worship of the Virgin, in whose honor the brothers sang lauds. The *Maestà* for the Laudesi was the first work on a monumental scale by the founder of the Sienese School. While influenced by Cimabue, the work also displays unprecedented Gothic accents in the elegant and light forms of the flattened bodies, in the precious decorative details of the throne and fabrics, traced with the precision of an illuminator, in the intense and refined colors and in the sinuous and undulating line of the golden border of the Virgin's mantle. The carved wooden throne on which the Madonna is seated is also inspired by Gothic architectural motifs from beyond the Alps: the sides have openings that resemble windows with three and two lights; the elegant seat rests on slender legs linked by arches; the back terminates in arches and pinnacles, from which hangs a precious woven cloth. The ornate frame has oculi with sacred figures: Christ in the medallion at the top of the altarpiece, followed by prophets, patriarchs and saints.

The work was probably originally located in what is now the Bardi Chapel in the right-hand transept of Santa Maria Novella, where the confraternity used to hold its services. The painting is also known as the *Rucellai Madonna* because it was moved to the Rucellai Chapel of the same church between the end of the seventeenth century and the beginning of the eighteenth.

DUCCIO DI BUONINSEGNA

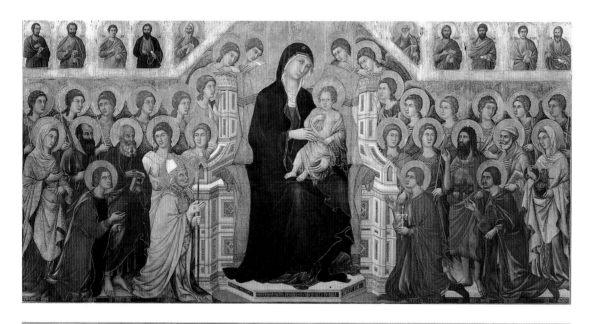

Maestà
panel, 211x426 cm
Museo dell'Opera del Duomo, Siena

On October 4, 1308 the Board of Trustees of Siena Cathedral commissioned Duccio to paint a monumental *Madonna Enthroned with Saints* to be placed on the high altar. They agreed to pay the artist sixteen florins a day, over and above expenses, and in the end the work cost the Board of Trustees a total of three thousand gold florins. The panel was finished on June 9, 1311, and a holiday was declared in the city so that the painting could be carried in triumph through the streets from the artist's workshop to the cathedral, in a solemn public procession in which the notables of the communal government took part. The Virgin represented by Duccio is the Mother of God, the city's protector and intermediary with God for the prayers of the faithful. And the citizens' mouthpieces are the four patron saints of Siena kneeling at the Virgin's feet in the foreground: from the left, Ansanus, Sabinian, Crescentius and Victor, easily identifiable by the inscriptions beneath. The monumental altarpiece, which was dismembered in the eighteenth century, originally represented the *Madonna and Child Enthroned between Saints, Angels and Ten Apostles* on the front, with each of the apostles set under an arch, along with *Scenes from the Life of the Virgin* in the crowning section and *Scenes from the Childhood of Christ* in the predella. On the back, the painting depicted *Scenes from the Public Life of Christ* in the lower part, *Scenes from the Passion* in the twenty six panels in the middle (still intact) and *Scenes of Christ after the Resurrection* at the top. The whole altarpiece was surmounted by cusps with angels.

Scenes from the Passion:
Last Supper, detail
panel, 46x53 cm
Museo dell'Opera del Duomo, Siena

Scenes from the Passion:
Entry of Jesus into Jerusalem, detail
panel, 100x57 cm
Museo dell'Opera del Duomo, Siena

In this panel the painter has set out to
present a detailed description of the
urban landscape and the figures that
animate the scene. Jerusalem is a city of
medieval appearance, ringed with
crenelated walls and studded with towers
and campaniles, as well as the lantern
and vaulted dome of a marble church.
Youths are climbing trees to break off
branches with which to greet the
procession, while other people line the
walls and a woman peers out from a
balcony (in fact there are no women at all
on the road).

Scenes from the Life of the Virgin:
Annunciation of Her Death
panel, 41·5x54 cm
Museo dell'Opera del Duomo, Siena

The *Annunciation of the Virgin's Death*
introduces the *Scenes from the Life of
the Virgin* that used to be located at the
top of the front part of the *Maestà*. It is
followed by the *Leave-Taking from John*,
Leave-Taking from the Apostles, *Death*,
Funeral and *Burial*. The panel
representing the *Annunciation of the
Virgin* has probably been lost. It must
originally have been placed at the center
and surmounted by the *Coronation* now
in the National Museum of Budapest.
The *Annunciation of the Virgin's Death*
is set in a bare interior, a sort of
architectural box. Seated in a simple room
with a raftered ceiling, Mary is distracted
from the book she is reading by the arrival
of the angel. Entering through the wide-
open door, the latter presents her with a
palm, symbol of death and of the paradise
that awaits the Mother of God. The gestures
are as simple and solemn as in a ceremony.

Giotto

Through his work, Giotto (Colle di Vespignano, near Vicchio di Mugello *c.* 1267-Florence 1337) brought about a radical renewal of Western figurative culture that had no precedent in the Christian era. Even the artist's contemporaries – including Dante Alighieri and Boccaccio – were conscious of his importance, seeing him as having resurrected an art that had been buried since the days of classical antiquity. With the passing of time, Giotto's significance has never faded and his biography has assumed the tones of a legend.

According to an ancient literary tradition dating back to the fourteenth century, Giotto son of Bondone had been a pupil of Cimabue, although there are no documents to support this claim. Although the question is still much debated, it seems very likely that Giotto was in Assisi at the end of the thirteenth century to fresco the *Scenes from the Story of Isaac* and then the *Scenes from the Life of Saint Francis* in the upper basilica of San Francesco. After this undertaking, Giotto maintained close relations with the Franciscans, going on to paint in other churches belonging to the order, at Rimini (San Francesco), Padua (Il Santo) and Florence (Santa Croce), leaving works that have been partly lost.

The innovative features of Giotto's art, where the scenes were set in a human and earthly dimension, were an expression of the spirit of rationality and self-determination displayed by the upper middle classes of the early fourteenth century. In fact Giotto carried out some of his fresco decorations for important bankers and merchants: in Padua, for instance, he painted the *Scenes from the Lives of Christ and the Virgin* in the chapel of Enrico Scrovegni (1303-05), and in Florence he decorated the chapels in Santa Croce belonging to the Bardi and Peruzzi families respectively (after 1320). In addition, Giotto was in demand at the principal Italian courts: those of the pontiff in Rome (Boniface VIII and then Clement V), Robert of Anjou in Naples and Azzone Visconti in Milan.

As his fame grew, Giotto also saw an improvement in his own social standing, assuming a distinguished role in civic life. In 1334 he was placed in charge of architectural undertakings in the city of Florence, overseeing the construction of civil, military and religious buildings. Appointed master builder of Florence Cathedral (1334), at the time dedicated to Saint Reparata, Giotto designed the bell tower that still bears his name.

The artist, now sought after by the most important patrons in Florence and elsewhere, set up a flourishing workshop that was to produce some of the greatest artists of the following generation. He died on May 8, 1337, and was buried in the cathedral.

General view of the nave looking toward the altar
Upper Basilica, Assisi

The ancient and still living tradition that assigns the *Scenes from the Life of Saint Francis* in the upper basilica to Giotto and his collaborators has been challenged by many art historians, who see them instead as the work of other artists (including the Roman painter Pietro Cavallini). What is certain is that no evidence clear enough to confute the traditional attribution has been presented and throughout the world the author of the scenes from the life of the Poor Man of Assisi is still identified with Giotto, the artist who introduced a new figurative language whose simplicity and communicative power were very different from the fixed iconography of Byzantine art.

The *Scenes from the Life of Saint Francis* run along the walls of the nave under the windows, while the spaces between the windows are filled with *Scenes from the Old and New Testament*: thus, in an organic and unified design, the life of St. Francis is presented in parallel to that of Christ and other figures from the Bible, such as Isaac. The scenes representing the life of the Poor Man of Assisi and the *tituli*, i.e. the inscriptions, that accompany and explain them (not very legible today), are drawn from St. Bonaventure's *Legenda major*, written between 1260 and 1263. If, as the biographer Giorgio Vasari claims (1568), it was Fra Giovanni di Muro who commissioned the cycle, then work on it could not have started before 1296, when the friar was elected general of the order. Giotto must have left the work in the hands of his assistants around 1300, when he was summoned to Rome by the pope.

Scenes from the Life of Saint Francis: The Dream of Innocent III, detail
fresco, 270x230 cm
Upper Basilica, Assisi

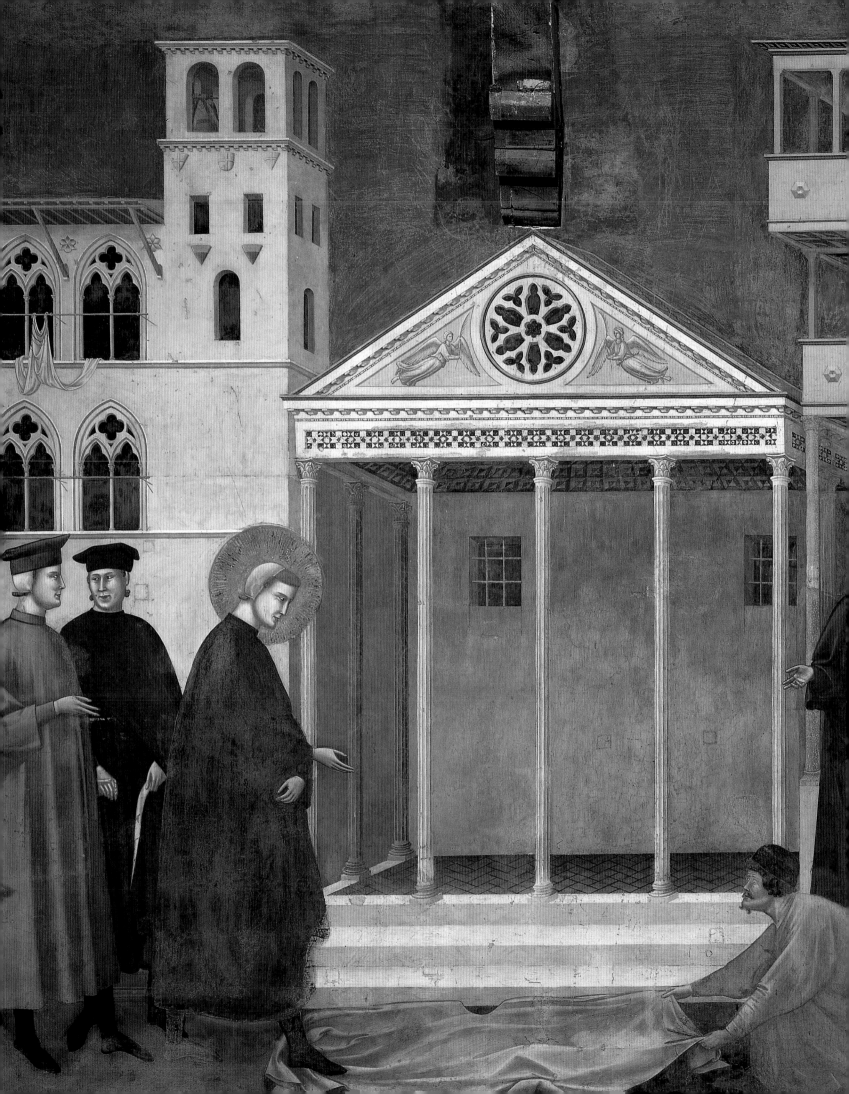

Scenes from the Life of Saint Francis: Francis Honored by a Simple Man
fresco, 270x230 cm
Upper Basilica, Assisi

The scene depicts an episode from the early part of Francis's life, but was one of the last – and therefore the most mature in its style – to have been painted by Giotto. It is set in a city street of the period, in front of an elegant portico. On the left stands the Torre del Popolo in Assisi, still incomplete (it would not be finished until 1305). The buildings in the background are set parallel to the figures in the foreground: the "simple man" kneeling on the ground, has a well-characterized face, with a thick head of hair, moustache and beard with two points. He is laying out his cloak for Francis, who is still dressed in "civil" clothes but already has a halo round his head.

Scenes from the Life of Saint Francis: The Expulsion of the Devils from Arezzo
fresco, 270x230 cm
Upper Basilica, Assisi

The scene represents St. Francis, kneeling on the left, as he exhorts his companion to drive out the devils cavorting in the sky above the city of Arezzo. On the right of the composition, which looks like the illustrated page of a fable, we see the citadel, ringed by walls, from which sprout multicolored towers, roofs, terraces and campaniles. Behind St. Francis and his companion stands the white apse of a church whose style is reminiscent of that of the parish church of Santa Maria in Arezzo.

Scenes from the Life of Saint Francis: The Preaching to the Birds
fresco, 270x200 cm
Upper Basilica, Assisi

This is one of the most celebrated episodes in the entire cycle. The intensity and poetry of the dialogue between Francis and the birds is underlined by the essentiality of the description: the saint and the birds are the absolute protagonists in a flat and bare landscape. The artist has included in the scene only those elements that are necessary to the story: St. Francis is accompanied by his ever-present traveling companion and the birds are given two trees to perch on. The birds – along with the sky – are the most heavily deteriorated parts of the picture, as the paint, for the most part applied to dry plaster, has come away.

General view
Scrovegni Chapel, Padua

In 1300, Enrico Scrovegni – a wealthy and influential citizen of Padua – bought a plot of land at the Arena, near the Roman amphitheater, to build himself a townhouse (now destroyed) with an adjoining chapel. This was founded in 1303 and consecrated two years later. It must have been within this period that Giotto – perhaps already in Padua, where he was summoned by the Eremitical Franciscans of the basilica of Il Santo – frescoed the chapel.

The main part of the cycle is made up of *Scenes from the Lives of Joachim and Anne, Mary and Christ*, arranged in three rows along the walls, from top to bottom. The socle at the bottom, painted to simulate marble panels, is decorated with monochrome allegorical figures representing the *Seven Virtues*, on the right, and the *Seven Vices*, on the left. The *Last Judgment* occupies the whole of the entrance wall, opposite the presbytery. On the ceiling, painted lapis-lazuli blue and dotted with gold like a starry sky, there are medallions depicting *Christ*, the *Virgin* and the *Prophets*, while the transverse decorative brands contain images of *Saints* and *Angels*.

In the presbytery, the altar is adorned with sculptures by Giovanni Pisano (p. 12): the *Madonna and Child* and two *Angels*. At the rear is set the tomb of the client, who died in 1336.

Scenes from the Lives of Joachim and Anne: Annunciation to Saint Anne
fresco, 200x185 cm
Scrovegni Chapel, Padua

Anne receives the news of her imminent conception from the angel in her own room, while a maidservant eavesdrops in the next room. The bedchamber is carefully described in all the details of its furnishings: the raftered ceiling, canopy around the bed, striped blanket, bench, chest and bellows.

The interior of the house is suggested by a sort of cube painted in perspective and open on one side to allow the observer to see what is going on inside: this is what is known as a "spatial box," in other words a three-dimensional container into which the figures are inserted, though with no respect for proportions.

Scenes from the Lives of Joachim and Anne: The Meeting at the Golden Gate
fresco, 200x185 cm
Scrovegni Chapel, Padua

After receiving the news from the angel, Joachim and Anne meet at Jerusalem's Golden Gate and kiss each other: with this act, Mary is miraculously conceived in Anne's womb. The sculptural figures of the elderly couple, embracing tenderly, form a "plastic pyramid" (Gnudi 1959) that is also the psychological fulcrum of the composition. A reference to the ancient Roman monuments of Rimini has been noted in the architecture of the Golden Gate.

Scenes from the Life of Christ:
Nativity
fresco, 200x185 cm
Scrovegni Chapel, Padua

The reclining Virgin is laying the Child wrapped in swaddling clothes in the manger with the help of a girl. The solemn gesture has the flavor of a ceremonial act. The light entering from the right lends volume to the figures, which are depicted in a summary fashion, most evident in the shepherd with his back turned and dressed in pink and Joseph wrapped in his yellow cloak. The elements of the composition are arranged in such a way as to create the optical illusion of a three-dimensional space: the architecture of the stable, the donkey with its head turned toward the manger, the way that the figure of Mary turns on itself and the angel bending forward to pay homage to the Redeemer all combine to create this effect.

Scenes from the Life of Christ:
Flight into Egypt
fresco, 200x185 cm
Scrovegni Chapel, Padua

This is one of the most intense frescoes in the Scrovegni Chapel. The barren and rocky landscape provides a dramatic setting for the scene and lends emphasis to the emotions of the characters and their role in the story. The noble and sculptural group of the Virgin sitting astride the donkey with the Child in her arms is set in isolation at the center, almost framed by the rocky spire in the background. Her gaze fixed on the distance hints at the dramatic destiny awaiting her son. At the sides, the ridges of the rock slope gently downward and seem to accompany the rest of the fleeing company, headed by St. Joseph and the angel above him.

GIOTTO

The two tribunes of the Scrovegni Chapel constitute an important precedent for the geometric perspective of the fifteenth century and testify to Giotto's interest in the representation of volumes in space.

Seven Virtues and *Seven Vices*: *Injustice* and *Despair*
fresco, 200x40; 200x60 cm
Scrovegni Chapel, Padua

The allegory of *Injustice* takes the form of a tyrant sitting on a structure that resembles an abandoned and dilapidated fortress. His feet rest on a piece of waste ground, dotted with saplings and bushes. Scenes of brutal aggression, the fruit of bad government, are represented on a small scale along the edge of the step that borders the ground.
Despair is contrasted with *Hope*. It is symbolized by a woman who has committed suicide, hanging herself from a wooden pole that is bowed down by the weight of her body. The woman has been instigated to commit this act of desperation by a demon.

Scenes from the Life of Christ: *Raising of Lazarus*
fresco, 200x185 cm
Scrovegni Chapel, Padua

The painting represents Jesus bringing back to life Lazarus of Bethany, the brother of Mary and Martha, four days after he had died and been laid in the tomb (John 11, 1-44): Christ, after ordering the removal of the stone that covered the tomb, cries to Lazarus to come out, which he does, still wrapped in his shroud. The scene is lent a more dramatic tone by the two bystanders in the middle: one with his arms raised in astonishment and the other reaching out doubtfully to ascertain the veracity of the miraculous event.
As in the other scenes in the cycle, the figures have solid and sculptural forms, with not very marked outlines and vivid but shaded colors.

Tribune
fresco, 150x140 cm
Scrovegni Chapel, Padua

At the sides of the presbytery, symmetrical to one another, are set two *trompe-l'œil* paintings of tribunes or small sacristies. The illusion of the openings in the wall is created by the use of a consistent perspective that assumes the observer to be standing at the entrance of the chapel.

Each tribune appears to be set under a pointed arch and to have a cross vault with a chandelier hanging from the center, with a rope and attached bell for raising and lowering it. Set in the rear wall is a window, through which an atmospheric sky of a pale and limpid color is visible: very different from the deep blue that serves as a backdrop to the scenes, this creates the illusion of a real window in the wall of the chapel.

GIOTTO

Madonna and Child Enthroned
(*Ognissanti Maestà*)
panel, 325x204 cm
Galleria degli Uffizi, Florence

The painting was commissioned from Giotto by the Humiliati for the church of Ognissanti in Florence. There is no record of the date, though it is generally thought to have been executed in the first decade of the fourteenth century. The work is believed to have been painted for the church's high altar, but it has recently been suggested that it was originally located on an altar situated to the right of the rood screen that used to split the nave into two parts, separating the "church of the congregation" from the chancel reserved for clergymen.

The Madonna is seated, with the Child on her lap, on a marble throne in the Gothic style, whose sides are represented in perspective, as are the seat and steps. Mary has a noble and majestic appearance and yet the figure is also solid and earthly: the body has volume and its curves (the breasts and knees) can easily be discerned through the clothing, thanks to the use of chiaroscuro. The plastic force of the figures and the structural solidity of the throne help to create an impression of planes receding into the distance.

Angels, patriarchs, apostles and saints are arranged one in front of the other, partly overlapping: they occupy a real and tangible space, an orderly and silent crowd of praying figures. The angels standing at the sides of the throne hold the crown, Mary's attribute as Queen of Heaven, and the pyx with the Host, an allusion to Christ's Passion. Each of the angels kneeling in the foreground holds a vase with a lily and red and white roses, symbols of purity, chastity and charity respectively.

Scenes from the Life of Saint Francis: The Verification of the Stigmata, detail
fresco, 280x450 cm
Bardi Chapel, Santa Croce, Florence,

Giotto worked in the basilica of Santa Croce for the Peruzzi as well as for another powerful family of bankers, the Bardi, for whom he frescoed the adjacent chapel with *Scenes from the Life of Saint Francis*, probably prior to his departure for Naples in 1328. In comparison with the scenes in Assisi, the style of this late work by the artist has more markedly Gothic connotations. The figures are less powerfully built than in the earlier cycles and the colors are softer and paler, as in this scene depicting the *Verification of the Stigmata*. Their expressions are more explicit and even pathetic, as can be seen in the face of the friar with joined hands, convulsed with grief, the affectionate gesture of the friar kissing the saint's hand and the curious and anxious examination of the saint's stigmata by the learned Messer Geronimo.

Simone Martini

We have only scanty information about the early activity of Simone Martini (Siena *c.* 1284-Avignon 1344), who was a pupil of Duccio di Buoninsegna. In fact Simone's first documented work is the *Maestà* in the Sala del Mappa-mondo of the Palazzo Pubblico in Siena, frescoed in 1315 and restored in 1321: the importance of the work suggests that the artist had already established a certain reputation.

In the second decade of the century, Simone moved between Siena and Assisi, where he frescoed the *Scenes from the Life of Saint Martin* in the lower basilica, which were complete by 1317. The same year, following the canonization of the king of Naples's brother, Louis of Toulouse, Simone was commissioned to paint the altarpiece with *Saint Louis of Toulouse Crowning Robert of Anjou* (now in the Gallerie Nazionali di Capodimonte, Naples). It is likely that for the occasion the artist went to the Angevin court in Naples, where he was invested with the honorific title of *miles* (knight).

While stepping up his activity in Siena, Simone also took on commissions for other Tuscan centers, painting polyptychs for Pisa (1319; in Santa Caterina) and for Orvieto (1320; now in that city's museum). In 1324 Simone – now forty years old – married Giovanna, daughter of the painter Memmo di Filippuccio. This also marked the beginning of a profitable collaboration between Simone and his brother-in-law Lippo Memmi.

In Siena Simone Martini was given the most important of public commissions, such as the fresco with *Guidoriccio da Fogliano* in the Palazzo Pubblico in 1330 (though the attribution of this work is still highly controversial) and the altarpiece with the *Annunciation* for Siena Cathedral in 1333. The painter showed an increasingly distinct preference for sinuous and rhythmic lines, luminous colors and refined details, in general revealing a propensity for a Gothic style of rare sophistication and extreme elegance.

Around 1336, Simone left Siena along with his family and assistants for Avignon, where he was made official painter to the papal court that had been transferred to the French city. Avignon, which had become an artistic and cultural center of international renown, had also attracted the poet Petrarch and his writings attest to the friendship he formed with the Sienese artist. In fact two of his sonnets celebrate the painting (now lost) in which Simone portrayed Laura, the woman whom the poet praised in his verses.

Maestà

fresco, 763x970 cm
Palazzo Pubblico, Siena

In 1315 Simone Martini carried out his most prestigious public assignment: the fresco of the *Maestà* that takes up the entire rear wall of the Sala del Mappamondo in the Palazzo Pubblico, a work commissioned by the government of the Nove. In 1321 the same artist restored (or "repaired" as they used to say at the time) the faces of several figures in the fresco, including the Virgin, the Child, the angels and two saints kneeling in the foreground, repainting them in a more linear style and paler colors.

The Virgin is seated on a gilded throne, whose light, graceful and refined structure is reminiscent of contemporary gold work, in which precious materials were worked in repoussé and engraved and then combined with translucent enamels. The sacred group is ringed by angels, archangels, apostles and saints, including the four patrons of the city of Siena, kneeling in the foreground. The scheme recalls that of Duccio's *Maestà*, which had been placed on the high altar of the cathedral in 1311. The sacred group, set against a backdrop of lapis-lazuli blue, is surmounted by a canopy of red cloth, with the black-and-white coat of arms of Siena alternating with the rampant lion emblem of the people along the border. The composition is surrounded by a frame with medallions depicting Christ giving his blessing, prophets, evangelists and saints.

The image has a profane and aristocratic tone that places an emphasis on preciosity, in the decorative details of the throne, the lavish clothing, the punched halos, the attributes that identify the figures and the pale and attractive faces. Demonstrating great familiarity with precious techniques and refined materials, the artist has used colored glass, raised and gilded surfaces, sophisticated punching and plaques of tin to bring out certain details, accentuating the effect of exquisite preciosity, as well as the luminosity of the composition. In this connection it is fascinating to note that the scrolls of the Child and of St. Jerome, represented in one of the medallions of the frame, are made of paper and inscribed in ink.

The large fresco dominates the hall in which the city government used to meet and it is explicitly exhorted to administer the state in accordance with principles of concord and justice in the inscription set on the step of the Virgin's throne.

Scenes from the Life of Saint Martin: His Renunciation of Arms; His Funeral; He Is Made a Knight (detail on facing page) fresco, 265x230, 284x230, 265x200 cm Lower Basilica, Assisi

In 1312 the Franciscan friar Gentile Partino da Montefiore, a powerful prelate and friend of the Angevins, appointed cardinal with the title of San Martino ai Monti, left a large sum of money to the friars of the mother house for the decoration of a chapel in the Lower Basilica. The work was carried out by Simone Martini and finished by 1317. The cycle includes *Scenes from the Life of Saint Martin of Tours*, an allusion to the cardinal's title.

The scenes have a lively and profane character, with worldly settings in which knights, squires, heraldic devices and refined architectural backdrops are attentively described, imbuing the paintings with a flavor of life at the courts of the time.

Martin of Tours was a soldier in the Roman army who, in 344, underwent a profound spiritual experience that induced him to give up arms and devote himself to a religious life. In four scenes of Simone's cycle of frescoes, however, the saint is presented not as a Roman *miles*, but as a medieval knight. In the scene where *He Is Made a Knight*, in fact, Martin is shown undergoing a solemn and aristocratic ceremony inside a medieval palace, accompanied by squires bearing arms and a falcon and feted by musicians and singers as was the custom at the courts.

In *His Renunciation of Arms*, Martin is still a medieval knight in his dress and hairstyle. The scene is set in a contemporary camp, where the treasurer is paying mercenary soldiers before they go into battle. The only figure dressed in a vaguely "ancient" manner is the emperor Julian, who is wearing a laurel wreath and seated on a *sedia curulis*.

The *Funeral* is the last of the *Scenes from the Life of Saint Martin*. It is set in a chamber whose architecture is in a refined and graceful Gothic style. The costumes, attitudes and features of the figures gathered around the corpse – clergymen, monks, and choirboys – are carefully depicted.

In the spatial organization of the scenes and the construction of the volumes Simone was influenced by the *Scenes from the Life of Saint Francis* painted by Giotto in the Upper Basilica. But where Giotto tended to draw the observer's attention to the heart of the action, Simone placed more emphasis on the description of the setting and the costumes.

SIMONE MARTINI

Annunciation
panel, 265x305 cm
Galleria degli Uffizi, Florence

In 1333 Simone Martini painted the *Annunciation* for the altar of Sant'Ansano in Siena Cathedral, in collaboration with his brother-in-law Lippo Memmi. The painting is dated and signed by both artists on the band at the bottom. *Saint Ansanus* and *Saint Giulitta* are represented on the wings of the polyptych and the *Prophets Jeremiah*, *Ezekiel*, *Isaiah* and *Daniel* in the medallions at the top, with scrolls referring to the mystery of the Incarnation. The central tondo situated above the dove of the Holy Spirit probably contained the Eternal Father.

The figures stand out against an even gold ground without any hint of a setting, so that they look like immaterial and precious personages in an ethereal and remote world. Between them stands a vase with long-stemmed lilies. On the right, the seated Virgin draws back uneasily as the arrival of the Archangel Gabriel interrupts her reading: she is an incorporeal and graceful figure, wrapped in a blue mantle whose sinuous form echoes her modest and bashful reaction. The archangel's wings are still spread and his cloak, made of a rare Scottish plaid, flaps in the wind. Kneeling on the floor of colored marble, Gabriel is holding an olive branch, symbol of peace, and pronouncing the words written in relief between the two figures: "Ave Gratia Plena Dominus Tecum."

The two figures have delicate complexions, fine features and slender and elongated forms. The composition, dominated by shades of yellow and gold and by a sinuous pattern of lines, attains unprecedented heights of elegance.

Pietro and Ambrogio Lorenzetti

The first reliable reference to Pietro Lorenzetti (Siena *c.* 1280-1348?) dates from April 17, 1320, when Bishop Guido Tarlati commissioned him to execute the polyptych for the high altar of the Pieve in Arezzo. Even before painting this picture, Pietro had gone to Assisi to start work on the *Scenes from the Life of Christ* in the left-hand transept of the lower basilica, finished in 1330.

Duccio, Giotto and the sculptor Giovanni Pisano were the chief influences on the development and maturation of the artist's personality. The sources tell us that Pietro was highly appreciated and much in demand at various centers in Tuscany. In his native city, the artist painted pictures for important ecclesiastical buildings, including altarpieces for the church of Mount Carmel (*Madonna between Saint Nicholas and the Prophet Elijah*, 1327-29, now in the Pinacoteca Nazionale di Siena) and for the cathedral (*Birth of the Virgin*, 1342, now in the Museo dell'Opera del Duomo) and frescoes for the hospital of Santa Maria della Scala. According to his biographer Giorgio Vasari (1568) the latter, unfortunately now lost, were what "launched" the artist's career.

Ambrogio too must have taken his first steps in the profession outside his hometown. In fact his earliest documented work – to have come down to us – is the *Madonna* formerly in the parish church of Vico l'Abate, signed and dated 1319. Ambrogio's interests appear to diverge somewhat from his brother's: where Pietro's works display a marked dramatic tension and an unconstrained handling of space, Ambrogio's have a speculative character and intellectual lucidity that are highly original. Ambrogio Lorenzetti (Siena doc. 1319-1348) also lived in Florence, which probably became his second home. The Sienese artist had no trouble finding acceptance in Florentine circles and in 1327 was able to enroll in the Arte dei Medici e degli Speziali, the official guild to which the city's painters belonged.

Returning to Siena, he reached the peak of his career in the thirties, appreciated not just for his artistic skills but also for his intellectual gifts. Moreover, with the departure of Simone Martini for Avignon (1336), the Lorenzetti brothers became the undisputed protagonists of the artistic scene in Siena. In 1338, to a commission from the government of the Nine, Ambrogio started to execute the frescoes with the *Allegories and Effects of Good and Bad Government* in a hall of the Palazzo Pubblico, the work for which the painter remains most famous today. In the adjoining room (where Simone Martini's *Maestà* used to hang), he also painted the so-called *Mappamondo*, i.e. a large map of the Sienese state that used to turn on a pivot and which survived up until the eighteenth century.

The activity and life of the Lorenzetti brothers were brought to an abrupt end by the outbreak of plague that dealt a crushing blow to the prosperity and aspirations of the city of Siena itself in 1348. On June 9, 1348, facing the imminent death of himself, his wife and his daughters, Ambrogio hastily wrote his last will and testament.

Pietro Lorenzetti
Scenes of Christ's Passion:
Crucifixion
fresco
Lower Basilica, Assisi

Dating from around 1320, Pietro Lorenzetti's *Scenes of the Passion* adorn the left transept of the Lower Basilica of Assisi.
The large scene of the *Crucifixion* is

PIETRO LORENZETTI

located on the left-hand wall of the transept. The three crosses stand against the background of a deep blue and even sky, with no hint of cloud. From them hang the white and luminous bodies of Christ and the two thieves. A vast crowd is gathered at the feet of the crosses, its individual members carefully characterized in their features, attitudes and dress. "Here the multitude has a face," commented Cesare Brandi (1958). And in fact it is possible to imagine the thoughts or emotions of each figure, often communicated to his or her neighbor through a gesture or a glance. Like the soldier who, placing a hand on the shoulder of his amazed companion, draws his attention to the group of mourning women.

Scenes of Christ's Passion: *Entry into Jerusalem*; *Road to Calvary*
fresco
Lower Basilica, Assisi

Both scenes are set against the background of the city of Jerusalem, which has the appearance of an Umbrian hill town, bristling with towers. In addition, each composition is dominated by a procession, the first a festive one accompanying Christ on his entry into the

city and the second a dramatic one leading him out of the gate in the direction of Mount Golgotha. The organization of the two scenes recalls the passion plays staged in the streets of Umbrian cities in the days leading up to Easter in which the whole of the population was involved.

In the *Entry into Jerusalem* two processions converge on the figure of Christ, static and almost regal in his long mantle of lapis-lazuli blue: on the left the retinue of apostles with Judas and Peter at their head and on the right the citizens emerging from the gate to greet him, while children lay their cloaks on the ground or climb an olive tree to detach branches.

In the *Road to Calvary*, the procession passes out of the city gate and then leaves

the road paved with bricks in a herringbone pattern to follow the rugged and lonely path leading to Golgotha. Christ – again the fulcrum of the scene – is carrying the heavy cross, foreshortened by its backward-leaning angle: thus the arms of the cross appear to be set parallel to the procession. The artist lingers over every minute detail of the scene, from the multicolored buildings to the beautiful armor worn by the soldiers and the naked bodies of the two thieves (one viewed from the front and the other from behind).

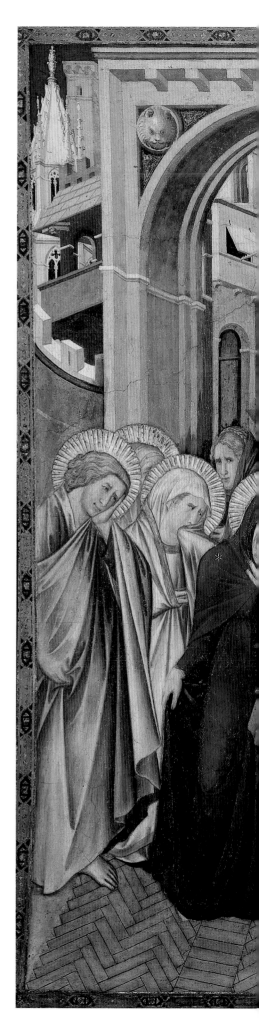

Pietro Lorenzetti
*Polyptych of the Virgin and Child
with Saints*
panel, 298x309 cm
Pieve di Santa Maria, Arezzo

Pietro Lorenzetti painted the polyptych
still on the high altar of the parish church
of Santa Maria in Arezzo (called the
Pieve) to a commission from Bishop
Guido Tarlati, under the terms of a
contract drawn up in 1320. The work,
signed "Petrus Laurentii me pinxit dextra
senensis," no longer has the predella,
columns and pillars that originally
accompanied it. At the center the
Madonna and Child face one another as if
absorbed in an intimate and private
dialogue: consisting of an exchange of
glances and veined with a hint of
melancholy, this is the pictorial equivalent
of a characteristic feature of the
contemporary sculptures by Giovanni
Pisano. The Virgin is wearing a minutely
embroidered dress lined with white vair
(we can even see the tails of the little
animals).
Various saints are arranged in two rows at
the sides of the holy group, while four
female saints are set in cusps on a third
row. The small tondi situated above the
pairs of arches contain heads of prophets:
facing toward the *Annunciation* in the
middle, they are an allusion to the
prophecy of the Incarnation of Christ.
This scene is set in a cubical room,
illusionistically foreshortened. The
structure is clearly derived from the
"spatial boxes" to be found in Giotto's
paintings.
The culminating point of the polyptych is
the cusp in the middle, where *Our Lady
of the Assumption* is represented in a
mandorla supported by cherubim.

Ambrogio Lorenzetti
Maestà and Saints
panel, 155x206 cm
Museo Civico di Palazzo Pretorio, Massa
Marittima

Ambrogio's *Maestà* had long been
relegated to an attic in the monastery of
Sant'Agostino, divided into five pieces,
when it was rediscovered in 1867.
Mentioned in the fifteenth century by
Lorenzo Ghiberti, the work was painted by
Ambrogio around 1335.

At the center, the Madonna and Child –
clasped in a tender embrace – are seated
on a throne, surrounded by angels and
saints arranged in ranks at the side.
Among the latter, we can see Cerbonius,
patron saint of Massa, on the far right,
accompanied by geese. On the three steps
of the throne are seated the Theological
Virtues, easily identifiable by their
attributes, the colors of their clothing and
the corresponding step, as well as by the
inscription on it: Faith is at the bottom,
dressed in white and contemplating the

Trinity in a mirror; she is followed by
Hope, dressed in green and gazing up to
heaven and at the top of the tower she is
supporting; at the center, finally, there is
Charity, holding an arrow and a heart and
wearing a pink robe of classical cut
through which we can see the curves of
her body. According to the critics, such a
representation of Charity refers to carnal
as well as spiritual love: as St. Bernard put
it: "there will never be Charity without
concupiscence, for we are men born from
the flesh."

Ambrogio Lorenzetti
*The Effects of Good Government
in the Town and the Country*
fresco, length *c.* 14 m
Palazzo Pubblico, Siena

Between 1337 and 1340, Ambrogio
frescoed the Sala dei Nove in the Palazzo
Pubblico of Siena with the famous cycle of
paintings that must originally have
intended as an allegory of *Peace* and *War*.
The title now commonly assigned to these

frescoes – *The Allegories and the Effects
of Good and Bad Government in the
Town and the Country* – was in fact
given to them for the first time in 1792 by
the scholar Achille Lanzi.
Entering the hall, the first thing you see on
the opposite wall is the *Bad Government*
(or *War*), in which both the city and the
countryside are devastated by destruction,
neglect and violence. The images are
contrasted, on the shorter wall to the
right, by the *Allegory of Good
Government* (or *Peace*, if you prefer)
and still further to the right (on the
entrance wall), by the serene and
reassuring image of the city of Siena and
its surrounding countryside with the
Effects of Good Government.
Good government has very positive effects
on city life, reflected in the tranquil and
productive climate represented in this
picture of Sienese life in the early
fourteenth century. In streets
and squares where buildings
are still being constructed and
renovated, each craftsman carries
out his activity in his own workshop
opening onto the road: a tailor is sewing,
a goldsmith has laid out his precious
merchandise, a cobbler is selling a pair
of shoes, a butcher has hung out his
salted meat, a teacher is talking to his
attentive pupils, anxious to learn, and
wool workers, weavers and carders are
intent on their work. In this serene view

of city life, where public order is
paramount, there is also room for
celebration: thus we see a procession
accompanying a young bride to her
wedding on the left and a round dance of
nine girls, accompanied by songs and the
beating of a tambourine. The harmony of
the music and the dance are an
embodiment of orderly civic life. The
lovely rural landscape of the Siena region
is caught by Lorenzetti in a bird's-eye
view: the hills, studded with villages,
castles and little churches, surrounded by
the geometric patterns of fields and riven
by watercourses, extend as far as the
horizon, where we are even offered a
glimpse of the sea. It is possible to
recognize vines, olives and fields of grain,
all fundamental resources of the Sienese
countryside: in fact the wheat is not just
being sown but also harvested, while
other fields are plowed.
Thus the painter presents an ideal vision
in which, among other things, there is no
hint of the revolts that troubled the
relations between town and country in the
fourteenth century.
"Every free man walks without fear / and
each sows as he works..." runs the
inscription in the scroll held by *Securitas*,
a winged, half-naked figure of a classical
flavor holding the figure of a hanged man
and hovering over the point where town
and country meet, setting the seal on this
timeless and mythical image of peace.

The Presentation in the Temple
panel, 257x168 cm
Galleria degli Uffizi, Florence

Ambrogio painted the picture for the altar of San Crescenzio in Siena Cathedral in 1342. The artist has set the scene in a church with a nave and two aisles, represented as a cutaway at the level of the main altar, with the chancel and ambulatory in the background. As the inscriptions on the scrolls held by the prophets at the top of the painting tells us, the composition combines two separate episodes taken from the Gospel according to Luke (2, 22-39): the presentation of Christ in the temple thirty days after his birth, for circumcision, and the purification of his Mother forty days after the birth. Behind the altar at the center the priest is holding a pair of doves ready for sacrifice. In front of Mary, the elderly Simeon, holding the Child in his trembling arms, predicts that a sword – i.e. a great sorrow – will pierce her soul, while alongside him the prophetess Anna declares her recognition of the Redeemer (as her scroll explains).

15 TH CENTURY

Gentile da Fabriano

T rained in the Marche, where he was born (Fabriano 1370-Rome 1427), but strongly influenced by the International Gothic of the Lombard region, Gentile commenced his career in Venice, where his presence is recorded from 1408. While in the lagoon city he painted important frescoes in the Sala del Maggior Consiglio of the Doge's Palace, which were finished by Pisanello in 1415 (now lost).

In 1414 Gentile went to Brescia and placed himself at the service of Pandolfo Malatesta, who in 1419 issued the painter with a safe conduct so that he could pay a visit to Pope Martin V in Rome. Leaving Brescia, he settled in Florence in 1420, living in a house rented from the wealthy merchant Palla Strozzi. It was for the latter that Gentile executed the sumptuous *Adoration of the Magi* – signed and dated 1423 – in the Strozzi Chapel in Santa Trinita (now in the Uffizi). The painting is a fine example of the courtly Gothic style, in which great emphasis is placed on the luxurious fabrics and gold work. Later, Gentile drew stimulating ideas from the works of Masolino and Masaccio, as is apparent from the solid construction of volumes in the *Quaratesi Polyptych* for San Niccolò in Soprarno (1425), a work that has now been split up among various museums.

In 1425, Gentile painted a fresco on the façade of the Palazzo dei Notai in Siena's Piazza del Campo: the work, now vanished, provided an important model for local artists. On his way to Rome, Gentile also stopped in Orvieto to fresco the *Madonna and Child* in the cathedral.

Gentile's presence in the papal city is documented from January 1427, though he may have arrived there a few months earlier. In the church of San Giovanni in Laterano, the artist painted a monumental monochrome cycle of *Scenes from the Life of the Baptist* and *Five Prophets*. His death later the same year prevented Gentile from completing the work, which was finished by Pisanello in 1432. Unfortunately very little remains of this undertaking, as the frescoes were destroyed two centuries later, when the church was renovated for the Jubilee of 1650.

Valle Romita Polyptych
panel, 280x250 cm
Pinacoteca di Brera, Milan

The earliest important work by Gentile to have come down to us is the so-called *Valle Romita Polyptych*, executed in Venice between 1405 and 1410 and then sent to the Marche, where it was placed in the church of the monastery of the Observants in Val Romita (now Val di Sasso) near the artist's birthplace Fabriano. The sumptuous polyptych, with its elegantly decorated framework, glittering gold and colors as brilliant as enamel, represents the *Coronation of the Virgin* in the central panel: Christ and Mary with the Eternal Father behind them hover against the background of a gold ground with a sunburst, above angels playing music and singers resting on a fanciful starry firmament.

In the side panels of the polyptych, *Saints Jerome, Francis, Dominic* and *Mary Magdalen*, standing on a paradisiacal sward studded with minutely depicted flowers, observe the miraculous apparition.

The scenes from the lives of the saints in the upper row also have the tone of a noble and precious fable: note, for example, how the *Killing of Saint Peter Martyr* (detail on facing page) is devoid of drama in spite of the subject and is dominated instead by the brilliant red of the killer's stockings.

GENTILE DA FABRIANO

Adoration of the Magi
panel, 303x282 cm
Galleria degli Uffizi, Florence

The painting, signed and dated (1423) on the frame, was commissioned from Gentile by the most prominent personage in Florence at the time, Palla Strozzi, who placed it on the altar of his own chapel in Santa Trinita. In this masterpiece, in keeping with the still vital tradition of International Gothic, the artist makes skilled and unconstrained use of different materials and techniques, in a worldly and sumptuous descriptive style where minute attention is paid to the outward appearance of things.

The composition should be read from the top left, beginning with the journey of the Magi who sight the star above Mount Vittoriale, reach Jerusalem (the walled city under the central lunette) and, finally, arrive at Herod's palace, which has the appearance of a menacing feudal castle with a moat and drawbridge. The journey ends in the foreground, near the stable in Bethlehem where the Magi pay homage to the newborn Redeemer. Here the Three Kings are the true protagonists of the scene: situated at the center, they are wearing sumptuous garments of gold and silver and have refined hairstyles. They are followed by a procession of figures on horseback dressed in the fifteenth-century style (among them, behind the youngest of the Magi, we can see the client and his son Lorenzo), accompanied by servants and heralds. The procession includes exotic animals as well as horses, deer and birds, recalling the hunting parties of which the Strozzi were so fond.

In the predella the *Nativity*, *Flight into Egypt* and *Presentation in the Temple* are depicted with an equally refined taste for narrative and the same meticulous technique. In these scenes, Gentile has used the sky as a backdrop, instead of a gold ground: a starry night in the *Nativity* and a sunlit day in the *Flight into Egypt*. The *Presentation in the Temple* – of which the original, reproduced here (pp. 66-7), is now in the Louvre – is set

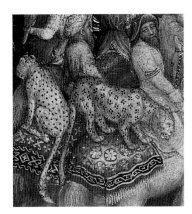

in a city square that looks like a fabulous and colorful vision of early fifteenth-century Florence, with the arcade on the right echoing the Spedale of the Innocenti built by Filippo Brunelleschi in 1418. Gentile's lively curiosity induces him to linger over precious details like the dresses of the two women on the left, as well as over humbler elements like the two beggars on the opposite side.

Adoration of the Magi, detail of the
predella showing the *Presentation
in the Temple*
Louvre, Paris

Pisanello

Antonio Pisano, called Pisanello, was born in Pisa some time prior to 1395, the date of his father Puccio di Giovanni's will in which he is named as sole heir, and died perhaps in Mantua before 1455. At the beginning of the fifteenth century Pisanello moved with his family to Veneto, perhaps to Verona. Bartolomeo Facio, a man of letters who lived at the same time as the painter, records in his writings that Pisanello received his training in Venice in the second decade of the century, working alongside Gentile da Fabriano on the lost frescoes in the Doge's Palace. A cultured and refined painter, Pisanello was active at some of the principal courts of Italy. We have no reliable information on the early part of Pisanello's career, though he may have executed the *Annunciation* for the Brenzoni Monument in San Fermo Maggiore at Verona around 1426.

Between 1431 and 1432, the artist was in Rome to finish the frescoes in San Giovanni in Laterano left incomplete by Gentile da Fabriano on his death. Returning to Verona, he painted the frescoes in the Pellegrini Chapel in Sant'Anastasia: all that survives today is the scene with the *Saint George and the Princess* (1433-38).

Following Gentile's death, Pisanello became the artist most in demand at the Italian courts. His style was very much in tune with the secular, elegant and chivalrous tastes of the peninsula's princes and their aristocratic and erudite entourages. In fact Pisanello worked as a painter, illuminator and medalist for Gian Francesco and Ludovico Gonzaga in Mantua, Lionello d'Este in Ferrara, Alfonso V of Aragon, king of Naples, Filippo Maria Visconti and Francesco Sforza in Milan and Sigismondo and Novello Malatesta in Rimini.

Pisanello was the most important Italian medalist of the fifteenth century: the earliest of his medals known to us today is the one portraying John III Paleologus, emperor of the East, struck at Ferrara in 1438 while the council of the Eastern and Western Churches was being held. Pisanello was a renowned portraitist, much in demand at the principal courts of Italy for his ability, in refined commemorative medals and paintings alike, to capture the essential traits of the sitter in a half-length profile. In 1441 he painted the *Portrait of Lionello d'Este* in competition with the Venetian artist Jacopo Bellini.

Active during the first half of the fifteenth century, Pisanello was the artist who most clearly represented the secular, courtly and chivalrous ideals of the Italian aristocracy in that period, with his ability to combine Humanistic cultural aspirations with a refined late Gothic style.

Saint George and the Princess, detail
fresco, 223x430 cm
Sant'Anastasia, Verona

Between 1433 and 1438, Pisanello frescoed the legend of St. George on the outer arch of the Pellegrini Chapel in Sant'Anastasia, from which it was detached in the nineteenth century. It is the artist's most celebrated work, reflecting his interest in exploring the real world at the same time as his fondness for a dreamlike and fabulous dimension

SANCTVS · GIORGIVS ·

linked to the world of the courts and chivalry.

In Pisanello's painting the warrior saint has just been told by the princess of the sad fate to which she has been condemned and is about to get back on his horse and set off to confront the terrible dragon that intends to devour the girl. The atmosphere is an enchanted one, charged with an unreal sense of expectation. Outside the walls of an elegant and ornate but deserted city, a gallows with two convicts hanging from it stands like an omen of death; a group of knights, off to one side on the left, and the animals in the foreground are motionless, as if frozen; the dwarf on horseback with a heavy helmet, who is supporting St. George's lance on the far right, is also immobile. The princess, a haughty and aristocratic figure with an elongated and graceful profile, embellished by her elegant hairstyle, stands stock still, waiting without showing any sign of emotion.

PISANELLO

Madonna of the Quaglia
(***Madonna with the Quail***)
panel, 67x43·5 cm
Museo di Castelvecchio, Verona

Datable to around 1420, the picture has
an iconographic motif that was very
widespread in the fourteenth and fifteenth
century, especially in Veneto: the
coronation of the Virgin set in the context
of the Madonna of Humility, i.e. in the
setting of the *hortus conclusus*, a walled
garden alluding to Mary's virginity. The
title by which the work is known derives
from the presence of a quail at the lower
right-hand corner of the composition: it
may be a reference to the Bible story of
the quails that arrived to feed the Jews
during their Exodus (*Exodus*, XVI, 13).
While still a young man the artist showed
a marked interest in the Gothic and
courtly fashion for the minute and
detailed depiction of flowers, animals,
jewelry, precious stuffs and furs (like the
ermine that lines Mary's cloak), here
associated with the elegant use of curved
lines throughout the composition.

Portrait of Lionello d'Este
panel, 29·5x18·4 cm
Accademia Carrara, Bergamo

At the court of Ferrara in 1441, Pisanello painted a portrait of Lionello d'Este, son of Marchese Niccolò III, in competition with the Venetian artist Jacopo Bellini. The marchese declared Bellini the winner, but his portrait has been lost, while Pisanello's has survived. The picture presents the subject in profile, against a hedge of wild roses (partly blackened by subsequent coats of varnish). The young man's gaunt and pale features, devoid of emotion, his elegant brocade overgarment adorned with silver-plated buttons and interwoven lace and his full head of hair tied at the back give the figure an aristocratic appearance, an impression that is underlined by the refinement of the background.

Born in 1407, after a long period as a military commander Lionello succeeded his father in that same year of 1441. A few years later, from 1444 onward, Pisanello struck six medals with effigies of the new marchese, once again in profile (the medal illustrated here is the one now in the Museo del Bargello in Florence), with stylized features and in a calm and solemn attitude. A cultured artists with links to Humanist circles as well as a refined goldsmith, Pisanello revived the illustrious numismatic tradition of the ancient Romans with his activity as a medallist.

Masolino

Tommaso di Cristofano Fini, called Masolino (Panicale in Valdarno 1383-Florence 1440), received his training in Florence, perhaps under Lorenzo Ghiberti, and was influenced by the goldsmith's art and late Gothic painting. Recorded in Florence for the first time in 1422, Masolino began to work in his own right the following year.

In the third decade of the fifteenth century Masolino, like Ghiberti, made himself the representative of a moderate renewal of art that set out to reconcile the fabulous and elegant tones of the Gothic with the solid grasp of perspective developed by Brunelleschi and applied, in the same years, by Donatello and Masaccio. In 1424 Masolino was entrusted with the task of frescoing the *Scenes from the Life of Saint Peter* in the chapel of Felice Brancacci in Santa Maria del Carmine. Shortly afterward he brought in his young fellow countryman Masaccio to assist him in the undertaking. The two artists went on to form a lasting partnership on an equal footing, in spite of their differences in age and above all in temperament. Departing for Hungary in 1425 as painter in the retinue of the condottiere Filippo Scolari, known as Pippo Spano, Masolino left the frescoes in the Brancacci Chapel unfinished and they were completed by Masaccio. Masolino may have arrived in Rome as early as 1427 and began to work for the court of Pope Martin V, where Gentile da Fabriano and Pisanello were also active. In the papal city Masolino was given the job of finishing several works commenced by Masaccio, who had in the meantime met a premature death: the polyptych of the *Madonna della Neve* for Santa Maria Maggiore and the frescoes with *Scenes from the Lives of Saint Catherine and Saint Ambrose* in San Clemente. The paintings in San Clemente were commissioned from him by Cardinal Branda Castiglioni, who took Masolino back with him to his fief in Lombardy, at Castiglione Olona near Varese. In the cardinal's birthplace, the Tuscan artist frescoed *Scenes from the Life of Saint John the Baptist* in the baptistery and the *Scenes from the Life of the Virgin* in the collegiate church (1435), works in which the narrative is handled in a gracious, worldly and even poetic manner.

The Fall of Adam and Eve
fresco, 208x88 cm

Scenes from the Life of Saint Peter: Raising of Tabitha and the *Healing of the Lame Man*
fresco, 255x598 cm
Brancacci Chapel, Santa Maria del Carmine, Florence

It was the wealthy silk merchant Felice Brancacci who commissioned Masolino, leading exponent of the courtly Gothic current, to paint the frescoes for his chapel in the Carmelite church in 1424. After about a year it was left to Masaccio – who had in the meantime joined Masolino in the work – to carry on with the decoration on his own until

Masolino's return in 1427. The frescoes were left incomplete, however, and only finished in 1485 by Filippino Lippi. The recent restoration (1988) has made the fifteenth-century frescoes far more legible, with the cleaning revealing the original tones of color as well as long forgotten details.

In Masolino's *Fall of Adam and Eve*, the first progenitors are shown under the tree of the knowledge of good and evil, with the serpent among its branches, represented with a human head. The two figures have elongated bodies and appear so light that they hardly touch the ground: their beauty is ideal and ethereal, without a hint of sensuality. They display no emotion, but are silent and expressionless, making no more than slight gestures with their hands. Gently illuminated by the light entering from the left, Masolino's Adam and Eve are exquisite characters in an unreal fairy tale that appears to leave no room for drama. The scenes with Masolino's *Fall of Adam and Eve* and Masaccio's *Expulsion from Paradise* (cf. pp. 76-7) form an introduction to the *Scenes from the Life of Saint Peter*, which include the *Raising of Tabitha* and the *Healing of the Lame Man*, painted by Masolino in collaboration with Masaccio. The *giornata*, or section of fresco painted in one day (delimited by the join in the plaster), that comprises the two well-dressed gentlemen walking elegantly and in step across an early fifteenth-century city square can be attributed to Masolino. Like manikins decked out in the latest fashion, the two young men are looking at each other silently, without establishing any real dialogue: the refined and stereotyped beauty of the two figures recalls that of Adam and Eve in the preceding scene and is typical of the International Gothic style that still held sway in Florence in the 1420s.

MASOLINO

Scenes from the Life of Saint John the Baptist: *Herod's Feast*
fresco
Baptistery, Castiglione Olona

While Masolino was in Rome Cardinal Branda asked the Florentine painter to accompany him to Castiglione Olona in Lombardy, where the high prelate had his fief. There he carried out various fresco decorations including the *Scenes from the Life of Saint John the Baptist* in the baptistery, executed around 1435. In this cycle Masolino gave free rein to his courtly style, producing a narrative with a fabulous flavor in which the rules of perspective that he had learned in Florence were used to create suggestive scenic effects.

The buildings to the left and the right of the scene with *Herod's Feast* have different vanishing points and provide the settings for two different moments in the story: on the one hand the feast proper, where several of Cardinal Branda's courtiers are portrayed among the guests, and on the other Salome presenting John's head to Herodias. The two women are represented in hierarchic proportion, the daughter smaller and more frail and the mother larger in size. The latter's elegant and sinuous profile is reminiscent of the princess in the fresco by Pisanello in Sant'Anastasia at Verona (p. 69). Finally, the two foreshortened buildings, especially the colonnade on the right, lead the observer's gaze toward the landscape, where the body of St. John is being buried in the distance, marking the last episode in the story.

Masaccio

M A S A C C I O

Son of the notary Giovanni Cassai, Tommaso (San Giovanni Valdarno 1401-Rome 1428?) was nicknamed Masaccio ("Hulking Tom") because of his slovenly and untidy ways, at least according to his biographer Giorgio Vasari (1568), who also described him as having a generous and open nature.

Moving to Florence, Masaccio was trained in the local, late Gothic artistic circles, but soon moved away from this style as he came under the influence of Giotto's painting, the sculpture of the early fourteenth century (Giovanni Pisano, Arnolfo di Cambio) and his own time (Donatello) and the experiments with perspective and architectural designs of Brunelleschi.

Launched on an independent career, Masaccio painted the triptych with the *Madonna and Child with Four Saints* in San Giovenale at Cascia near Reggello, dated 1422. The artist embarked on a lasting relationship of collaboration with the older Masolino (p. 72), who also came from the Valdarno in Tuscany. The first fruit of this partnership was the *Madonna and Child with Saint Anne* for Sant'Ambrogio (now in the Uffizi), perhaps executed in 1424. Shortly afterward, the two artists were collaborating again on the *Scenes from the Life of Saint Peter* in Felice Brancacci's chapel in Santa Maria del Carmine, though from 1425 onward Masaccio worked on them alone as Masolino had left for Hungary. The frescoes are a milestone in Western art, marking the shift in painting toward the new conception of space and humanity typical of the early Renaissance.

In 1426, Ser Giovanni di Colino commissioned Masaccio to paint a polyptych for the Carmelite church in Pisa, a work that has now been dismembered and dispersed among museums in various parts of the world. His stay in Pisa – in the same year that Brunelleschi was there – gave Masaccio an opportunity to study the sculpture of Nicola and Giovanni Pisano and the ancient marbles in the Camposanto.

Masaccio may have painted the fresco of the *Holy Trinity* in Santa Maria Novella for Domenico Lenzi, who died on January 19, 1426. It has been suggested that Brunelleschi was directly or indirectly involved in the rigorous perspective construction of the painted architecture.

At the end of 1427 Masaccio went to Rome, where he again worked alongside Masolino until dying at the age of only twenty-seven about a year later. Hearing of the death of his young friend, Brunelleschi in Florence said "Masaccio is a very great loss for us" (Vasari 1568).

Expulsion from Paradise, detail
fresco, 208x88 cm
Brancacci Chapel, Santa Maria del
Carmine, Florence

The frescoes painted by Masaccio in the Brancacci Chapel (cf. also Masolino, pp. 72-3) constitute a fundamental chapter in the history of European art, in so far as they were the first translation of the ethical, secular and rational principles of Humanism into pictorial terms. The protagonist of Masaccio's scenes, in fact, is a realistic and heroic humanity, set in a natural space that can be rationally measured by means of perspective. Over the course of the fifteenth and sixteenth century, the artists of subsequent generations (including Michelangelo) came to the Carmelite church to study and copy the frescoes, which had marked the beginning of the Renaissance in Florentine painting.

Visitors have always been struck by the figures of Adam and Eve in the *Expulsion from Paradise*, heroic protagonists of the tragic story of the moment when humankind assumed painful responsibility for its own choices. Exhausted by despair and shame, the first man and woman stumble blindly, their faces and bodies contracted and twisted. So real and tangible is their nudity that it is almost crude. Their shadows trailing behind them, Adam and Eve leave the Garden of Eden forever. During the recent restoration (1988), the leaves painted over the genitals of the two figures in the seventeenth century were removed.

*Scenes from the Life of
Saint Peter: The Tribute Money*,
detail
fresco, 255x598 cm
Brancacci Chapel, Santa Maria del
Carmine, Florence

The Tribute Money is the most famous of
the *Scenes from the Life of Saint Peter*.
Masaccio painted it in 1427, in thirty-two
giornate (the paint had to be applied to
fresh plaster and therefore only one
section was applied each "day"). It
depicts a story from the *Gospel according
to Matthew* (XVII, 24-7) and subdivides it
into three episodes all in the same setting:
Christ in the middle, surrounded by the
apostles, tells Peter to get the money
exacted from those wishing to enter the
temple at Capernaum and pay it to the
Roman tax collector, who has his back to
us; on the left we see Peter following
Jesus's instructions and taking the coin
from the mouth of a fish he has caught in
the lake; finally, on the right, Peter hands
the tribute money to the tax collector.
The scene is steeped in a solemn and
austere atmosphere, laid out in a lucid
perspective that comprises every detail:
the mountains receding into the
background, the flat and foreshortened
clouds, the flattened disks of the haloes,
the arrangement of the figures in a half-
circle in the middle and the difficult pose
of Peter crouching over the fish. Christ is
the fulcrum of the composition and is
located at the vanishing point of the
perspective construction. The apostles
gathered around Jesus, whose compact
and sculptural forms give them the severe
and majestic appearance of ancient
philosophers and orators, look very
different from the refined young men out
for a stroll depicted by Masolino in the
same cycle (p. 73): they belong to two
distinct worlds that coexisted but had still
not met, the courtly Gothic of Masolino
and the early Renaissance in Masaccio.

MASACCIO

Scenes from the Life of Saint Peter: The Baptism of the Neophytes; Saint Peter Healing the Sick with His Shadow
fresco, 255x162, 230x162 cm
Brancacci Chapel, Santa Maria del Carmine, Florence

In the scene where St. Peter baptizes the new converts, Masaccio dwells upon the naked bodies of the men waiting to take part in the sacred ritual. The figure of the young man on the right, trembling with cold, was much admired in the fifteenth and sixteenth centuries. The interest shown by Masaccio in the human body was something that he shared with the contemporary sculptor Donatello. The painter set several of the *Scenes from the Life of Saint Peter* in the urban environment of early fifteenth-century Florence. An example is the scene where Peter heals the sick with his shadow, set in a street flanked by contemporary buildings: a rusticated palace, two houses with protruding upper stories (called "jutties") and the facade of a church with a column in the classical style. The saint's retinue contains a number of portraits of living people: the man with the red cap has been identified as Masolino, the old man with a white beard at the back as Donatello and the young man to the left of St. Peter as Masaccio's brother Giovanni, called Scheggia. The two derelicts in the foreground, waiting full of hope for the miraculous healing, offer a glimpse of the realities of human existence that was unheard-of at this time.

*Pisa Altarpiece: Madonna and
Child Enthroned with Angels*
panel, 135·5x73 cm
National Gallery, London

Pisa Altarpiece: Crucifixion
panel, 83x63 cm
Gallerie Nazionali di Capodimonte, Naples

The two panels formed part of the
polyptych painted by Masaccio in 1426
for an altar of the church of Santa Maria
del Carmine at Pisa. The monumental
work, originally about five meters tall, was
dismembered over the course of the
sixteenth century. So far, eleven of the
numerous sections of which it was made
up have been identified in various
museums. The *Madonna and Child* in
London was the central panel, while the
Crucifixion was set above it, in the cusp.
In the *Madonna and Child*, Masaccio
adopted the solemn and sculptural scheme
of Giotto's *Ognissanti Maestà* (p. 38) but
used perspective to transform it into a
rational setting. The lutes played by the
two angels seated in the foreground are
foreshortened in the direction of the
Virgin, as if to guide the observer's gaze
into the depths of the painting. Only in the
Child has the artist experimented with
foreshortening the halo so that it looks like
a disk set in a plane parallel to the floor.
The *Crucifixion* has an extremely low
point of view, intended to compensate for
the altarpiece's original position, high
above the observer: in fact Christ's head
looks as if it is sunk into his collar bones.
The dramatic scene, which focuses on the
agony of the three figures, is depicted in an
essential fashion, devoid of any reference to
the surroundings. At the center Mary
Magdalen is depicted from behind, kneeling
and covered with a flame-red cloak. She
appears to be uttering a piercing scream,
with her arms flung upward and outward:
despite the fact that we cannot see her face,
her body is so powerfully expressive that it
is considered one of the most moving
figures in the whole of Italian art.

Donatello

Donatello (Florence 1386-1466) was one of the leading figures – along with Brunelleschi and Masaccio – of the Florentine Renaissance. Of humble origin, Donato di Niccolò di Betto Bardi, called Donatello, became one of the most renowned artists in early fifteenth-century Florence. A friend of Brunelleschi, Paolo Uccello and Masaccio and with ties to intellectuals like Leon Battista Alberti, Donatello was to constitute an indispensable model for subsequent generations, comparable to the artists of classical antiquity.

A pupil and collaborator of Lorenzo Ghiberti, Donatello became involved in the fervent work on the city's religious heart: for the cathedral and the campanile next to it, Donatello carved a series of marble sculptures that kept him occupied up until the 1430s. At the same time, he executed several sculptures for the niches on the exterior of the church of Orsanmichele, belonging to the Florentine guilds, including the *Saint George* for the Guild of Armorers and Sword Makers (*c.* 1416-17). In 1423, Donatello was commissioned to execute the gilded bronze relief of *Herod's Feast* for the font of Siena Baptistery, for which he later made two statuettes of *Virtues* and three *Putti*. From 1425 to 1433 he worked in partnership with the sculptor and architect Michelozzo, with whom Donatello spent two years in Rome (1430-32). This gave Donatello the opportunity to study late classical, early Christian and Romanesque art.

Back in Florence, he was again at work in the cathedral, executing the *Cantoria* or *Singing Gallery* (1433-38) and the cartoon of the *Coronation of the Virgin* for one of the stained-glass windows set in the oculi around the dome (1434-37). In the same years Donatello found a friend and regular client in Cosimo de' Medici the Elder, ruler of the city: it was for Cosimo that Donatello executed the stucco reliefs for the Old Sacristy of San Lorenzo, built by Filippo Brunelleschi.

In 1443 Donatello moved to Padua, staying there until 1454. The visit was of fundamental importance, allowing the artist to export the style of the Florentine Renaissance outside the borders of Tuscany, introducing it not only to the region of Veneto but also to other cities in the north where the artist carried out commissions, such as Mantua, Modena and Ferrara. In Padua, the artist worked on the high altar of the basilica of Sant'Antonio (1446-49) and on the *Equestrian Statue of Gattamelata* (1447-53).

When he returned to Florence in 1454, though now elderly and infirm, he continued his sculptural activity unflaggingly, producing several masterpieces of an intensely dramatic character. These included the bronze panels with *Scenes from the Passion* that were later inserted in the pulpits of San Lorenzo, perhaps the last commission from his patron and friend Cosimo de' Medici. Dying in the December of 1466, Donatello was buried in San Lorenzo, the Medici church, near the tomb of Cosimo the Elder who had died two years earlier.

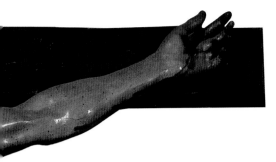

Crucifix
wood, 168x173 cm
Santa Croce, Florence

For the Franciscans of Santa Croce, Donatello carved a wooden *Crucifix* of great dramatic force, in which Christ, his head drooping and body rigid, appears to have just breathed his last breath after a long and unbearable agony. According to the anecdote recounted by the sixteenth-century biographer Giorgio Vasari, when Filippo Brunelleschi saw Donatello's work he remarked with a hint of disappointment that his friend "had put on the cross the body of a peasant, not the body of Jesus Christ which was most delicate and in every part the most perfect human form ever created." So Brunelleschi carved the *Crucifix* in Santa Maria Novella (reproduced on facing page), which left Donatello stupefied with admiration for the perfect harmony of its forms and proportions.

Like other wooden sculptures dating from the fourteenth and fifteenth centuries, Donatello's *Crucifix*, carved out of pear wood, has jointed arms so that it could easily be transformed into the deposed Christ during Holy Week. The restoration (1974) has also shown that the artist added two metal sleeves at the wrists, to lengthen the arms he had already carved, demonstrating the deftness with which he was able to adapt a variety of techniques to suit his own expressive requirements.

Saint George
marble, ht. 209 cm
Museo Nazionale del Bargello, Florence

In 1416 the Guild of Armorers and Swordsmiths commissioned from Donatello a statue of its patron saint – George – to be placed in the corporation's niche on the outside of the church of Orsanmichele in Florence. The resulting work marks an important crossroads between Gothic sculpture and that of the early Renaissance.

The saint, who once gripped a metal and perhaps gilded sword, is represented as a proud and courageous young warrior, his mind focused on the task before him. His body, enclosed in armor, is a compact volume with consistent proportions, erect and with his feet splayed and firmly planted on the ground. Unlike the worldly knight depicted by Pisanello in Verona (p. 69), this *Saint George* has the appearance of an austere Christian hero, conveying a sense of moral integrity, readiness for action and trust in divine assistance.

The relief underneath the statue represents the saint's most celebrated exploit: his killing of the dragon about to devour a princess. For this scene, the artist did not foreshorten the volumes in depth, but adopted an extremely low relief (known to his contemporaries as *stiacciato*, or "flattened relief"), in which the figures in the foreground emerge strongly but those in the background are increasingly compressed.

DONATELLO

Cantoria (Singing Gallery)
marble and mosaic, 348x570 cm
Museo dell'Opera del Duomo, Florence

Between 1433 and 1438 Donatello carved the *Cantoria* or *Singing Gallery* for Florence Cathedral, a companion piece to the one that was being executed by Luca della Robbia over the same period (pp. 102-3). The two balconies, used to house the organs and singers during religious services, were located above the entrances to the cathedral's two sacristies until 1688.

Taking his inspiration from late classical and early Christian sarcophagi, Donatello conceived the front of the singing gallery as a portico in which child-angels, with the joyful features of little fauns, dance frenziedly on a flowery sward. The slender columns of the loggia and the back wall are faced with mosaic, created by filling small channels with gilded and colored glass paste. The surfaces were intended to glint in the flickering light of the candles and lamps that illuminated the church. The semidarkness of the arcade, the mosaic, the colored pieces of marble set in the architectural framework and the white putti with their fluttering robes bestow a luminous vitality on the work. Donatello achieved an effect of great dynamism, a figurative and ornamental exuberance that appears antithetical to the static harmony of Luca's singing gallery.

In his creation of a solution for the singing gallery of the cathedral that was original in its structure, technique and iconography, the artist exploited the ideas that he had derived from his study of Hellenistic, late classical, early Christian and Romanesque models during his stay in Rome between 1430 and 1433.

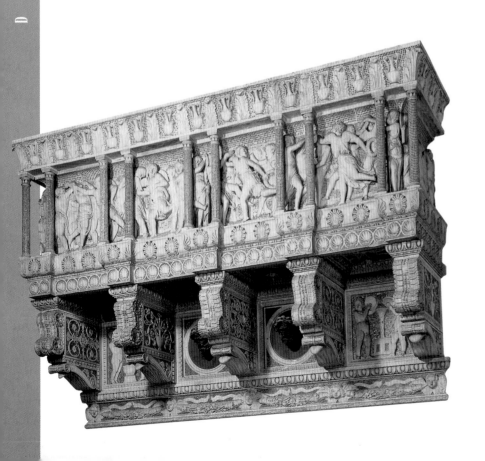

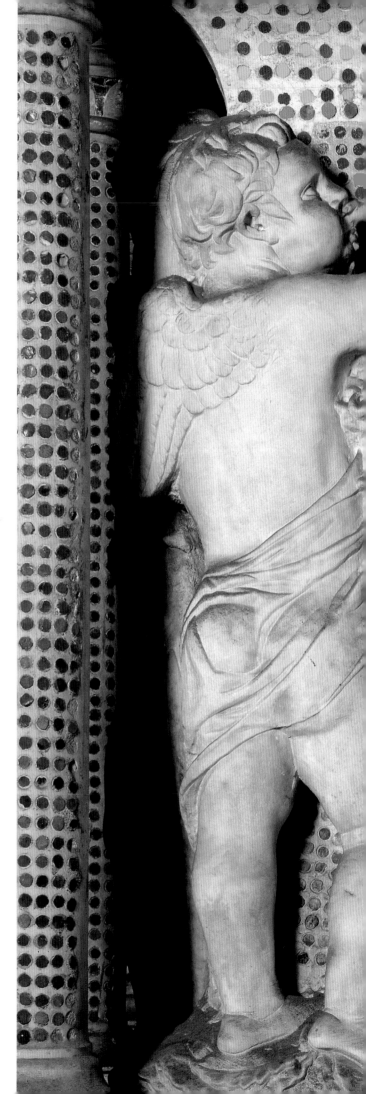

DONATELLO

ALTAR OF IL SANTO

Deposition
marble, 139x188 cm
Miracles of Saint Anthony:
Miracle of the Ass in Rimini;
Miracle of the Repentant Son
gilded bronze, 57x123 cm each
Basilica of Il Santo, Padua

In 1446 Donatello was given the task of making the high altar for the basilica of Sant'Antonio in Padua. The monumental altar, made up of bronze sculptures in full relief and reliefs along the four faces of the base, was broken up and stripped of its architectural structure in the sixteenth century. So the order in which the surviving sculptures and reliefs were placed in the nineteenth century does not correspond to the original appearance. It is likely that the statues in full relief were originally situated under a sort of tabernacle with the *Madonna and Child* at the center and the six saints at the sides. These statues were set on a quadrangular step and the reliefs, including the *Miracles of Saint Anthony* and the *Deposition*, inserted along its four sides.

The latter is of particular interest since, unlike the others, it was carved out of colored marble. The scheme of the composition is derived from the Roman sarcophagus decorated with the *Death of*

Meleager (Louvre, Paris). Once again, however, Donatello has departed from the ancient model to produce an original solution that renders the scene more dramatic. In the Paduan relief the women, depicted behind the men in attitudes of extreme grief, mark the height of the tragedy. The emotional tension is accentuated by the lack of space in the scene and by the density of the polychrome decorations on the sarcophagus and the rear of the wall. *The Miracles of Saint Anthony*, by contrast, are arranged inside architectural backdrops represented with a lucid central perspective: in this way the scenes

emphasize the miraculous event depicted at the center, around which the figures crowd in excited attitudes. In the *Miracle of the Ass in Rimini*, the protagonist is a mule kneeling in front of the Host held up by St. Anthony. The saint and the mule are located in isolation in front of the central apse of a church with a nave and two aisles. The astonished onlookers crowd around to get a better view of the miracle, gesticulating wildly and pushing their way through the doors and between the columns. The animation of the figures is so great that they overflow the limits imposed by the composition, even clambering onto the pillars in the foreground.

David
bronze, ht. 158 cm
Museo Nazionale del Bargello, Florence

Executed by Donatello shortly before his departure for Padua (1443) or during the following decade, probably for Cosimo de' Medici the Elder, *David* is represented as a young man with long hair in an attitude of repose. He is holding a stone in one hand and a long sword with a blunt tip in the other, while his foot rests on Goliath's severed head. According to the Bible story, David killed the brutal leader of the Philistines with a stone thrown from his sling, but the sculptor chose not to show the weapon. The bronze figure of *David* is the first nude in postclassical art: the artist's interest in the beauty and harmony of the human body was awakened by ancient Greek, Hellenistic and perhaps even Etruscan models. Other allusions to the world of pagan mythology are the figure's refined footwear and hat, resembling the talaria and petasus worn by the god Hermes, while a relief on one side of Goliath's winged helmet represents an idol on a triumphal chariot drawn by cupids, an image that appears to have been derived from an ancient gem. The work was intended to be located in the middle of a space and this is the position in which it was recorded in a document dating from 1469, set on top of a carved column at the center of the courtyard of Palazzo Medici.

DONATELLO

The Magdalen
wood with gold highlights, ht. 188 cm
Museo dell'Opera del Duomo, Florence

The *Magdalen*, carved by Donatello after
his stay in Padua (1454-55), used to be
located in Florence Baptistery. The saint is
represented in penitence, with her body
covered solely by her long hair, an
iconographic motif that had been
widespread in Tuscany since the end of
the thirteenth century. Her lined face and
hollow cheeks, toothless mouth, sunken
eyes and gaunt and bony limbs are signs
of the fasting and privation to which she
has subjected herself. The figure seems to
have difficulty staying upright, almost
worn out by weakness and fatigue. Even
though the sculptor dwells in such great
detail on the woman's physical decline
and thus the fleeting nature of her beauty,
he is still capable of conveying her inner
tension through her austere and trusting
expression, her hands about to join in
prayer and the moving dignity of the
figure. Like other sculptures of saints
and prophets by Donatello, Mary
Magdalene is represented as an ascetic
figure, whose strength stems from the
profundity of her faith.

Lorenzo Ghiberti

Lorenzo Ghiberti (Florence 1378-1455) was a versatile artist with a wide range of interests: in fact he was a sculptor, goldsmith, painter, designer of cartoons for stained-glass windows, architect and collector of antiquities, as well as a writer. His work reflects the personality of an artist who was able to successfully reconcile different cultures, such as the late Gothic style of Northern Europe, with the perspective and plastic ideas of the early Renaissance.

Ghiberti commenced his artistic education in the workshop of his stepfather, the goldsmith Bartolo di Michele, displaying great natural gifts. In 1401 Ghiberti took part in the competition for the second door of Florence Baptistery and, judged the winner, was given the commission. The enterprise occupied the artist's energies up until 1424. It proved such a success that the artist was entrusted with the execution of the baptistery's third and last door, which later came to be known as the *Porta del Paradiso* or *Porta d'oro* (1425-52). While working on the monumental doors, he executed a bronze sculpture of *Saint John the Baptist* in 1412 for the Arte di Calimala, or guild of merchant bankers, to be placed in a niche on the outside of Orsanmichele. This was the first large bronze statue in full relief to have been produced since antiquity. Ghiberti executed other sculptures (*Saint Matthew, Saint Stephen*) for the niches of Orsanmichele that showed the influence of Donatello's contemporary works.

In order to carry out public commissions on such a scale, Ghiberti assembled a large group of assistants who were able to learn, experiment with and refine the "lost-wax" technique of casting bronze, which had fallen into disuse since ancient times, in their master's workshop. Ghiberti's pupils and collaborators included Donatello, Paolo Uccello, Pollaiolo and perhaps Luca della Robbia.

After 1424 Ghiberti was active in Venice and Rome. He also made two gilded bronze reliefs for the baptismal font of Siena Cathedral representing *Scenes from the Life of Saint John the Baptist* (1417-25), an undertaking in which he was assisted by Donatello.

After 1447, Ghiberti spent the last years of his life writing the three volumes of *I Commentari* (i.e. "memorable things"). The second of these books is particularly interesting as it comprises the earliest autobiography of an artist known to us today.

Sacrifice of Isaac
gilded bronze, 44x40 cm
Museo Nazionale del Bargello, Florence

In 1401 Lorenzo Ghiberti won the competition to make the second bronze door of the baptistery of Florence Cathedral. The contest – which entailed the execution of a quatrefoil panel in gilded bronze representing *The Sacrifice of Isaac* in relief – was also entered by

Filippo Brunelleschi, who had served his apprenticeship as a goldsmith and worked as a sculptor before he became an architect (going on to build the celebrated dome of Santa Maria del Fiore). The "competition pieces" of Ghiberti and Brunelleschi (whose panel is illustrated on this page) are the only ones to have come down to us, evidently because both were greatly admired. Thus it is only natural for us to compare them.

In the first place Ghiberti demonstrated a total mastery of the technique, managing to cast the panel in a single piece and using a minimum of material. In addition, the judges must have appreciated the harmonious composition devised by the artist, perfectly in keeping with the shape of the frame and carefully balanced in its parts. The rock extends diagonally from top to bottom, splitting the scene into two distinct sections: on the one hand we see two servants waiting with a donkey, on the other Abraham about to sacrifice his son Isaac in obedience to God's command, when an angel appears and reaches out to prevent the terrible deed. The subject is by its nature dramatic, but Ghiberti handles it in a serene and relaxed manner, as is apparent from the elegant figure of Abraham, still in a Gothic style, and the harmonious nude body of Isaac which, together with the decoration of the sacrificial altar, harks back to classical art.

Brunelleschi, on the contrary, has interpreted the episode from the Bible in a more dramatic key, placing the accent on the emotions of the characters and thus making the story more relevant to his own time. In fact the artist has chosen to represent the crucial moment in which the angel checks Abraham's hand, causing him to turn his head abruptly. It is clear the tragedy has been averted at the very last instant.

So what was really at stake in the competition held in 1401 was the choice between two different figurative principles: Ghiberti's mythical and idealized interpretation in line with the late Gothic tradition and the new dynamic and dramatic conception of human history proposed by Brunelleschi.

North Door and Gates of Paradise
Baptistery, Florence

In 1425 Ghiberti was commissioned to make the third and last door of the baptistery in Florence, following the success he had achieved with the second. The first door had been executed by Andrea Pisano in the fourteenth century and is made up of panels with *Scenes from the Life of Saint John the Baptist*. The second (*North Door*), executed by Ghiberti after he had won the competition of 1401, comprises *Scenes from the New Testament*. The last door, finished by Ghiberti in 1452, presents *Scenes from the Old Testament*. For the latter the artist adopted a scheme different from that of the earlier ones, choosing to divide the two leaves of the door into larger and less numerous quadrangular panels (ten instead of twenty) and represent more than one episode in each. The panels of each leaf are surrounded by a frame with figures from the Bible: among them are portraits of Ghiberti himself and his son Vittore. The entire door (whose original panels, replaced in situ with copies, are now in the Museo dell'Opera del Duomo), is framed by a frieze with fruit, flowers and animals, with a gilded eagle,

emblem of the guild known as the Arte di Calimala which had commissioned the work, at the top. The bronze wings of the door are gilded with an extremely resistant amalgam of mercury that bestows a special sheen on the surface, as has been revealed by the restoration currently under way. This feature has earned the door the name of the *Golden Gate*, in addition to that of the *Gates of Paradise*.

Gates of Paradise: Scenes from the Story of Cain and Abel; Meeting between Solomon and the Queen of Sheba (pp. 98-9); Scenes from the Life of Joseph the Patriarch (p. 100)
gilded bronze, 79·5x80 cm each
Museo dell'Opera del Duomo, Florence

Over the many years that it took him to carry out the enterprise (almost three decades), Ghiberti changed and developed his style, nurturing a marked interest in perspective and in Donatello's *stiacciato* (cf. p. 85). In the early panels, in fact, such as the ones with the *Scenes from the Story of Cain and Abel*, the artist inserted the episodes and personages in a paratactic manner without organizing the composition in a logical, consistent and unitary fashion. In the later panels, however, the sculptor laid out the scenes on the basis of a predetermined and rational perspective design, giving greater relief and plastic emphasis to the volumes in the foreground than to the ones further back. Thus in the *Scenes from the Life of*

Joseph the Patriarch – one of the most highly appreciated even in the sources – the episodes are arranged in sequence, with the first ones set amidst the landscape in the background and then the others among the buildings. On the mountains at the top, Joseph is taken out of the well and sold by his brothers to the Ishmaelites, who take him to Egypt. In the foreground, inside the circular building, the harvest is being stored in Egypt's granaries in order to cope with the great famine predicted by Joseph in his interpretation of the pharaoh's dream. On the left, Joseph's cup is found in the bag of his brother Benjamin. Finally, in the background, Joseph, now raised to the highest honors by the grateful pharaoh, forgives his brothers and embraces Benjamin. The story places the emphasis on the figure of Joseph, whose wisdom and mercy allows him to bring prosperity and well-being to the people of Egypt and to his own brothers. In this there may be an allusion to the figure of Cosimo the Elder, who had returned from exile to Florence in 1434 and become the ruler of the city. Unlike the others, the panel with the *Meeting between Solomon and the Queen of Sheba* presents a single episode, and one that implicitly refers to a recent event: the council of the Eastern and Western Churches held in Florence in 1439 and which concluded with a decree of union between the two groups, signed in Santa Maria Novella. In the composition, the two figures meet and hold hands as if in a marriage celebrated against the backdrop of a temple with a nave and two aisles. At the sides, an orderly and silent crowd observes the solemn event.

L O R E N Z O   G H I B E R T I

Gates of Paradise:
Scenes from the Life of Joseph
the Patriarch
Museo dell'Opera del Duomo, Florence

Luca della Robbia

Luca (Florence 1399/1400-1482) was the son of Simone di Marco della Robbia, a dealer in woolen cloth. In fact the family surname probably derives from *rubeus*, the crimson color used to dye cloth. In 1432, Luca enrolled in the Guild of Stone and Woodworkers, even though he had already been a member of the Wool Guild for some time. In the same year of 1432 he received the commission to carve the *Cantoria* or *Singing Gallery* in Florence Cathedral, to serve as a companion to the contemporary one by Donatello. The unanimous admiration and appreciation aroused by the singing gallery earned Luca a series of commissions for the cathedral and the adjacent campanile. In 1436 Luca was cited by Leon Battista Alberti in the preface to his treatise *De Pictura* as one of the artists who were formulating the new Renaissance style in Florence, along with Brunelleschi, Masaccio, Donatello and Ghiberti.

At the end of the decade, Luca gave up sculpting in marble to develop the technique of glazed terracotta, which entailed applying colored glazes mixed with lead, tin and silica to make the surface of the fired clay shiny and resistant. The earliest work by Luca della Robbia making use of this technique to have come down to us is the tabernacle of the church of Sant'Egidio (now in Santa Maria at Peretola), dating from 1441. Luca della Robbia's glazed terracotta, in which the colors white and blue predominate, was also much appreciated by Filippo Brunelleschi. It may have been through the good offices of Brunelleschi himself that Luca came to execute the *Angels Holding Candles* in full relief and the lunette with the *Resurrection* (1442-44) and the *Ascension* (1446-51) for the cathedral, while he made the tondi in relief representing the *Evangelists* for the Pazzi Chapel in Santa Croce (1445-50). At the end of the forties he began to collaborate with the architect and sculptor Michelozzo on works commissioned by Piero de' Medici, such as the ceiling of the *studiolo* in Palazzo Medici (now dismantled and on show at the Victoria and Albert Museum in London) and the Tempietto of San Miniato al Monte.

Owing to its brilliant colors and low cost in comparison with materials like marble and bronze, the glazed terracotta developed by the della Robbia family was much in demand. It was used primarily as a decoration for people's homes and to make coats of arms and reliefs set on the exteriors of public buildings, hospitals and the headquarters of the city's guilds. On his death in 1482, Luca della Robbia bequeathed a profitable business to his family that was to survive for over a century, gradually assuming the characteristics of a factory.

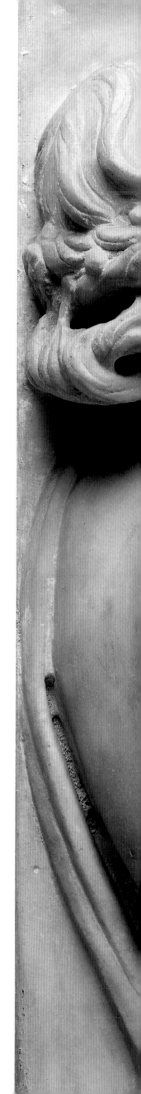

Cantoria or Singing Gallery
marble, 348x570 cm
Museo dell'Opera del Duomo, Florence

In the 1430s, while Filippo Brunelleschi was completing the dome of Florence Cathedral, Luca della Robbia and Donatello were commissioned to carve the *cantorie* or singing galleries to be located in the same building. These galleries were intended to house the organs that were used to accompany the singers during services. A comparison of the two works, removed from their original locations in 1688, offers a fascinating insight into the different personalities of the two great Renaissance artists.

Luca's *Cantoria* (1431-38) is the artist's earliest documented work and the most famous of all those that he produced in marble. The gallery has an architectural structure of classical inspiration, divided into ten quadrangular compartments, six on the parapet and four between the brackets that support the balcony. They are carved in relief with boys, girls and angels singing, playing instruments and dancing. The subject illustrates Psalm 150 of King David, whose verses, inscribed on the horizontal cornices, are an invitation to praise the Lord through song and music. The figures are carefully depicted, puffing out their cheeks to play the wind instruments, concentrating on finding the right tone of voice or bending their heads to listen to the music of the string instruments. Both reliefs and architectural structure are perfectly finished. The cleanness of the surfaces, the calm classicism of the forms and the limpid delight of the boys and girls convey a sense of balance and serenity, the fruit of a profound spiritual harmony.

Luca's *Cantoria* contrasts with and complements the exuberant and unrestrained dynamism of Donatello's (cf. pp. 86-7). Both artists set out to represent the joy of the young people that stems from their love of God. But where Luca shows a propensity to idealize that sentiment in an "Apollonian" spirit, Donatello displays a more dramatic and emotional temperament, which has been defined as "Dionysiac."

Madonna della Mela
(*Madonna with the Apple*)
glazed terracotta, 70x52 cm
Museo Nazionale del Bargello, Florence

From the 1440s onward, Luca della
Robbia gradually gave up working in
marble to devote himself to glazed
terracotta: the technique, which the artist
himself had developed, proved
increasingly popular. Originally in the
Medici collections, the *Madonna della
Mela* derives its name from the apple in
the Child's hand. The *Madonna and Child*
was the subject most in demand for
tabernacles and portable altars in glazed
terracotta used for private devotion.

Generally, they consisted of white figures
on a blue ground, in an allusion to purity,
divine light and heaven.
The glazed-terracotta Madonnas produced
in a great variety of iconographic versions
by Luca and then by his son Andrea were
commissioned not only by merchants,
bankers and intellectuals, but also by
confraternities, monastic orders and
hospitals. The fact is that the sense of
gentle and affectionate humanity that
pervades such figures was well suited to
the needs of a simple and direct devotion,
something sought by all types of client.

Resurrection
glazed terracotta, 200x260 cm
Santa Maria del Fiore, Florence

The positive reaction to his *Cantoria*
earned Luca della Robbia several other
important commissions from the
Cathedral Vestry Board. In particular, he
was entrusted with the two lunettes
representing the *Resurrection* (1442-44)
and the *Ascension* (1446-51) – located
under the two singing galleries – and the
bronze door of the Sacristy of the Masses,
executed later on and with the help of
collaborators.
The *Resurrection* has white figures on a
cobalt blue ground embellished with a
few gilt details that were applied after
firing, such as the haloes, rays, hems of
the clothing and hair. In addition, the
artist has retouched the clouds with paint.
This was the first time that Luca had used
the technique of glazed terracotta for a
work on a large scale. The lunette was
made in pieces and then assembled *in
situ*, like a sort of jigsaw puzzle. This was
made necessary by the limited size of the
kilns used to dry and fire the reliefs. In
addition, the production of the reliefs in
more than one piece made it easier to
correct any mistakes and to transport the
work to the place where it was to be
installed.

The Flood and the Retreat of the Waters, detail
detached fresco, 215x510 cm
Chiostro Verde, Santa Maria Novella, Florence

The fresco is part of a cycle with *Scenes from Genesis* painted mostly in green earth in one of the cloisters of the Dominican monastery of Santa Maria Novella, begun around 1425 by various artists. In the *Flood*, painted by Paolo Uccello after 1439, the scene is dominated by the hull of Noah's ark, presented in perspective and receding toward the horizon where the storm is raging. The wind drives the clouds and shakes the branches of the trees. The half-naked figures of desperate men are trying in vain to break into the hermetically sealed ark or trying to save

Paolo Uccello

Paolo (Florence 1397-1475) was the son of Dono, a barber-surgeon from Pratovecchio, and Antonia, who came from a noble family in Perugia. The byname Uccello ("Bird") may have been an allusion to the artist's passion for these creatures, which he kept in his home and liked to portray in his pictures.

A pupil of Ghiberti, he had begun to work independently as early as 1415, though we know nothing of his output during this period. In 1425 Paolo Uccello went to live for a while in Venice, where he produced cartoons for stained-glass windows and mosaics in St. Mark's. Back in Florence, he showed a growing interest in the recent works of his friend Donatello and of Masaccio. Spurred by this to carry out graphic experiments with foreshortening, Paolo adopted linear perspective as a means of representing a fantastic world of poetic charm and geometrical abstraction that demonstrated the artist's fascination with the Gothic manner.

In 1436 he was commissioned to fresco the *Equestrian Monument to Sir John Hawkwood*, the English mercenary who had won the battle of Cascina (1364) for Florence, in the left-hand aisle of the cathedral. Again for the cathedral, Paolo executed the cartoons of three stained-glass windows for the drum of the dome and the pictorial decoration of the clock face on the inside of the front wall (1443).

He may have painted the three panels with *The Battle of San Romano* (1435-40) for Cosimo de' Medici the Elder. The *Scenes from the Life of Noah* that Paolo frescoed in green earth in the cloister of Santa Maria Novella, where he had already worked ten years earlier, were particularly highly praised by his contemporaries for their daring use of foreshortening.

In 1445 Paolo Uccello set off for Padua, where Donatello had been working for some time on the altar of Il Santo. Here Paolo frescoed a monumental series of *Illustrious Men* in Palazzo Vitaliani (now lost) which were much admired by Andrea Mantegna.

Between 1465 and 1469 Paolo made repeated visits along with his son Donato to the court of Federico da Montefeltro at Urbino. The now elderly and ailing artist spent his last years in Florence, with Donato by his side, while his daughter Antonia, also a painter, became a nun.

themselves in makeshift vessels. The artist uses perspective as a means of bestowing the fantastic and visionary tones of a nightmare on the scene. As well as the ark itself, each element is subjected to an extreme and artificial foreshortening: the bolts of lighting, the trees, the ladder, the *mazzocchi* (fifteenth-century headgear of circular shape and with a checked

pattern) and even the mule carrying a young woman and her slumped companion on its back.

Battle of San Romano
panels, 182x317; 182x323; 180x316 cm
National Gallery, London; Galleria degli
Uffizi, Florence; Louvre, Paris

Masterpieces of the early Florentine
Renaissance, the three panels were
probably commissioned by Cosimo de'
Medici the Elder after 1435 for a
stateroom in the family palace. The battle
depicted by the painter took place in
1432 in the vicinity of the tower of San
Romano in Valdelsa (Tuscany) between
Florentine troops led by Niccolò da
Tolentino and Micheletto Attendolo da
Cotignola and the Sienese army
commanded by Bernardino Ubaldini della
Ciarda. In the picture in London Tolentino
is leading his own army into battle against
the Sienese; the crucial moment of the
encounter is represented in the panel in
the Uffizi, originally located in the middle
of the sequence, where Niccolò da
Tolentino unhorses Bernardino della
Ciarda; finally, in the painting in the
Louvre, Cotignola advances with the rest
of the Florentine troops to finish off the
already hard-pressed Sienese.
There is nothing violent and cruel about
Paolo Uccello's interpretation of the
battle. On the contrary, he has given it an
epic and fabulous tone and set it in an
abstract and surreal atmosphere. The
horses and knights are in frozen poses,
like manikins incapable of displaying
emotion and condemned to eternal
immobility. In the background a hunting
scene is set in a hilly landscape, which
rises up to block any view of the horizon
and the sky. In the foreground, each
element is subordinated to an insistent
and contrived scheme of perspective: note
the broken halberds, shields and bodies
lying on the ground, in the pattern of a
foreshortened checkerboard. Thus Paolo
Uccello did not adopt perspective as a
means of describing reality in a more
lucid and rational manner, but of
transfiguring it into a fantastic and
enchanted world that still spoke the
language of International Gothic.

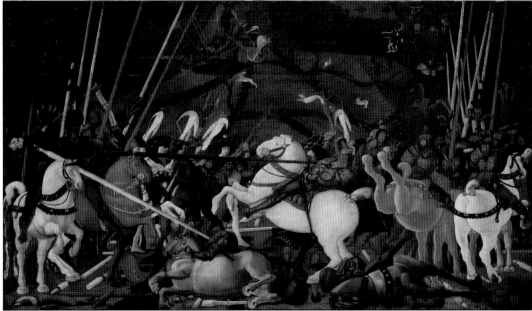

Fra Angelico

The life of Fra Giovanni da Fiesole – in the world, Guido di Pietro (Vicchio di Mugello, *c.* 1395-Rome 1455) – rapidly took on legendary tones: just a century after the artist's death, the biographer Giorgio Vasari (1568) dubbed the Dominican friar and painter "angelic" for his piety and inclination to mysticism. Commentators built up this legend even further in the nineteenth century.

Born at Vicchio di Mugello to the north of Florence at the end of the fourteenth century, Guido di Pietro took his vows at the monastery of San Domenico in Fiesole around 1418, assuming the name of Fra Giovanni. Trained in the late Gothic manner and influenced by the illumination and gold work of Northern Europe, Fra Angelico's cultural interests and artistic style had a great deal in common with those of the sculptor Lorenzo Ghiberti, with whom he collaborated on the *Linaiuoli Altarpiece* (1433; Museo di San Marco, Florence): in fact the two artists made themselves champions of a balanced and intelligent reform of art, opting for solutions that would reconcile the old and the new, the elegant late Gothic style imported from France and the rigorous use of perspective and modeling promoted by Donatello and Masaccio. These were combined with an attention to minute detail drawn from Flemish art.

In 1438, Fra Angelico moved to the convent of San Marco in Florence, which was being renovated under the supervision of the architect Michelozzo. Thus the artist was given the task of decorating the monastery, painting the altarpiece for the high altar of the church (1438-43; *San Marco Altarpiece*; Museo di San Marco, Florence) and frescoes in the friar's cells. He had several assistants in the undertaking, including Benozzo Gozzoli (pp. 128-31).

Summoned to Rome by Eugenius IV in 1446 to paint in the Vatican palaces, Fra Angelico was then commissioned by his successor, Nicholas V, to fresco the pope's private chapel with *Scenes from the Lives of Saints Lawrence and Stephen*. In 1447 the artist temporarily interrupted his stay in Rome to go to Orvieto, where he frescoed the chapel of San Brizio in the cathedral with the help of the members of his workshop.

Returning to Florence, Fra Angelico was appointed prior of the monastery of San Domenico at Fiesole in 1450, a post that he held until 1452. After declining the commission to paint a cycle of frescoes in Prato Cathedral (which was then given to Fra Filippo Lippi, p. 124), he left for the papal see again. He died in Rome in February 1455 and was buried in the Dominican church of Santa Maria sopra Minerva. A few weeks later Pope Nicholas V followed him to the grave.

The Naming of John the Baptist
panel, 26x24 cm
Museo di San Marco, Florence

The small panel was probably part of a predella, but so far it has not been possible to reconstruct the rest. The scene represents Zacharias who, struck dumb, writes down the name to be given to his newborn son. It is an early work by Fra Angelico, who was trained as an illuminator in the late Gothic tradition and therefore devotes a great deal of attention to a meticulous depiction of the details of the flowered sward, the foliage of the trees and the gilded ornaments of the clothing. At the same time, however, it is clear that the painter was influenced by the more innovative of contemporary works of art: the pose adopted by Zacharias, for instance, is a free citation of the crouching figure of St. Peter in Masaccio's *Tribute Money* (p. 78).

Deposition from the Cross
panel, 185x176 cm
Museo di San Marco, Florence

The painting was commissioned by the wealthy merchant Palla Strozzi, who wanted it for the sacristy in the family church of Santa Trinita, for which he had already ordered Gentile da Fabriano's *Adoration of the Magi* (pp. 64-7). When Fra Angelico started work on the picture in the 1430s, the cusps and predella had already been painted by Lorenzo Monaco, a Florentine artist in the late Gothic mold who died in 1425.

At the center of the *Deposition* stands the cross, from which Joseph of Arimathea, Nicodemus and St. John (all three of them with haloes) are taking down Christ's body. The other man with a black cap may be a portrait of Michelozzo di Bartolomeo, Cosimo the Elder's favorite architect and the man placed in charge of the renovation of the monastery of San Marco. On the left we see the holy women, while several men dressed in fifteenth-century clothes look on from the right, including the kneeling figure of the

client's ancestor, the Blessed Alessio Strozzi.

Although set in a late Gothic frame divided into three by pointed arches, the scene has a unified setting consisting of a springtime landscape. A clear and crystalline light, entering from the left, plays over the ramparts of the castles, the walls of the city, the steep slopes of the hills, the boughs of the trees and finally the white body of Christ. Overall, the calm and solemn composition and the brilliant and vivid palette suggest a serene contemplation of the Gospel story, in which the drama of Christ's death is balanced by the hope of his resurrection.

The eye of the observer is able to range all the way to the pale blue sky flecked with white clouds, over a countryside divided into fields by hedges and dotted with buildings of a wholly Tuscan appearance. An attempt has been made at their identification: the town ringed with walls may be based on a view of Cortona, while the building with the battlemented tower on the left is reminiscent of Trebbio Castle, then the property of the Medici.

FRA ANGELICO

Deposition from the Cross,
details
Museo di San Marco, Florence

s nobila Triolinian

ETERFVNDO CAVE NE SILEATVR AVE

Annunciation
fresco, 230x297 cm
Museo di San Marco, Florence

The *Annunciation*, located in the second corridor on the second floor of the monastery of San Marco (now a museum), is perhaps the most celebrated of all the frescoes painted by Fra Angelico round about 1440 for the Dominican community in which he lived.
The sacred event takes place under a portico, whose architecture resembles that of the cloister of Michelozzo's monastery. The portico faces onto a walled garden filled with flowers, an interpretation of the *hortus conclusus* that symbolized Mary's virginity in the Middle Ages. The sobriety and clarity of the architectural style reflect the feelings of Mary, who accepts the news of her impending motherhood with astonishment but serenity and composure. The outspread wings of the angel, who is bowing in reverence, are brightly colored and dotted with gold. The atmosphere is solemn and peaceful, silent and tranquil.

FRA ANGELICO

Baptism of Christ
fresco, 179x148 cm
Museo di San Marco, Florence

The fresco, like others in the cells of San Marco, was painted by Fra Angelico's assistants to their master's design. In fact, it must have been the friar who conceived the landscape viewed in perspective from above and extending to the horizon, where unreal colors light up the sky on the arrival of the dove: thus the narration assumes tones appropriate to a miraculous event.

Christ Mocked
fresco, 187x151 cm
Museo di San Marco, Florence

The picture represents the sufferings of Christ before being sentenced to crucifixion in a synthetic and allusive manner: the profile of a man spitting, the hands slapping him or striking him with a rod. At the center, in a raised position against the backdrop of a green panel, sits Christ dressed in a white tunic and blindfolded, wearing the crown of thorns and holding the symbols of his martyrdom: the reed and the sponge. Below the step, the weeping Virgin is seated in sorrowful meditation. Beside her, St. Dominic is absorbed in reading the account of the Passion in the Holy Scriptures.
While the scene has a limpid and rational layout, it conveys the abstract atmosphere of a vision alluding to an unfathomable mystery but one that is filled with spiritual meaning.

kneeling deacon saint, in a secluded courtyard where the two soldiers with their backs to us have discreetly averted their gaze. The artist lingers over the description of the clothes, the objects and the classical architecture, while the observer's eye is drawn into the pontiff's private chambers through the deserted cloister in the background.

A contrived and spectacular perspective dominates the episode with *Saint Lawrence Distributing Alms*, which symbolizes the Church's dispensing of the gifts of divine grace to the Christian community. The saint is placed at the center of the composition, in front of the elegant portal of a basilica through which we can see the nave. The alms he is distributing are the fruit of the gifts he has just received from the pope. Around him the beggars, destitute and disabled, wait their turn with dignity. The refined gold highlights of the saint's robe contrast with the modesty of their clothing, but in comparison with the derelicts represented by Masaccio in the Brancacci Chapel twenty years earlier (p. 80), Fra Angelico's display a dignity and an almost otherworldly resignation.

Scenes from the Life of Saint Lawrence: *Saint Lawrence Receiving the Gifts of the Church*; *Saint Lawrence Distributing Alms*
fresco, 271x205 cm each
Nicholas V's Chapel, Vatican

In 1447 Fra Angelico was called to Rome by Pope Nicholas V to fresco the *Scenes from the Lives of Saints Lawrence and Stephen* in the pontiff's private chapel. A Humanist, lover of literature and the arts and the advocate of a policy that attempted to reconcile ancient Roman culture with that of Christianity, Nicholas V saw the two martyred saints as the founders of the Christian Church on the ruins of the pagan world.

The artist set the scenes in a Rome where buildings of the late imperial era stand alongside Renaissance buildings. His style, sober and rigorous in the Florentine works, took on a courtly and monumental tone in the Vatican apartments.

In the scene in which *Saint Lawrence Receives the Gifts of the Church*, Pope Sixtus II (in reality a portrait of Nicholas V) and his assistants lavish gifts on the

Filippo Lippi

Of humble origin and orphaned while still a boy, Filippo Lippi (Florence *c.* 1406-Spoleto 1469) took his vows at the monastery of Santa Maria del Carmine in 1421. Masaccio was painting the Brancacci Chapel at the time and he was able to watch him work. In 1430 he was first mentioned in the monastery records as a painter.

In 1434 Filippo went to Padua, where he executed works in the basilica of Il Santo and in the Palazzo del Podestà, all of which have now vanished. During his stay there he encountered the antiquarian taste of the local cultural circles and studied Flemish paintings in the collections of the nearby city of Venice.

In Florence Filippo painted altarpieces for the chapels of some of the city's most important churches, such as Santo Spirito, San Lorenzo and Sant'Ambrogio. He was also much appreciated as a painter of works intended for private devotion (including portable altars, small arched panels and tondi, most of them representing the *Madonna and Child*, *Annunciation* or *Nativity*).

In 1452 the commune of Prato entrusted Lippi with the fresco decoration of the chancel of the cathedral, after the job had been turned down by Fra Angelico. In May 1454, Lippi settled in Prato and with the help of Fra Diamante and local craftsmen executed the *Scenes from the Lives of Saint Stephen and Saint John the Baptist*, as well as the design for the stained-glass window, an undertaking which he did not complete until 1465. In the meanwhile he was appointed chaplain to the nuns of Santa Margherita at Prato in 1456. It was here that he met the nun Lucrezia Buti, with whom he eloped and who bore him a son, Filippino. Cosimo de' Medici the Elder took a personal interest in Filippo Lippi's situation, as he was one of his favorite artists: in 1461, through the good offices of the Medici, Pope Pius II gave Filippo and Lucrezia permission to marry, releasing them from their vows.

In 1466 Lippi was commissioned to fresco the *Scenes from the Life of the Virgin* in the apse of Spoleto Cathedral. Moving to the Umbrian city, Filippo set about the task with the assistance of – among others – Fra Diamante and his son Filippino. Dying in Spoleto in 1469, he was buried in the cathedral, where Lorenzo the Magnificent had a sepulchral monument erected to him: made to a design by Filippino, it was inscribed with commemorative verses by Politian.

Coronation of the Virgin
panel, 200x287 cm
Galleria degli Uffizi, Florence

Completed in 1447 by Filippo Lippi, the monumental altarpiece – now lacking its original frame – was located on the high altar of the church of Sant'Ambrogio. The work was commissioned by Francesco Maringhi, governor and procurator of the church, who is represented on the right alongside St. John the Baptist. On the opposite side the painter has portrayed himself in the guise of the Carmelite friar in an informal and pensive attitude. Along with St. John the Baptist, the protector of Florence and particularly dear to the client, we see St. Ambrose, to whom the church is dedicated.

The composition is orchestrated in an original way, laid out in a range of different planes and foreshortened views. At top center the Virgin is being crowned by God the Father, instead of Christ as was the tradition. On the platform at the foot of the throne, a group of saints is kneeling on the marble floor, some of them gazing toward the observer. Saints and angels are arranged in three rows on each side of the imposing structure of the throne. The scenes are set against a backdrop of diagonal light and dark blue bands, which recalls the drape of an awning. The sacred scene assumes the characteristics of a contemporary and mundane representation.

FILIPPO LIPPI

Annunciation
panel, 155x144 cm
Galleria Nazionale di Palazzo Barberini,
Rome

Painted around the same times as the
Maringhi *Coronation*, the picture was
originally located in the oratory of the
Bardi Larioni family at Pian di Ripoli in
the environs of Florence. The donors,
portrayed in a separate group on the
right, may be Alessandro de' Bardi and
Lorenzo di Ilarione de' Bardi: their
presence is unusual as it was rare for
clients to be represented in sacred scenes
of a narrative character, within the same
setting and in such lively and natural
attitudes.
The scene takes place in an elegant
fifteenth-century chamber, with a marble
floor and columns, painted ceilings, finely
inlaid furniture and gold embroidered

fabrics. The female figures climbing the
stairs beyond the door on the right may
be an allusion to the virgins who in
medieval legend attended the ceremony of
Mary's presentation in the temple.

Madonna and Child and Scenes from the Life of Saint Anne (*Bartolini Tondo*)
panel, diam. 135 cm
Galleria Palatina, Florence

The work, executed by Filippo Lippi
around 1453, is one of the earliest tondi
of the Renaissance. These circular
pictures were painted to be hung in
private homes and were usually
commissioned to celebrate marriages or
births.
The Virgin is represented in the

foreground seated on an elegant chair
with the Infant Jesus in her lap. He is
holding up the seed of a pomegranate,
symbol of Christ's Passion. Behind the
sacred group opens a series of rooms in
which two *Scenes from the Life of Saint
Anne*, Mary's mother, are set: the
meeting between Joachim and Anne
(an episode that actually took place at
the Golden Gate in Jerusalem) is
depicted on the staircase; in the
bedchamber, located closer to the
foreground, Anne has given birth to Mary
and several women are gathered around
her bed. The daylight entering through
the windows imparts an intimate and
domestic atmosphere to the rooms. The
female figures, painted in vibrant and
sinuous lines, are animated by
spontaneous gestures like that of the
young mother in the red cloak, to which
her child clings, begging to be picked up.

Benozzo Gozzoli

B enozzo di Lese, known as Benozzo Gozzoli (Florence *c.* 1421-Pistoia 1497), received a sound academic education and then served an apprenticeship with Fra Angelico, becoming his most important assistant on the decoration of the convent of San Marco. In 1444 he signed a contract committing him to collaborate for at least three years on the execution of Lorenzo Ghiberti's *Gates of Paradise* (p. 96). But in 1447, before the contract had expired, Benozzo accompanied Fra Angelico to Rome to work at the court of the newly elected Pope Nicholas V.
On Fra Angelico's death (1455), Benozzo embarked on a prolific and independent career, working largely outside the walls of Florence, in the smaller towns and cities of Tuscany and especially those of Umbria and Lazio in the Papal States.
Between 1450 and 1452 he executed numerous works at Montefalco: the cycles of frescoes he painted for the churches of San Fortunato and San Francesco aroused particular interest. After another stay in Rome, where he painted standards to commemorate the election of Pope Pius II Piccolomini (1458), Benozzo returned to Florence where, in 1459, Cosimo de' Medici the Elder and his son Piero commissioned him to fresco the chapel of the new family palace. This is Benozzo's masterpiece, whose fame has surpassed that of the artist himself.
From 1464 to 1467 Gozzoli was in San Gimignano, where he painted frescoes in the main chapel of Sant'Agostino. Moving to Pisa, he devoted most of his time up until 1484 to frescoing the north wall of the Camposanto with *Scenes from the Old Testament*. In 1494, with the arrival of King Charles VIII of France and the expulsion of the Medici from Florence, Benozzo returned home, but only for a few years. In fact he soon moved to Pistoia where his two children were already living and where he continued to work up until his death in 1497, perhaps from the plague.

Journey of the Magi
fresco
Palazzo Medici Riccardi, Florence

In the spring of 1459 the Medici entrusted Benozzo Gozzoli with the task of frescoing the chapel in the new family palace designed for them by Michelozzo. In this small private place of worship, which the illustrious family also used for official political meetings, Benozzo represented the *Journey of the Magi*.
The journey of the Three Kings is depicted in a single scene that covers all the walls, starting from the right, where Jerusalem has the appearance of a walled Tuscan city. It concludes on the left, on the walls of the rectangular apse where, in the setting of a garden ringed with rosebushes, the angels are worshiping the Child born in Bethlehem, an event that is represented in the picture of the *Nativity* on the altar (the original by Filippo Lippi is now in Berlin). The processions of the three Magi are set against the backdrop of a fertile, hilly landscape in the springtime, with Tuscan and fifteenth-century characteristics: alongside the hunting scenes

with men and animals in pursuit of deer, there are even wild beasts like leopards attacking their prey. In the retinue of the youngest Magus it is possible to recognize several portraits of members of the Medici family: Cosimo is riding a finely caparisoned mule, Piero is on a white horse and wearing a red cap, his brother Giovanni is standing, dressed as a halberdier and, behind the group, Carlo – Cosimo's natural son – has a headband wrapped around his black hair. The boy with a prominent nose in the group in the background may be a portrait of Piero's still young son, Lorenzo the Magnificent (Acidini, 1993). Just above him is Benozzo himself, with his name inscribed in gold letters on his red hat.

The recent restoration (1988-92) has revealed the high technical quality of the work, the preciousness of the materials used (lapis lazuli, pure gold) and the fine detail in which the artist has depicted the landscape, animals, clothing and jewelry. In a work intended to celebrate the family that commissioned it and to stir a sense of wonder in their guests, like a jewel casket opened up to reveal its precious contents, Benozzo has combined the perspective of the early Renaissance and the limpid light and poetic enchantment of Fra Angelico's colors with the worldly taste of the International Gothic and the meticulous description of Flemish art.

Piero della Francesca

Piero was born around 1416 in the upper valley of the Tiber on the border between Tuscany, Umbria and the Marche (Sansepolcro 1416/17-1492). Son of the cobbler Benedetto de' Franceschi and Romana di Perino from Monterchi, Piero assumed the patronymic "della Francesca."

The young artist probably served an apprenticeship in the Florentine workshop of Domenico Veneziano and in 1439 was working as his assistant on the frescoes with *Scenes from the Life of the Virgin* (now vanished) in the church of Sant'Egidio.

Returning to Sansepolcro, he maintained links with his hometown all his life, in spite of frequent and prolonged stays at the courts of Central and Northern Italy. At Sansepolcro, Piero held various public posts and received a number of artistic commissions. As early as 1445 he was entrusted with the task of painting the *Madonna della Misericordia* for the altar of the confraternity of the same name, though it was not finished until 1462.

In the meanwhile, Piero began to frequent the Montefeltro court at Urbino and paid visits to several centers in the Marche and Emilia Romagna (Ferrara, Rimini, Ancona, Pesaro and Bologna), where many of the works he left have now been lost. In Rimini he frescoed *Sigismondo Malatesta and His Patron Saint* (1451) in the Tempio Malatestiano: the building had been renovated to the design of the architect and treatise writer Leon Battista Alberti, whom the painter got to know on that occasion.

After 1452 Piero della Francesca began to fresco the main chapel of San Francesco in Arezzo with *Scenes from the Legend of the True Cross*, one of the greatest masterpieces of the Italian Renaissance and a condensation of the artistic developments of the preceding decades. In 1458 Piero went to Rome, to the court of Pope Pius II, for whom he painted pictures in the Vatican Palaces that have now disappeared.

Returning to Sansepolcro, he held several public appointments in his hometown and the Arezzo region while establishing close ties with Federico da Montefeltro. He made repeated stays at the latter's court in Urbino, a crossroads for works, artists and intellectuals from various parts of Italy and Europe. Piero's principal works for the duke of Urbino date from the sixties and seventies: the *Flagellation*, the *Portraits of Federico da Montefeltro and Battista Sforza* and the *Brera Madonna*.

Before his death in 1492, the painter dedicated the last years of his life to writing a couple of treatises: the *De prospectiva pingendi*, which explains the application of perspective to painting in logical and mathematical terms, and the *Libellus de quinque corporibus regularibus*, in which the author theorizes about an ideal and perfect world of harmony where visible forms and volumes are reduced to regular solids.

Legend of the True Cross: Constantine's Dream
fresco, 329x190 cm
San Francesco, Arezzo

The *Legend of the True Cross* in the church of San Francesco at Arezzo is one of the greatest masterpieces of European art, on a par with Giotto's frescoes in Assisi and Padua, Masaccio's in Santa Maria del Carmine at Florence, Michelangelo's in the Sistine Chapel and Leonardo's *Last Supper* in Santa Maria delle Grazie at Milan. Based on Jacobus de Voragine's *Golden Legend*, the scenes tell the story of Christ's Cross, built out of the wood of the tree that grew on Adam's tomb and then hidden, rediscovered, stolen and finally brought back in triumph to Jerusalem: a story spanning centuries that is recounted through the paintings on the walls of San Francesco in a unitary, majestic and solemn fashion, bound together by the thread of the immanent and mysterious presence of God, guiding the Cross to victory over paganism. These are themes and allusions that in the time of Piero and the probable client Giovanni Bacci – who had links with cultured ecclesiastic circles – reflected the widespread call for a crusade to defeat the Turks who were battering on the gates of Christendom. Piero was entrusted with the commission after the death of Bicci di Lorenzo (1452), who had already frescoed the ceiling with the *Four Evangelists*, the intrados of the arch with two *Doctors of the Church* and the outer wall of the entrance arch with the *Last Judgment*. The date of completion of the work is uncertain, but must have been 1466 at the latest.

Over the centuries the cycle of frescoes has survived the ravages of time, infiltrations of water, earthquakes, the damage caused by Napoleon's troops when they were stationed in the church, modern-day pollution and a number of incompetent earlier interventions. But it is only thanks to the latest restoration, which lasted about fifteen years and has just been completed, that the masterpiece can be said to have been saved. The thorough diagnostic investigations that were carried out prior to the intervention have revealed that Piero adopted other techniques alongside fresco – including oil – that were customarily used for panel painting. But unlike Leonardo in his *Last Supper* (pp. 216-9), Piero had mastered them sufficiently to be able to prevent subsequent alterations: for instance, he did not use white lead, which tends to darken in wall paintings. The restoration proper entailed consolidating the walls, removing encrusted material, filling in gaps with reversible methods where possible and putting a definitive halt to the disastrous phenomenon of sulfation in the plaster (i.e. the conversion of calcium carbonate into calcium sulfate, or gypsum, which then crumbles away, taking the fresco with it). Today, it is possible for us to fully appreciate the quality of the painting in the *Legend of the True Cross*, which has regained its luminosity and clarity and produced some surprises, such as the bright red of the drapes and the brilliance of the skies. An example of this is the scene with *Constantine's Dream* (reproduced here from a photograph taken prior to the restoration), hitherto considered one of the most celebrated nocturnes in the history of art: in reality the apparition of the angel to the emperor takes place against the backdrop of a dawning sky in which the stars are still visible, something which had previously been obscured by the layers of oxidized varnish.

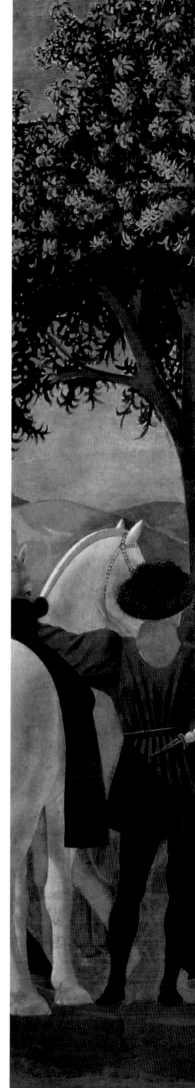

PIERO DELLA FRANCESCA

Legend of the True Cross:
The Adoration of the Sacred Wood
and the Meeting of Solomon
and the Queen of Sheba
fresco, 336x747 cm
San Francesco, Arezzo

After thousands of years the tree that
grew on Adam's tomb was cut down to
provide timber for the construction of
Solomon's temple. Proving unsuitable,
however, the Sacred Wood was used to
build the bridge over the river Siloe. As
the Queen of Sheba comes to the bridge
she kneels, recognizing the wood
destined to become the cross on which
the Savior would die. Received by

Solomon, the queen reveals her
premonition to him. The scene is that of
a ceremony conducted in a slow and
subdued manner, as was the custom at
fifteenth-century courts.

Legend of the True Cross:
The Battle of Heraclius and
Khosrow
fresco, 329x742 cm
San Francesco, Arezzo

Khosrow, king of the Persians, has
gained possession of the Cross and used
it to adorn his throne. Heraclius,
emperor of the East, then leads the

Christian army into a violent battle
– represented as a modern crusade –
against the Persians. Defeated, Khosrow
is forced to kneel by the Christians in
front of his sacrilegious throne, with the
Sacred Wood alongside it.

Madonna del Parto
detached fresco, 260x203 cm
Monterchi (Arezzo)

Inside a tent held open by two angels, the austere and solemn Madonna is touching her swollen belly, which protrudes from the pleated opening of her maternity dress and in which she carries her Son, the Word incarnate. The Virgin's gesture is slow and grave, like that of a sacred ceremony. The iconography, rare in Italian art, lends itself to suggestive interpretations (Calvesi, 1989) which refer to a passage in *Exodus* (XXVI, 1-14): the tent is the Church, the house of God, and the Virgin inside it is the tabernacle, the ark of the covenant constructed by Moses, a prefiguration of the ciborium of the Mass that houses the body of Christ.

After its recent restoration (1992) the fresco, detached in the past and completed at the top in a rough and ready manner, has been moved for reasons of conservation, but it is likely that it will soon be returned to its original location, the chapel of the cemetery of Monterchi that was once known as Santa Maria a Momentana.

Resurrection
fresco, 225x200 cm
Museo Civico, Sansepolcro

Around 1460, Piero frescoed the *Resurrection* in the Palazzo dei Conservatori of Borgo Sansepolcro, now the seat of the Museo Civico. The subject was particularly dear to the inhabitants of the Tuscan town, in that the origins of

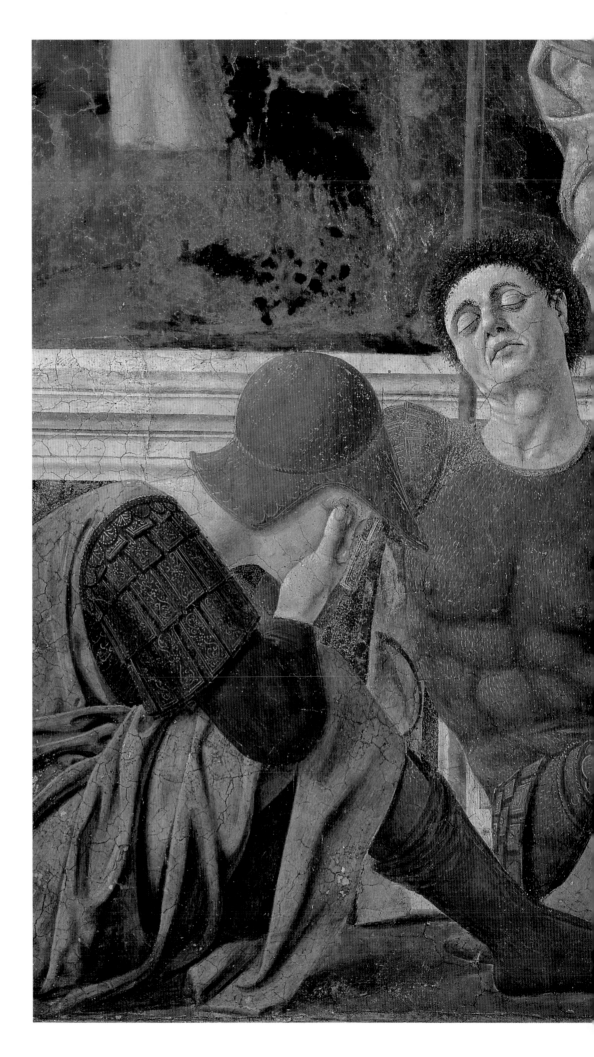

Sansepolcro ("Holy Sepulcher" in Italian)
were linked to the legend of a sacred relic
brought back from the Holy Land by two
pilgrims in the eleventh century.
Piero's composition is solemn and
mysterious, steeped in an atmosphere of
silent immobility. The hilly landscape
behind is bathed in the rosy light of dawn,
extending bleak and bare on the left of the
Savior and green and lush on the opposite
side, an allusion to the Resurrection as
renovatio mundi, i.e. as a cosmic
renewal of nature, and to Christ as a
symbol of life triumphing over darkness.
Piero has laid out the scene from two
different points of view: one at the level of
the sarcophagus and the other
perpendicular to the head of Christ,
whose appearance is majestic and
imposing.
The soldier sleeping with his head resting
on the edge of the sarcophagus has
traditionally been recognized as a portrait
of the artist.

The Flagellation
panel, 59x81·5 cm
Galleria Nazionale delle Marche, Urbino

The *Flagellation* is a painting that still
leaves many questions open with regard
to its meaning and to the identity of the
three figures represented. However, it
seems probable that the picture refers to
some contemporary event, which has
been interpreted in various ways: to cite
just two examples, the assassination of
Oddantonio, the brother of Duke Federico
da Montefeltro of Urbino, and the crusade
invoked by Pope Pius II following the fall
of Constantinople to the Turks. Such
interpretations are of course linked to the
date of the work, for which the experts
have made proposals varying from the
1440s to the early 1460s.
The true protagonist of the painting is the
perspective: the scene is laid out on the
basis of a rigid framework that organizes
the space defined by the architecture
according to precise numerical
proportions. The figures participate in the
event with imperturbable calm, immersed
in the atmosphere of lucid and abstract
equilibrium suggested by the composition
as a whole. The architecture, painted and
adorned in the antique manner, is
inspired by the theoretical studies and
buildings of Leon Battista Alberti, whom
Piero had met at Rimini in 1451.

*Portraits of Battista Sforza
and Federico da Montefeltro*
panels, 47x33 cm each
Galleria degli Uffizi, Florence

The two portraits are part of a diptych
painted on both sides: on the back are set
allegorical triumphs of the duke and
duchess that celebrate Federico's military
and political skills and Battista's moral
and Christian virtues.
The sitters are represented in profile in
the manner of ancient medals and appear
to be looking out of a window at a bird's

eye view of a landscape extending to the
horizon. The light that picks out the
minutest details, from the precious and
transparent pearls worn by Battista to the
imperfections in Federico's features,
creates shadows and reflections in the
landscape, among the foliage of the trees,
along the watercourses and on the ridges
of the hills.
Battista's face has a waxy pallor, and this
has led critics to suspect that the image
was painted from the death mask of the
woman, who died in 1472. This
hypothesis is supported by the Latin

inscription that accompanies the triumph
on the back, based on classical funeral
orations. This means that the diptych
would have been painted after 1472.
In this work Piero unites his propensity to
represent volumes in perspective, defined
by a clear and transparent light and by
limpid and pure colors, with a marked
interest in the qualities of the surfaces of
things, from the tiniest to the biggest,
from the closest to the most distant. This
interest was probably stimulated by the
artist's study of the Flemish paintings that
he saw at the court of Urbino.

PIERO DELLA FRANCESCA

Madonna and Child with Angels and Saints and Duke Federico da Montefeltro (*Brera Madonna*)
panel, 248x170 cm
Pinacoteca di Brera, Milan

Saints and angels, imperturbable and majestic in appearance, are arranged in a circle around the enthroned Virgin, like works of architecture constructing a circular space around a central axis. Federico da Montefeltro, duke of Urbino and client of the picture, is kneeling in prayer in the foreground, portrayed in profile. Painted between 1472 and 1474 for a church in Urbino, this *Sacra Conversazione* is set inside a church against the background of an apse with panels of colored marble and a coffered ceiling. From the conch hangs an ostrich's egg, symbol of the Virgin's Immaculate Conception and at the same time heraldic device of the Montefeltro family. The presence of St. John the Baptist may be an allusion to Battista Sforza, Federico's consort who had died in childbirth in 1472, while the sleeping Child, in itself a prefiguration of Christ's death, has also been interpreted as a reference to the birth of Guidobaldo, heir to the ducal throne. Finally, Federico's military dress could be a celebration of his conquest of Volterra on June 18, 1472. Through the reference to contemporary events, however, the composition can be seen as a sort of solemn consecration of the power of Federico da Montefeltro, recognized and legitimized by the Virgin as well as by the angels and saints who accompany her.

Antonio Pollaiolo

ntonio Benci, called Pollaiolo (Florence 1431/32-Rome 1498), was a gold- and silversmith, a sculptor highly skilled in the casting of bronze, a painter and an engraver, who headed one of the most important and versatile workshops in Florence. His father Jacopo Benci, a poulterer (*pollaiolo* in Italian), had noticed the artistic talents of both his sons and had sent the elder of the two, Antonio, to study with a goldsmith and the younger, Piero, with a painter.

Most of Antonio's early works were in gold or silver, such as the upper part of the silver *Cross-Reliquary* for the altar of Florence Baptistery (1457-59; now in the Museo dell'Opera del Duomo, Florence). He made several church ornaments in silver for the baptistery, as well as twenty-six designs for the embroidery of the precious vestments of San Giovanni (1469-83). As a painter, Antonio often worked in collaboration with his brother Piero on compositions in which it is difficult to distinguish the contributions of the two artists: an example is the altarpiece with *Three Saints* for the Cardinal of Portugal's chapel in San Miniato (1466; Uffizi, Florence).

In the seventies Antonio worked for Federico da Montefeltro, duke of Urbino, who in 1473 wrote Lorenzo the Magnificent a letter warmly recommending Pollaiolo. Lorenzo came to esteem him highly too and it was for him that the artist executed the small bronze of *Hercules and Antaeus* (Bargello, Florence). His contact with the cultivated and refined atmosphere of the Medici circles led Antonio to realize a series of works on a small scale (paintings and sculptures): intended for the setting of a study, they were appreciated by scholars and collectors of rare objects of the highest quality. Thus Antonio showed a preference for mythological themes drawn from ancient models or suggested by exponents of the neoplatonic ideas that were so much in vogue in Florence at the time, such as Marsilio Ficino.

In 1484 Antonio moved to Rome, where with the collaboration of his brother Piero he executed the sepulchral monuments for Popes Sixtus IV (1484-93) and Innocent VIII (1492-98), both in St. Peter's. Following his death in 1498, he was buried in San Pietro in Vincoli, where his brother's body had been laid to rest two years earlier.

Hercules and Antaeus
small bronze, ht. 45 cm
Museo Nazionale del Bargello,
Florence

Executed around 1475, the work used to be in the collection of Lorenzo the Magnificent. It represents Hercules engaged in one of his most famous labors: the hero is suffocating Antaeus and lifting him off the ground, as contact with his mother Gaea, the Earth Goddess, rendered him immortal. The tightly clasped bodies exhibit a centrifugal tension, moving in different directions and invading the surrounding space in a dynamic way. In fact the sculpture has no privileged point of view but invites the observer to look at it from all sides and explore the careful study of anatomy in movement.

In choosing to make a small bronze, Pollaiolo revived an antique genre that had been much in vogue at the courts of imperial Rome and at the same time created the prototype of a production that was to prove extremely popular in the sixteenth century.

ANTONIO POLLAIOLO

Battle of the Nudes

engraving on copper, 38x59·5 cm
Gabinetto Disegni e Stampe degli Uffizi,
Florence

The subject of the print is unknown, but it
may have been a sort of exercise in the
representation of bodies in movement
based on an ancient sarcophagus. In fact,
the naked figures engaged in hand-to-
hand fighting are shown in a variety of
poses and from different points of view:
thus the artist is exploring possible
solutions for depicting the tension and

movement of the human body and
creating a three-dimensional effect. This
effect derives not just from the use of light
and shade, but also from the agile and
forceful, vibrant and restless line,
emphasized by the technique of engraving.
Signed at top left, a number of copies of
the print were distributed and used to
train artists in Florence over the last few
decades of the fifteenth century. Before
1468, moreover, one of them was in use
in the Paduan workshop of Squarcione,
the teacher of Andrea Mantegna.

Portrait of a Woman

panel, 47·6x34·5 cm
Museo Poldi Pezzoli, Milan

Like a number of other paintings by
Antonio Pollaiolo and his brother Piero,
this portrait represents a woman in
profile against a neutral background. The
young woman has her hair tied back and
held by a *frenello*, consisting of a rope of
pearls fixed to a gold braid that binds and
covers the tresses, keeping them in place
with a transparent veil that reaches down
to the ears. The sitter is well characterized

and the fixity of her pose seems to be only
apparent, momentary. Her expressive eye
looks as if it is about to turn, her lips to
open, her neck to tilt. The profile is
defined by a supple and vibrant line,
which hints at the vital energy inherent in
the form.

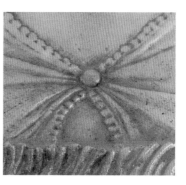

Andrea del Verrocchio

I n 1457, after serving an apprenticeship in a goldsmith's workshop, Andrea di Michele (Florence 1435-Venice 1485) became the partner of Francesco di Luca Verrocchio and adopted his surname. His experience of working with gold left the artist with a marked interest in surface finishes and in the skilful and flexible use of different techniques and materials.

Verrocchio was one of the favorite artists of the Medici family, who were his almost exclusive clients or intermediaries with illustrious personages or public institutions. A number of important works executed for the church of San Lorenzo, in a refined and somewhat artificial decorative style, were commissioned by the Medici: the lavabo in the Old Sacristy (*c.* 1465), the tomb of Cosimo de' Medici the Elder (1464-67) and the tomb of Piero and Giovanni de' Medici (1472), father and son of Lorenzo the Magnificent respectively. For the Medici the artist also made the bronze *David* that Lorenzo and his brother Giuliano later donated to the Florentine Signoria (Bargello, Florence). The Tribunale di Mercatanzia commissioned the bronze sculpture representing the *Incredulity of Saint Thomas* for the niche on the outside of the church of Orsanmichele from Verrocchio in 1466, but the artist did not start work on it until 1483.

Verrocchio was the head of a flourishing workshop, in which his young pupils had the opportunity to experiment with a wide range of techniques under the skilled guidance of an artist whose principal objective was that of formal perfection.

A man of many facets and interested in a wide variety of techniques, Andrea del Verrocchio was also a painter, but few pictures have survived that can be attributed to him with certainty. One of them is the *Baptism of Christ* (Uffizi, Florence), where it is also possible to recognize the hand of Leonardo da Vinci, his pupil at the time. In fact Verrocchio taught a number of distinguished painters, including Botticelli, Ghirlandaio and Perugino.

In 1483 he left for Venice, where he had already spent time in the past. He was commissioned by the Venetian Senate to execute an *Equestrian Statue of Bartolomeo Colleoni*, to be set up in the Campo dei Santi Giovanni e Paolo. The work was finished by Alessandro Leoni, as Verrocchio died in Venice in 1485. The artist's body was taken back to Florence and buried in Sant'Ambrogio.

Winged Putto
bronze, ht. 67 cm
Palazzo Vecchio, Florence

The winged putto clutching a dolphin is one of Verrocchio's most joyful and lively works. Dating from the early eighties, the bronze was executed for the garden of the villa of Careggi, owned by the Medici. Very different from the vigorous dynamism and powerful energy of Antonio Pollaiolo's sculptures (pp. 147-9), it is the light naturalness and the graceful animation of this cupid poised in the air that allows it to maintain its precarious balance on just one foot.

Lady with Primroses
marble, ht. 60 cm
Museo Nazionale del Bargello, Florence

As this sculpture demonstrates, Verrocchio's works are able to convey the subtle and pulsating dynamism of nature and of human emotions, an effect that is enhanced by the way light plays over their perfectly polished surfaces. Carved between 1475 and 1485, the *Lady with Primroses* was the first portrait bust ever to be sculpted complete with arms and hands. The format quickly proved extremely popular, especially in painting, where it was used by several of Verrocchio's pupils, including Ghirlandaio, Botticelli and Leonardo. The identity of the woman portrayed is unknown, though some have suggested that she was Ginevra Benci, whose portrait Leonardo also painted in a picture now in Washington (National Gallery of Art), or Lucrezia Donati, a woman courted by Lorenzo the Magnificent.

Incredulity of Saint Thomas
bronze
Museo di Orsanmichele, Florence

The bronze group of the *Incredulity of Saint Thomas*, executed by Verrocchio to a commission from the Tribunale dei Mercatanti (1466) for one of the niches on the outside of the church of Orsanmichele, was unveiled in 1483. Recently restored, the work is composed of two distinct figures closely linked together by dialogue and action. Thus the dramatic encounter between Christ and St. Thomas is presented in an unprecedented and original fashion, as if it were a scene on the stage. In fact, situated to one side on the threshold of the tabernacle, Thomas twists almost all the way round to touch the wound in Jesus's side: the apostle's fingers approach hesitantly, betraying his emotion, but have not yet touched Christ, who is waiting patiently at the center of the niche.

This is perhaps Verrocchio's finest work as far as the technical quality and formal result are concerned. The sculptures are made by the lost-wax process, an ancient technique that had been revived and perfected by Ghiberti and Donatello. The two statues, conceived as imposing bas-reliefs, have no backs, and each has been made from a single casting of the molten metal. Once cool, the two bronzes were "cleaned," that is polished, completed and enriched with details with meticulous care by the artist and his assistants. Particular attention has been paid to the drapery, falling in deep and undulating folds, and to Christ's face, where the curls of his soft hair are symmetrically parted around the head. The artist has used the idealized beauty of the figures to convey a vibrant sense of their emotions.

Sandro Botticelli

Alessandro Filipepi, called Botticelli (Florence 1445-1510), was one of the principal representatives of Florentine art and culture in the years of Lorenzo the Magnificent's rule. After an apprenticeship with a goldsmith, Sandro entered the workshop of Filippo Lippi and then that of Verrocchio. Quickly gaining an entry to Medici circles, Botticelli, along with Ghirlandaio, Perugino and Cosimo Rosselli, was sent by Lorenzo the Magnificent to Rome in 1481 to fresco the Sistine Chapel with *Scenes from the Lives of Moses and Jesus Christ*. Returning to Florence with his prestige enhanced by the work in Rome, the artist devoted himself to a series of allegorical paintings that reflected the refined culture of neoplatonic inspiration which held sway at Lorenzo the Magnificent's court. One of Botticelli's regular clients was Lorenzo the Magnificent's cousin, Lorenzo di Pierfrancesco, for whom the artist probably painted the *Spring* and *Birth of Venus*, as well as a series of illustrations of Dante's *Divine Comedy* in tempera on parchment (1490-96; the drawings are now divided between museums in Berlin and the Vatican Library).

At the end of the eighties, Botticelli turned his attention increasingly to devotional paintings (altarpieces and chamber works), couched in pathetic and dramatic tones. Toward the end of the century, the artist and his younger brother Simone fell under the sway of Girolamo Savonarola, prior of the convent of San Marco, who used his fiery sermons to denounce the corruption of the Church and the luxury of the Medici, urging people to return to a more sincere form of devotion and austere way of life. Paintings like the *Mystic Adoration* dated 1501 (National Gallery, London) represent the apocalyptic images conjured up in the friar's sermons, in a deliberately simplified and old-fashioned style.

In 1504, the now elderly Botticelli was called to sit on the board set up to decide on a location for Michelangelo's *David*, but in spite of such prestigious appointments the artist received fewer and fewer commissions. He died in 1510, a lonely old man.

La Primavera (*Spring*)
panel, 203x314 cm
Galleria degli Uffizi, Florence

The *Primavera* is one of the most celebrated paintings of the Italian Renaissance, long admired for its qualities of harmony, elegance and beauty. Yet Botticelli's masterpiece is also one of the most problematic paintings in the history of Western art and opinions are still divided on the interpretation of the subject and its meaning. Datable to the penultimate decade of the fifteenth century, the picture is recorded for the first time in an inventory drawn up in 1498, which describes it as hanging in a room of the Florentine palace of Lorenzo the Magnificent's cousin Lorenzo di Pierfrancesco de' Medici, although we do not known the occasion for which the work was executed.

On the basis of an interpretation put forward some time ago (Warburg, Gombrich and others), the scene should be read from right to left, commencing with the livid and capricious figure of Zephyr. The latter – the biting wind that ushers in spring in March – carries off the nymph Chloris and, after possessing her, turns her into Flora, the eternally fertile goddess of spring who is scattering flowers. The dominant figure in this imaginary garden is Venus, chaste goddess of love, framed by a bush of myrtle, her sacred plant. Above her, blindfolded Cupid shoots an arrow at the dancing figures of the three Graces, their bodies draped in transparent veils. Finally Mercury – recognizable by his *petasus* or pointed hat and his winged sandals – holds back the clouds with his rod or *caduceus*.

In fact the scene is set in a garden without shadows, where no bad weather will ever enter, nor night ever fall, and where everything appears eternally perfect. In the background stand orange trees, laden with flowers and golden fruit, which recall the mythic apples of the Hesperides, another symbol of eternity. The figures, ethereal in their elegant poses, rest their feet on the grass without trampling it, as if suspended in the air. The dark green meadow and the white dress of Flora are dotted with numerous flowers, whose colors are brightened up by the use of tempera mixed with oil: a total of five hundred species of plants have been identified in the painting, of which around a hundred and ninety bloom between March and May in the countryside and gardens of Florence (Levi D'Ancona).

La Primavera (Spring), detail
Galleria degli Uffizi, Florence

Madonna del Magnificat
(*Madonna and Child with Angels*)
panel, diam. 118 cm
Galleria degli Uffizi, Florence

More or less contemporary with the
Primavera, the picture is the best-known
of the tondi painted by Botticelli. The
title derives from the *incipit* of the
prayer to the Virgin inscribed on the
page of the book in the foreground.
The figures adapt to the circular shape of
the frame: they bend and curve and the
circle is closed by the joined hands of
the two angels who are crowning Mary.
The scene appears to have been further
distorted, as if it were an image reflected
in the convex surface of a mirror, a
sophisticated optical trick.
The artist has used other refined
technical devices to embellish the work,
such as gold to bring out precious
details and enhance the picture's
luminosity.

The Birth of Venus
canvas, 184·5x285·5 cm
Galleria degli Uffizi, Florence

In the painting Venus, born from the foam
of the sea, floats to the shore naked and
standing on a shell, driven by the waves
and the winds, represented by two winged
spirits – perhaps Zephyr and Aura –
clinging to each other. Waiting to receive
the goddess is a female figure with sprays
of roses and myrtle (plants sacred to
Venus) wound around her bust and
holding out the mantle woven by the three
Graces, strewn with flowers: in fact, the
figure has been identified as one of the
three sisters (though others have seen her
as one of the Hours, the nymphs in
Venus's retinue). Like the *Primavera*,
painted a few years earlier, the *Birth of
Venus* was intended for a cultivated and
refined public, capable of grasping its
literary, philosophical and iconographic
references, drawn from both ancient and
contemporary sources, and thus of
understanding the coded message carried
by the allegory. In fact, the composition is
linked in its themes and iconography to
the neoplatonic culture that held sway in
the circles of Lorenzo the Magnificent.
In the middle of the sixteenth century the
painting was recorded in the Villa di
Castello, formerly the property of Lorenzo
of Pierfrancesco de' Medici, the cousin of
Lorenzo the Magnificent and the probable
client of both the *Birth of Venus* and the
Primavera.

SANDRO BOTTICELLI

Lamentation over the Dead Christ
panel, 107x71 cm
Museo Poldi Pezzoli, Milan

Botticelli painted the picture at the end of
the fifteenth century, at a time when the
influence of Fra Girolamo Savonarola was
very strong in Florence. The Dominican
friar, burned at the stake in 1498, had
been the inspirer of the popular uprising
four years earlier that had led to the
expulsion of the Medici and the
establishment of the Republic.
Savonarola's fiery sermons had stirred
deep spiritual feelings and a desire for
repentance in many tormented souls.
Botticelli – who with his brother Simone
had become a close follower of the friar
(or a *piagnone*, "weeper," as they were
called at the time) – was also caught up
in this climate of fervent asceticism and
austere moral rigor, prompting him to
paint dramatic and touching works like
this one. The artist's sentiments were in
any case in tune with those of the client, a
certain Donato di Antonio Cioli,
illuminator of manuscripts and convinced
piagnone.

Calumny
panel, 62x91 cm
Galleria degli Uffizi, Florence

This small allegorical painting recalls the
celebrated *Calumny* painted by the Greek
artist Apelles after he had been falsely
accused of betraying his protector King
Ptolemy IV. The original having been lost,
the work was known in the fifteenth
century from the descriptions of it in the
literary sources, in particular Lucian's *De
Calumnia* of which several translations
had appeared over the course of the
century, including the most recent one of
1496.
In an architectural setting decorated with
sculptures and reliefs, we see King Midas
with his ass's ears on the right, tempted by
Suspicion and Ignorance. Opposite him
stands Rancor, clinging to the arm of
Calumny. The latter, dragging off the
Slandered, is accompanied by Envy and
Deceit, who is plaiting her hair. Finally,
Repentance turns her gaze, half concealed
by a black veil, toward naked Truth.

Domenico Ghirlandaio

D omenico Bigordi, called Ghirlandaio (Florence 1449-1494), son of the goldsmith Tommaso, was a pupil of Andrea del Verrocchio, along with Sandro Botticelli and Perugino. With these two and Cosimo Rosselli, he went to Rome in 1481 to fresco the *Scenes from the Lives of Moses and Christ* in the Sistine Chapel for Pope Sixtus IV. In Florence, Ghirlandaio worked for the circle of merchants and bankers with links to Lorenzo de' Medici the Magnificent: he painted the frescoes with *Scenes from the Life of Saint Francis* and the altarpiece of the *Nativity* for Francesco Sassetti's private chapel in Santa Trinita (*c.* 1480-85); for Giovanni Tornabuoni (Lorenzo the Magnificent's uncle) he frescoed the main chapel of Santa Maria Novella with *Scenes from the Lives of Mary and Saint John the Baptist* and drew the cartoon for the stained-glass window (1486-90). In 1482 he was entrusted, along with Botticelli, Perugino and Pollaiolo, with the fresco decoration of the Sala dei Gigli in Palazzo della Signoria, but Domenico was the only artist of the four to actually carry out the commission. In his compositions (frescoes, altarpieces, tondi for private devotion), Ghirlandaio often inserted contemporary Florentine scenes and figures, especially personages belonging to Lorenzo's circle. A faithful and vivid portraitist as well as an attractive and elegant narrator, Ghirlandaio celebrated the personalities, customs and surroundings of the upper middle classes in late fifteenth-century Florence. The artist's paintings reflect the prosperity, taste and culture of the time and have preserved their image for posterity.

He was able to rely on the support of an efficient workshop, whose members included his brothers Davide and Benedetto and his brother-in-law Bastiano Mainardi. Dying of the plague in 1494, Ghirlandaio was secretly buried at night in the graveyard of Santa Maria Novella. The painter left his workshop to his brothers and his son Ridolfo, who also became a painter.

Scenes from the Life of Saint Francis: The Confirmation of the Rule
fresco
Sassetti Chapel, Santa Trinita, Florence

In 1485 Domenico Ghirlandaio and his assistants completed the frescoes in the chapel of Francesco Sassetti, one of the most prominent personalities in the Florence of Lorenzo the Magnificent. The *Confirmation of the Rule* is the most celebrated scene in the cycle of frescoes representing *Scenes from the Life of Saint Francis*, the client's patron.

The episode, in which Pope Honorius III approves the Franciscan rule, is relegated to the background, so that the observer's attention is directed toward the figures in the foreground who are watching the event as if it was a performance on a

stage. Francesco Sassetti and his young son Federigo are portrayed on the right, alongside Lorenzo the Magnificent and Antonio Pucci, gonfalonier of justice and Sassetti's brother-in-law. On the opposite side we see the client's other sons, Galeazzo, Teodoro and Cosimo. The figures climbing the stairs, on the other hand, are Lorenzo's three sons, Giovanni, Piero and Giuliano, following their tutor, the scholar and poet Politian. Behind them come two more tutors, perhaps Luigi Pulci and Matteo Franco. The scene is not set in thirteenth-century Rome but in fifteenth-century Florence: in fact the episode takes place under an open loggia on Piazza della Signoria, onto which face the City Hall (Palazzo Vecchio) and the Loggia dei Priori (now Loggia dei Lanzi). Thus the picture served as an opportunity to celebrate Florence under the rule of Lorenzo the Magnificent and its notables.

Adoration of the Shepherds
panel, 167x167 cm
Sassetti Chapel, Santa Trinita, Florence

Ghirlandaio's masterpiece, dated 1485, is located on the altar of the Sassetti Chapel in Santa Trinita and completes its pictorial decoration. Following the example of contemporary Flemish painting, the artist has lingered over every detail of the scene, filling it with a sense of wonder and enchantment. The lively and joyous narrative is accompanied by symbols and metaphors. The three stones in the foreground allude to the client's name, Sassetti ("Pebbles"). The sarcophagus that acts as a manger, the pillars that support the roof and the triumphal arch through which the procession of the Magi passes are crumbling ruins that testify to the grandeur of the now superseded pagan world. Thus in the landscape beyond the stable we can see ancient Roman monuments like Hadrian's Mausoleum and the Torre delle Milizie on the left and on the right the spherical Dome of the Rock of Jerusalem, symbolizing the cities of the Romans and the Jews which will be succeeded by the city of Christ.

Perugino

Born in the vicinity of Perugia, Pietro Vannucci, called Perugino (Città della Pieve *c.* 1450-Fontignano 1523), went to Florence, where he frequented Verrocchio's workshop and was enrolled in the association of painters known as the Compagnia di San Luca in 1472.

In 1481 he went to Rome to participate in the fresco decoration of the Sistine Chapel alongside Domenico Ghirlandaio, Sandro Botticelli and Cosimo Rosselli. Perugino played a dominant role in this undertaking, painting the majority of the scenes in the cycle depicting the *Lives of Moses and Christ*: one of the most important of these scenes is that of *Christ Delivering the Keys to Saint Peter*. Over the following years, Perugino moved back and forth between Florence, Perugia and Rome, carrying out major public commissions.

In 1493 Perugino married Chiara, daughter of the Florentine architect Luca Fancelli, and stepped up his activity in the Tuscan city. The works of the last decade of the century have a religious tone verging on sentimentalism, reflecting the tastes of the Florentine upper middle classes at the time, troubled by the political uncertainties and social anxieties arising out of Girolamo Savonarola's subversive preaching. Typical of this are the *Pietà* and *Agony in the Garden* (Uffizi, Florence) for the Ingesuati of the monastery of San Giusto fuori le Mura (destroyed in 1530) and the *Lamentation over the Dead Christ* (1495; Galleria Palatina, Florence) for the church of Santa Chiara. At the same time, Perugino carried out several commissions for ecclesiastical and monastic buildings in Northern Italy, including the monumental altarpiece for the Charterhouse of Pavia, now dismembered (1496-99). In these years of prolific activity, one of the members of Perugino's workshop – in Perugia and Florence – was the young Raphael.

Returning from a journey to Venice, where he had been called to paint in the Doge's Palace, Perugino received the prestigious commission to fresco the Collegio del Cambio (1496-1500) in Perugia, where he went back to live permanently in 1502. But, after so much success, the painter's reputation went into rapid decline toward the end of his career. Consequently Perugino spent the last years of his life working in peripheral regions of Umbria. He died of the plague in 1523.

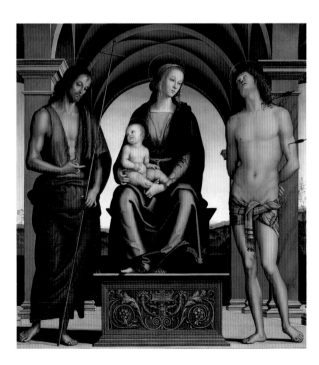

Madonna and Child Enthroned between Saints John the Baptist and Sebastian
panel, 178x164 cm
Galleria degli Uffizi, Florence

Signed and dated 1493 on the pedestal at the base of the Virgin's throne, the picture was painted by Perugino for a chapel in the church of San Domenico at Fiesole. Framed from below, the composition has a monumental and harmonious but at the same time stark structure. The figures are set in the foreground, as solemn and simple as the architecture behind them. The light caresses the surfaces of the pillars, the soft drapery and the tender flesh tones, in a suspended atmosphere of silent religious meditation. The exquisite body of St. Sebastian – reproduced here in the detail as well – was much praised by Perugino's contemporaries and his physical beauty is intended to be a reflection of the inner beauty of his soul.

Lamentation over the Dead Christ
panel, 214x195 cm
Galleria Palatina, Florence

Perugino painted this *Lamentation*, signed and dated 1495, for the convent of Santa Chiara. In the scene at the center Mary tenderly embraces the body of her Son, taken down from the Cross. The bystanders show that they share in her sorrow by their composed and sympathetic attitudes, but without any violent expressions of despair or horror. Tears run down the faces of Mary and the other women without marring their harmonious beauty, evoking an even greater sense of compassion in the observer. The landscape that stretches to the horizon in the background serves to accentuate the subdued but contained sadness of the scene: the serene acceptance of the drama on the part of the figures is reflected in the lyrical and idyllic tones of the landscape, depicted in loving detail in the manner of Flemish artists. This atmosphere cleansed of passions recalls that of the paintings of Fra Angelico, who was held up by Girolamo Savonarola at the end of the fifteenth century as a model for the development of an artistic style that could be used to bolster people's faith.

Prudence and Justice with Six Sages of Antiquity; The Eternal Father with Prophets and Sibyls
frescoes, 293x418; 229x370 cm
Collegio del Cambio, Perugia

Between 1496 and 1500 Perugino frescoed the Audience Chamber of the Collegio del Cambio in his native city. The Collegio del Cambio, which had its seat in the Palazzo dei Priori, was a public institution that supervised exchange and settled disputes of an economic nature. On the basis of a program drawn up by the Humanist Francesco Maturanzio, Perugino and his assistants frescoed the chamber with a complex cycle of encyclopedic scope whose fundamental theme was exaltation of the Virtues: the Cardinal Virtues (Prudence, Justice, Fortitude and Temperance) and the Theological Virtues (Faith, Hope and Charity), presented as the foundation of civil society and a mark of continuity between the virtues of antiquity and those of Christianity. For instance, Prudence and Justice are seated on clouds above the six sages of antiquity who best represent them, Fabius Maximus, Socrates, Numa Pompilius, Furius Camillus, Pittacus (detail on facing page) and Trajan. In another lunette on the wall opposite, prophets and sibyls guided by the Eternal Father act as intermediaries between pagan civilization and the episodes from the Gospels (*Nativity* and *Transfiguration*) represented at the back of the room.

Pintoricchio

Bernardino di Betto (Perugia *c.* 1452-Siena 1513) was nicknamed Pintoricchio ("Little Painter") owing to his small stature. He was a painter of frescoes and panels and an illuminator, whose style was an expression of a refined taste for decoration that combined antiquarian tastes for rare literary subjects, minute and detailed descriptions and sophisticated techniques.

Pintoricchio received his artistic training in Perugia, where he was born, and began to collaborate with Perugino. It was with the latter, in 1481, that Bernardino went to Rome to help with the frescoes of *Scenes from the Lives of Moses and Jesus Christ* in the Sistine Chapel. Introduced to influential circles in Rome, he worked for important members of the papal court, including Manno Bufalini and the Della Rovere family. In addition, while keeping up his activity in Perugia, he entered the service of Popes Innocent VIII Cybo and Alexander VI Borgia.

It was the Borgia pope who assigned Pintoricchio the most demanding task of his entire career between 1492 and 1494: the stucco and fresco decoration of the pope's apartment in the Vatican, whose iconographic program drew on Christian doctrine, the culture of antiquity and hermetic texts.

Returning to Perugia, Pintoricchio was commissioned to paint the altarpiece for the church of Santa Maria degli Angeli, known as the *Fossi Altarpiece* (now in the Galleria Nazionale dell'Umbria), in 1496. This sumptuous and refined work, rich in decorative inventions and minute descriptions, proved a great success. Active in various Umbrian cities, Bernardino frescoed the Baglioni Chapel in Santa Maria Maggiore at Spello, where – just as Perugino had done in the Collegio del Cambio – the painter included a self-portrait, along with his signature and the date 1501. In 1502 Cardinal Francesco Todeschini Piccolomini commissioned Pintoricchio with the fresco decoration of the library of Siena Cathedral, with *Scenes from the Life of Enea Silvio Piccolomini*. As in previous undertakings, the artist availed himself of the collaboration of apprentices and young artists, including Raphael. Finished in 1507, the cycle marked the last glorious chapter in fifteenth-century art.

Jesus Disputing with the Doctors
fresco
Baglioni Chapel, collegiate church of
Santa Maria Maggiore, Spello

In 1501 Pintoricchio finished the frescoes in the chapel of Prior Troilo Baglioni in Santa Maria Maggiore. Under the lunettes of the vault representing the Sibyls are set three scenes from the Childhood of Christ: the *Annunciation*, *Jesus Disputing*

with the Doctors, the *Adoration of the Shepherds* (reproduced here at right). The scene of *Jesus Disputing with the Doctors*, on the central wall, has a sweeping perspective converging on the elegant central-plan building in the background. This theatrical setting is influenced by the works of Perugino, and in particular the fresco of *Christ Giving the Keys to Saint Peter* in the Sistine Chapel. Pintoricchio also dwells lovingly on the various refined details that enrich the narration. The figures in the foreground have generic and standardized features, with the exception of a few personages on the left, including the client Troilo Baglioni dressed in dark robes.

Scenes from the Life of Enea Silvio Piccolomini: Enea Silvio Leaves for the Council of Basel
fresco
Libreria Piccolomini, Siena

The frescoes in the Libreria Piccolomini adjoining Siena Cathedral are Pintoricchio's masterpiece. At the request of Cardinal Francesco Todeschini Piccolomini, Pintoricchio decorated the library with scenes from the life of the client's uncle Enea Silvio Piccolomini, Humanist and pope from 1458 to 1464 under the name of Pius II. The scenes are couched in epic and celebratory tones and have a mock architectural setting that creates the effect of an open loggia supported by pillars with painted decorations in the antique manner. The ceiling consists of a central rectangle – with the Piccolomini coat of arms at the center – surrounded by vaults and pendentives with refined "grotesques," i.e. fanciful motifs derived from stuccoes of the imperial age (including those in Nero's *Domus Aurea*), a type of decoration that was much in vogue in Central Italy from the end of the fifteenth century onward.

Luca Signorelli

Born around the middle of the fifteenth century in the vicinity of Arezzo, Luca Signorelli (Cortona *c.* 1445-1523) received his training from Piero della Francesca, though he also came under the influence of Florentine artists like Verrocchio and above all Pollaiolo. After spending the early part of his career (from which few works have survived) between Arezzo, Città di Castello and Urbino, he frescoed the sacristy of the basilica of Loreto between 1477 and 1480 with paintings that testify to the artist's propensity to place the emphasis on dramatic action and theatrical gestures. In 1481 Luca went to Rome to collaborate with Perugino on the *Scenes from the Lives of Moses and Jesus Christ* in the Sistine Chapel.

In 1484 he painted the *Saint Onouphrius Altarpiece* for Perugia Cathedral (Museo dell'Opera del Duomo), a picture that marked the beginning of the artist's maturity. Moving to Florence, Luca started to work for the Medici and their cultural circle of neoplatonic inspiration. Examples of the captious and sophisticated influences exercised by this environment are provided by the *Madonna and Child* now in the Uffizi and the *Education of Pan* (formerly in the Kaiser Friedrich Museum, Berlin), executed around 1490 for Lorenzo the Magnificent. From that time on, Signorelli was active in various Tuscan centers, including Volterra and Siena.

After the death of Lorenzo (1492) and the collapse of Medici rule following the political and cultural crisis that overcame Florentine society, Signorelli left the Tuscan city and went back to work in Umbria and the Marche (Urbino, Città di Castello). Between 1497 and 1498 he frescoed the *Scenes from the Life of Saint Benedict* in the great cloister of the monastery of Monteoliveto Maggiore near Siena. The artist interrupted this

work in 1499 to undertake the most important enterprise of his career: the imposing cycle of frescoes based on the Apocalypse in the chapel of San Brizio in Orvieto Cathedral (1499-1502), a commission that had first been entrusted to Fra Angelico (p. 112).

After the cycle in Orvieto, the artist was unable to keep pace with the artistic innovations coming out of Florence and Rome at the beginning of the new century and thus spent the final part of his career working in provincial centers (Cortona, Sansepolcro, Arezzo, Arcevia), falling back on an eclectic and tired style, at times verging on the archaic.

Frescoes in the chapel
of San Brizio
Cathedral, Orvieto

On April 5, 1499, Luca Signorelli signed a
contract with the Vestry Board of Orvieto
Cathedral for the completion of the

frescoes on the ceiling of the chapel of San Brizio. Over fifty years earlier, in 1447, Fra Angelico had begun the enterprise with the help of various collaborators, including Benozzo Gozzoli, frescoing two cells of the vault with *Christ the Judge* and *Prophets*, but had then interrupted the work. The imposing cycle is unquestionably Luca's finest work and after the recent restoration has regained its brilliant colors and full expressiveness.

The Preaching and Deeds of the Antichrist; *The Damned*
fresco
chapel of San Brizio, Cathedral, Orvieto

With the assistance of a well-organized team of collaborators, Luca Signorelli completed the most grandiose cycle of scenes from the *Revelations* ever to be painted in Italy in the space of just over three years (1502). The theme and atmosphere of these frescoes can be understood in the light of the dramatic events that shook people's consciences and faith as well as the world of politics at the end of the century. In the *Preaching of the Antichrist*, the false prophet who at the Devil's prompting instigates people to heap their wealth at his feet may be an allusion to Girolamo Savonarola, the Dominican friar who inspired the republican insurrection of 1494 in Florence and who was condemned to be burned at the stake four years later. Luca Signorelli himself – portrayed here in a black cloak and cap – and Fra Angelico in a Dominican habit look on from the edge of the spectacular and prodigious scene. The *Preaching of the Antichrist* is the first of the majestic scenes that decorate the walls: it is followed by the *End of the World*, the *Resurrection of the Flesh*, the *Damned*, the *Blessed*, *Heaven* and *Hell*. In the scene of the *Damned* the tangle of naked bodies in contorted poses, tortured by livid and grotesque demons in the setting of a desert, demonstrates Signorelli's interest in the foreshortened representation of anatomies as well as his ironic and grotesque imagination. Michelangelo (pp. 224-43) was to use this theatrical image with its tones of pathos and devilry as a rich source of figurative ideas.

Andrea Mantegna

Born in the territory between Vicenza and Padua, Andrea Mantegna (Isola di Cartura 1431-Mantua 1506) was the son of a carpenter. He went on to become the pupil and adoptive son of Francesco Squarcione, a mediocre painter but able teacher who instructed his disciples to study the models of antiquity and the works of Florentine artists in Padua and Venice, and Donatello in particular.

In 1448 Mantegna received his first important commission: together with Nicolò Pizolo, he frescoed part of the Ovetari Chapel in the Eremitani Church at Padua with *Scenes from the Lives of Saint James and Saint Christopher*: completed in 1456-57, the innovative character of their style was so shocking that it even aroused the anger of his former teacher Squarcione. The chapel, unfortunately largely destroyed in the last war, marked the beginning of the Renaissance in Northern Italy. The daring use of perspective and the monumental and classical tone had a powerful influence on the artists of the time.

In 1453 Andrea married the sister of Giovanni Bellini, Nicolosia, and from then on the two painters were bound not only by family ties but also by an artistic relationship. Between 1456 and 1459, Mantegna painted the altarpiece for the basilica of San Zeno in Verona, which – echoing the scheme of Donatello's High Altar in Il Santo – was the first altar painting in the north of the peninsula in a fully Renaissance style.

Immediately afterward, Mantegna moved to Mantua, where he became the official artist of the Gonzaga court. In 1459 he was joined in the Lombard city by the architect and treatise writer Leon Battista Alberti. Kept hard at work on paintings, decorations for festivities, set designs and engravings, Andrea left Mantua only for two brief visits to Pisa (1467) and Florence (1468) and for a longer stay in Rome, where he frescoed a chapel in the Belvedere for Pope Innocent VIII (1489-90; destroyed).

In Mantua, he decorated the so-called Camera degli Sposi (Wedding Chamber) in the Castello di San Giorgio, urban residence of Ludovico Gonzaga and his family, between 1465 and 1474. Mantegna also executed a series of pictures for the Gonzaga representing *The Triumphs of Caesar* (1486-1501; Hampton Court). At the end of the century he started to paint the panels requested from him by Marchesa Isabella d'Este for her study in Mantua Castle. Having completed the *Parnassus* and *Minerva Driving Out the Vices* (Louvre, Paris), Andrea was finishing the design for *The Fable of the God Comus* when he died in 1506.

Saint Zeno Altarpiece
panel, 480x450 cm
basilica of San Zeno, Verona

The work is the first altarpiece in a fully Renaissance style to have been painted in Northern Italy. Mantegna executed it between 1456 and 1459 for the high altar of the Veronese church of San Zeno to a commission from Abbot Gregorio Correr.

Mantegna took the model for his unusual conception from Donatello's altar of Il Santo (pp. 88-9), whose original appearance can now be reconstructed on the basis of the painting in Verona. Inside a monumental frame of classical form is set a *Sacra Conversazione*, with the Virgin and Child on a throne at the center surrounded by angels and, at the sides, sculptural and imposing figures of

saints, absorbed in meditation and reading. In spite of the tripartite frame the scene is unified by its setting: the figures are situated inside a sort of architectural canopy with a quadrangular plan and decorated with reliefs and moldings drawn from the figurative repertory of antiquity. The foreshortened view of this portico includes the columns of the wooden frame, which overlap with the

ones painted in the foreground. The saints at the sides and the Virgin in the middle are set inside a sort of spatial box represented in perspective from a low point of view, which corresponds to that of the observer.
The predella is a nineteenth-century copy while the original panels are now in the Louvre and the Musée des Beaux-Arts at Tours.

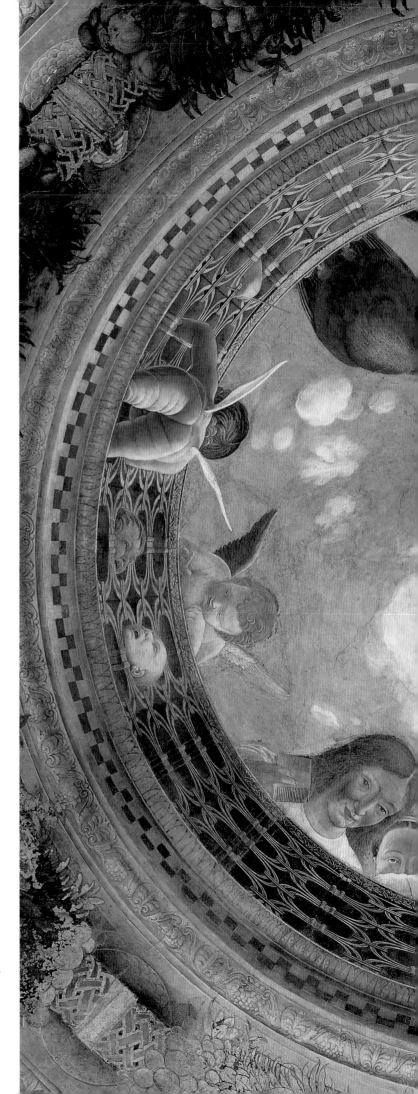

Camera degli Sposi (*Wedding Chamber* or *Camera Picta*)
frescoes and seccoes
Castel San Giorgio, Mantua

Moving to Mantua where he was
appointed official painter to the court of
the Marchesi Gonzaga, Mantegna
undertook his most demanding pictorial
enterprise: the decoration of the so-called
Camera degli Sposi in Castel San Giorgio.

The room, which housed the private
archives of Marchese Ludovico Gonzaga,
was also used to entertain guests. On view
to princes, ambassadors and illustrious
foreigners, Mantegna's fresco decoration
(1465-74) of the room's ceiling and walls
was therefore intended as a celebration of
the lord of Mantua and his family in the
sumptuous setting of his court.
The artist has painted an illusory
architecture that simulates a portico

opening onto the outside on each of the four walls, two of which present scenes of life at court and members of the Gonzaga family. The painted pillars of the portico support a vault decorated with mock stuccoes, opening illusionistically onto the sky at the center through an oculus. Thus Mantegna has expanded the actual space of the room, breaking through the walls and playing a subtle game with the real and painted architecture.

In the scene frescoed on the north wall – the main one (reproduced on pp. 184-5) – a view of a courtyard with an elegant enclosure of polychrome marble opens at the height of the mantelpiece: in it we see the court and family of Ludovico Gonzaga and Barbara of Brandenburg, the *sposi* or "husband and wife" to whom the chamber is dedicated. The figures are immobile and impassive, as if posing for a solemn ceremony in which everything is arranged according to a rigid hierarchy: Ludovico Gonzaga and his consort Barbara are seated in the middle, surrounded by their children; the youngest are placed next to their mother; Gianfrancesco and Rodolfo – the eldest – immediately behind their parents, along with their tutors; their daughter Barberina is behind, accompanied by her nurse. The family group is completed by the marchese's councilor, Marsilio Andreasi, who is whispering the latest news to his lord, by the dwarf near Barbara of Brandenburg and by the dog under Ludovico's chair.

The Dead Christ
canvas, 68x81 cm
Pinacoteca di Brera, Milan

Mantegna's interest in perspective led him to produce virtuoso effects such as those in the *Dead Christ*, datable to between the eight and the nineth decade of the fifteenth century. In a scene of great emotional impact, the pale and bloodless body of Christ is laid out on a slab of stone at the height of the observer's gaze, ready to be daubed with the ointment in the jar to his left. The observer, therefore, is made to feel part of the group of mourners, on the left, along with the weeping figure of the Virgin.

Saint Sebastian
panel, 275x142 cm
Louvre, Paris

Probably executed for the Gonzaga (1480-85), the painting presents St. Sebastian transfixed by the arrows of his martyrdom and bound to the column of a classical ruin. The beauty of the martyr's harmonious body is not marred by the wounds, whereas the refined decorations of the archeological relic bear the marks of abandonment, shattered and overgrown with vegetation. Thus the young man's elegant foot, resting on a piece of ancient marble, is echoed by the foot of a statue reduced to a mere fragment. The Christian martyr who has accepted the supreme sacrifice is presented as a noble and austere hero, victorious in his faith over the ruins of pagan civilization.

Antonello da Messina

The son of a stonecutter, Antonello (Messina *c.* 1430-1479) spent the years from 1445 to 1455 in Naples as a pupil of the painter Colantonio. In Naples, alternately under the rule of the houses of Anjou and Aragon, Antonello found himself in a cultural environment open to Flemish, Provençal, Burgundian and Valencian influences introduced by the artists and works that arrived there from various parts of Europe.

We know nothing of the works produced by the artist in Messina over the following decade, even though the documents testify to an intense activity in Sicily and at Reggio Calabria. Between 1465 and 1470 Antonello may have gone to stay on the mainland again, perhaps in Rome, during which time he came into contact with the art of Piero della Francesca: this can be deduced from the earliest of his paintings to have come down to us, such as the *Crucifixion* in Bucharest and the *Ecce homo* in the Metropolitan Museum, in which the minute description of Flemish inspiration is clarified and subordinated to the new conception of perspective and light formulated in Central Italy.

In 1475 Antonello was in Venice, where he painted the *Saint Cassiano Altarpiece* (Kunsthistorisches Museum, Vienna) and *Saint Sebastian* (Staatliche Gemäldegalerie, Dresden). Leaving Venice after about a year, he went to Milan and placed himself for a short time at the service of Duke Galeazzo Maria Sforza. Antonello's stay in Venice and Milan had a fundamental influence on the course of art history, as it marked the encounter between the synthesis of light and space developed by the artist from Messina and the tonal and lyrical color of Giovanni Bellini (p. 194). Antonello's work provided an essential lesson for Bellini, Carpaccio, Giorgione and Titian.

Antonello was back in Messina by the September of 1476. He died in 1479, leaving his son Iacobello the task of finishing the *Pietà* now in the Prado.

Saint Jerome in His Study
panel, 46x36 cm
National Gallery, London

Of uncertain date (proposals range between 1455 and 1475), the small painting represents St. Jerome seated in his study, presented as a sort of raised platform with two walls covered with shelves set inside a Gothic church. We observe the scene, rationally laid out according to a central perspective, through the portal in the foreground of the scene. It is possible to make out the straight lines engraved on the surface of the panel which the artist has used to construct the composition. The atmospheric light, warm and sunny, lends a sense of unity to the whole and at the same time brings out the details, something that Antonello had learned from Flemish painting. The artist achieved certain effects of brilliance and transparency through skillful use of the technique of painting with oils, arousing the admiration of his contemporaries.

ANTONELLO DA MESSINA

Our Lady of the Annunciation
panel, 46x34 cm
Galleria Nazionale della Sicilia, Palermo

In the painting, dating from around 1475, the Virgin is represented in the act of responding to the news brought by the angel, whose presence can only be imagined outside the composition. The girlish figure of the Virgin, swathed in a blue mantle against a dark background, is reduced to pure form, to a sort of architecture set in a three-dimensional space: the cloak recalls the structure of a pyramid in which the oval face of the woman rotates toward the outside of the picture. Mary's right hand advances in the direction of the observer, passing beyond the prominent edge of the lectern. We can almost feel the air circulating around those solid hands, lucidly constructed out of subtle plays of light and shade, just as it is ruffling the pages of the book.

Portrait of a Man
(*Trivulzio Portrait*)
panel, 36x27·5 cm
Museo Civico d'Arte Antica, Turin

Antonello was one of the greatest portrait painters of the fifteenth century. Together with Giovanni Bellini, the artist from Messina introduced the new scheme of the half-length, three-quarters portrait, of Flemish derivation, as a substitute for the formula of the portrait in profile, widely used in Veneto.
The *Trivulzio Portrait* (so-called because it used to belong to the collection of the same name in Milan) is one of Antonello's masterpieces. It is dated 1476 and was therefore painted during the artist's stay in Venice or immediately afterward. The man's features (the bristling eyebrows, cheeks shadowed with stubble, lines around the mouth) look almost as if you could touch them. The depiction of physiognomic traits is combined with a study of the sitter's psychology, apparent in his glad eye and slight smile. The overall structure of the portrait is imposing and succinct, enhanced by the light that enters from the left, imparting a sculptural effect to the image.

*Madonna and Child with Saints
Nicholas, Mary Magdalene, Ursula
and Dominic*
(*San Cassiano Altarpiece*)
panel, 115x63 (central panel);
56·8x36·6 cm (wings)
Kunsthistorisches Museum, Vienna

While Antonello was in Venice, in 1476,
he painted the *San Cassiano Altarpiece*,
a masterpiece that has regrettably only
come down to us in a fragmentary state.

However, its original appearance can be
reconstructed from an old print. The
vertical structure of the composition and
the imposing architectural setting are
derived from an altarpiece painted by
Giovanni Bellini for the church of Santi
Giovanni e Paolo (or San Zanipolo),
unfortunately lost. On the high throne the
Madonna is seated against a barely
unfolded piece of violet cloth: her head
is covered by a veil that stands out like a
white sphere surrounded by precious

fabrics. The light, while emphasizing the
details (note the glass of water in
St. Mary Magdalen's hand) and caressing
the surfaces (St. Nicholas's golden balls,
and even the Child's legs), also
constructs the forms and imparts an
overall unity to the composition. The way
that the Virgin's hand advances toward
the observer serves to create a greater
sense of depth in the sacred group: it is a
device that Antonello resorted to
frequently.

Giovanni Bellini

Born to a family of painters, Giovanni Bellini (Venice 1433?-1516?) was the leading figure in Venetian art in the closing decades of the fifteenth century and at the beginning of the following one. Over his long career, Bellini marked a turning point in Venetian painting, hitherto still linked to Byzantine gilding and schemes and to Gothic rhythms and refinements.

In Venice, Giovanni received his training and carried out his initial activity in the workshop of his father Jacopo, of whom he may have been an illegitimate son. After the early works of the sixties, influenced by the Paduan Andrea Mantegna, who was married to his sister Nicolosia, the Venetian artist developed a contemplative manner all of his own, reflected in the warm and tonal handling of color. The arrival of Antonello da Messina in Venice in 1475 had a fundamental impact on Bellini's style.

On the death of his father in 1470 or 1471, Giovanni started to collaborate with his brother Gentile on the decoration of the Doge's Palace. In 1483, now aged fifty, Giovanni was declared the official painter of the republic. Unfortunately we have few reliable records of Bellini's activity, at least up until 1500. Between the 1470s and 1480s Bellini painted several works of crucial importance to the history of Venetian art, including the *San Giobbe Altarpiece* and the triptych still in Santa Maria dei Frari.

From the nineties onward Bellini relied on the collaboration of a large group of assistants in order to cope with an ever increasing number of commissions. At the turn of the century Bellini adopted a style consonant with the new developments in Venetian art, which was coming more and more under the sway of Giorgione as time went by. An example of this is the *San Zaccaria Altarpiece* (1505).

From 1496 to 1505 Giovanni carried out a series of commissions for the Gonzaga court and collaborated on the pictorial decoration of the study of Isabella d'Este, marchesa of Mantua. In 1514 he was paid for *The Feast of the Gods*, painted for Alfonso d'Este's study in Ferrara (National Gallery, Washington).

In the meantime, on February 6, 1506, the German artist Albrecht Dürer had written a letter from Venice to his friend Willibald Pirkheimer in which he declared that the now aging Bellini was still the best painter in the city.

*Coronation of Mary between
Saints Paul, Peter, Jerome and
Francis (Pesaro Altarpiece)*
panel, 262x240 cm (central panel)
Museo Civico, Pesaro

Embalming of Christ
panel, 107x84 cm
Pinacoteca Vaticana, Rome

Probably painted in the early seventies,
the altarpiece used to be located on the
high altar of the church of San Francesco
in Pesaro. The work marks the artistic
maturity of Giovanni Bellini, who was the
dominant figure in Venetian art up until
the first decade of the sixteenth century.
Still in its original frame, the altarpiece is
made up of the *Coronation of the Virgin*
in the central panel, eight figures of saints
on the lateral pillars, and a predella with
six scenes from the lives of saints and a
Nativity in the middle. The picture with
the *Embalming of Christ* now in the
Pinacoteca Vaticana was originally set at
the top and was temporarily reunited with
the rest of the altarpiece for an exhibition
held in 1988.

The main painting is conceived as the
opening of a double window, one framed
by the other, looking onto a space that
extends into the background as if viewed
through a telescope. The landscape is
dominated by a castle that looks like one
of the fortresses in the Marche (the
region in which Pesaro is located) and
has been identified by some as the Rocca
di Gradara. Quite apart from any
connection with reality, however, the
building with its towers and walls has a
symbolic significance and alludes to the
heavenly Jerusalem, whose gates have
been opened by Christ in the Virgin's
womb, or to the ivory tower, a Marian
attribute referring to the Immaculate
Conception.

The time that Bellini spent in the Marche
to carry out this commission probably
gave him the opportunity to study the
works of Piero della Francesca, from
which the Venetian artist learned the
rigorous use of geometric perspective
and sense of luminous spatiality.

GIOVANNI BELLINI

Madonna and Child Enthroned with Saints Francis, John the Baptist, Job, Dominic, Sebastian and Louis of Toulouse (*San Giobbe Altarpiece*)
panel, 471x258 cm
Gallerie dell'Accademia, Venice

Bellini painted the monumental altarpiece for the Franciscan church of San Giobbe in Venice. The commission probably coincided with the terrible outbreak of plague that struck the city in 1478-80, and on such occasions St. Job and St. Sebastian – along with St. Roch who is not present in the painting – were invoked to overcome the epidemic. The scene, viewed from below, is set inside the majestic apse of a church that looks like a continuation of the actual space. The protagonist is the Virgin, who is seated in a regal attitude on a tall throne: she is at the vertex of an imaginary pyramid at whose base are ranged the saints, at the sides, and the angels playing musical instruments in the middle. The inscription on the gold mosaic of the vault of the apse describes Mary as a "chaste flower of virginal purity." This is an allusion to the Immaculate Conception of the Mother of God, a doctrine upheld and defended by the Franciscans even before it was officially recognized by the Church. Notwithstanding the complex theological references and the solemnity of the architectural structure, the artist has given lively and varied poses and attitudes to the figures around the throne, allowing them to convey restrained but intense emotions in response to the mysterious manifestation of Mary. The warm and golden luminosity of the colors helps to create an atmosphere of profound humanity.

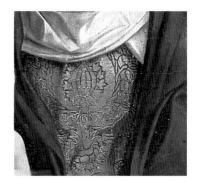

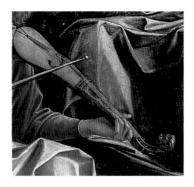

Portrait of Doge Loredan
panel, 61·5x45 cm
National Gallery, London

This is Giovanni Bellini's most celebrated portrait, in which he showed himself to have been one of the most sensitive and refined European painters of the fifteenth century. It is a formal effigy of Leonardo Loredan, doge of Venice from 1501 to 1521. Of slender build but strong-willed and irascible, Loredan is presented in an impassive and proud pose consonant with his political role. The scheme of the portrait – half-length, frontal and set behind a parapet that pushes the sitter back from the foreground – recalls the one already introduced by Antonello da Messina (p. 191) and inspired by Flemish models. Against a blue ground, the noble personage turns his evasive and haughty gaze in the direction of the light, which softens the features of his face and brings out the precious refinement of his clothing and his ceremonial cap, both made of white and gold brocade.

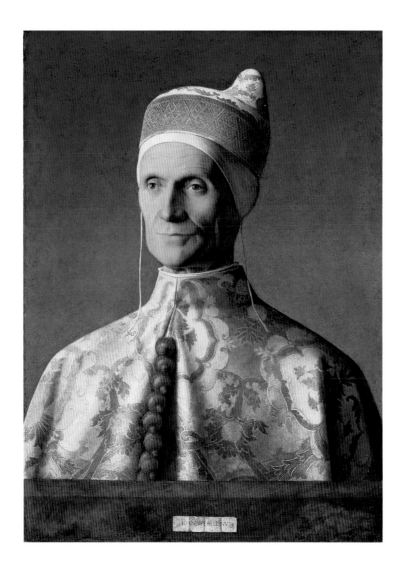

Sacred Allegory
(*The Allegory of the Souls
in Purgatory*)
panel, 73x119 cm
Galleria degli Uffizi, Florence

The meaning of the so-called *Sacred
Allegory* is much disputed, though the
small picture was undoubtedly intended
for the private home of a cultivated client
who frequented intellectual circles where

questions of Humanism, theology and
philosophy were debated. On a sort of
marble terrace stand the figures of several
saints (Paul with a sword, Joseph with a
beard, and Job and Sebastian wearing
nothing but loincloths). The latter are
advancing slowly and looking at the Virgin
seated on the throne on the left, as *sedes
Sapientiae*, with two Virtues alongside. At
the center, around the tree (an allusion to
the Tree of Life) are set several children

(the one seated with a fruit in his hand is
probably the Infant Jesus). In the
landscape, we see St. Anthony of Egypt in
his hermitage amidst the rocks. The sense
of mystery is enhanced by the presence of
an Arab walking by the water and, in the
background, a herdsman and a centaur
on the bank.
The scene, ambiguous and cerebral in its
significance, is pervaded by a quiet and
solemn atmosphere that extends to the

landscape as well, with the surrounding
nature reflected in the surface of the
lake. The warm light of evening lends a
soft and mellow tone to the colors.
Independently of the line, color is used
as a means of translating the reality of
nature into poetry, of transforming
intellectual contemplation into elegiac
sentiment. This is the principal legacy
that Bellini bequeathed to his pupils and
followers.

Vittore Carpaccio

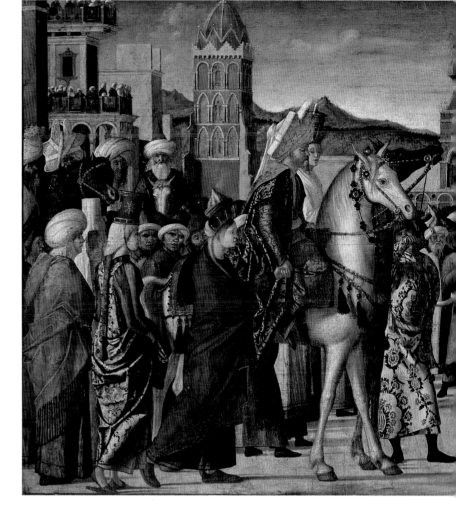

T he son of Pietro Scarpaza, Vittore (Venice *c.* 1460/65-1525/26) was in the habit of signing his work with the Latinized form of his name, "Carpathius," from which his byname Carpaccio is derived. It is not known where Vittore received his training, although it has been suggested that he was a pupil of Giovanni Bellini's brother Gentile. However, his work reveals the marked influence of Antonello da Messina. Carpaccio spent almost all of his life within the walls of the Serenissima, with the possible exception of a journey to Rome that the artist may have made in his youth to study the use of perspective in Central Italian art.

Between the end of the fifteenth century and the first few decades of the next, Carpaccio was the most renowned author of the gigantic canvases (or *teleri*) depicting narrative scenes that were hung in the Scuole, as the seats of confraternities and guilds were called. The earliest dated painting by the artist is from 1490 and represents the *Arrival in Cologne* from the series of *Scenes from the Legend of Saint Ursula* he executed for the Scuola di Sant'Orsola (*c.* 1490-98). The success of these pictures earned the artist commissions for other narrative cycles for the Venetian Scuole. The finest of these and the only one still *in situ* is the series of scenes he painted for San Giorgio degli Schiavoni (*c.* 1502-08). Under the direction of Gentile Bellini, Carpaccio contributed several paintings to the cycle of *Miracles of the True Cross* (1494) for the hostel of the Scuola di San Giovanni Evangelista and the lost series of *Scenes from the Life of Pope Alexander III* in the Sala del Maggior Consiglio of the Doge's Palace (*c.* 1507-11). In 1508 Giovanni Bellini had him appointed to the commission set up to decide how much Giorgione should be paid for the frescoes on the outside of the Fondaco dei Tedeschi.

In the last fifteen years of his life, Carpaccio received a growing number of commissions for altarpieces, most of them for churches in the Venetian provinces. Carpaccio was also described by contemporary sources and his sixteenth-century biographers as an excellent portrait painter. The fascinating *Knight in a Landscape* (Thyssen-Bornemisza Collection, Madrid), dated 1510, is a precocious example of a full-length portrait.

The Triumph of Saint George
canvas, 141x360 cm
Scuola di San Giorgio, Venice

Belonging to the series of nine large canvases painted by Carpaccio for the Scuola di San Giorgio, the work represents the saint at the moment when, after dragging the dying dragon to the city of Silena, he gives it the *coup de grâce* before the princess, the king and queen on horseback and the dignitaries and musicians of the court. The Christian knight stands alone at the center of the composition, admired by the pagan population dressed in Saracen clothing, who then agree to convert and be baptized. The setting emphasizes the epic and celebratory tone of the picture through the use of a central perspective, for which he had made a detailed study (reproduced above) in pen and ink beforehand (Gabinetto Disegni e Stampe degli Uffizi, Florence). In the painting the grid of the perspective confers a spectacular quality on the scene, which is imbued with fabulous and exotic tones through the description of the costumes, buildings, and rituals.

*Scenes from the Life of
Saint Ursula: The King of Brittany
Receiving the Ambassadors*
canvas, 275x589 cm
Gallerie dell'Accademia, Venice

The cycle of canvases with *Scenes from
the Life of Saint Ursula*, painted by
Carpaccio for the Scuola di Sant'Orsola
between 1490 and 1498, is the earliest
work by the artist to have come down to
us. The series of paintings, cunningly
orchestrated and spectacular in their
effect, represents the ancient, as well as
adventurous and romantic, legend of
Ursula, Christian daughter of the king of
Brittany and betrothed to the pagan Ereus,
son of the king of England. According to
the *Golden Legend* of Jacobus de
Voragine, the girl imposed several
conditions on her marriage: she wanted
eleven thousand virgins as ladies-in-
waiting, asked her husband-to-be to

convert to Christianity and finally postponed the marriage for three years so she could make a pilgrimage to Rome. Ereus agreed and joined Ursula on the pilgrimage. Everything seemed to be going fine until the young couple were attacked on their return journey from the papal city and killed by the Huns in Cologne.

As is clear from the first episode of the cycle, Carpaccio has emphasized the moments and situations in the story that gave him the opportunity to represent magnificent public ceremonies, formal diplomatic meetings and disembarkations at splendid ports. In the painting, King Maurus of Brittany receives the English ambassadors who have come to ask the hand of his daughter Ursula for the heir to the throne of England. On the right, the king, overcome by the request and fearful of offending such a powerful ruler, confides in his daughter.

**Scenes from the Life of
Saint Ursula: The Leave-Taking
of the English Ambassadors**
canvas, 280x253 cm
Gallerie dell'Accademia, Venice

In a large and sumptuous room of the palace, adorned with polychrome marble inlays in the Venetian manner, King Maurus delivers to the ambassadors his written response to the king of England's request, agreeing to the marriage of his daughter Ursula to the English prince Ereus but laying out the conditions imposed by the young woman.

16TH CENTURY

Leonardo da Vinci

The illegitimate son of the notary Ser Piero di Antonio, Leonardo (Vinci, near Florence, 1452-Château de Cloux, near Amboise, 1519) was apprenticed by his father to Andrea Verrocchio in Florence. He remained in his workshop until 1476, but then left to work on his own. Around 1481 Leonardo started to paint the altarpiece with the *Adoration of the Magi* (Uffizi, Florence) for San Donato at Scopeto, but did not finish it as the following year he moved to the court of Ludovico il Moro in Milan. Sent there by Lorenzo the Magnificent, Leonardo presented himself to the duke of Milan bearing the gift of a silver lyre in the shape of a horse's skull, which he played with great skill according to his biographers. During his first stay in Milan, Leonardo painted the altarpiece entitled the *Virgin of the Rocks* (1483; Louvre, Paris) for San Francesco Grande (the church was later destroyed) and the fresco of the *Last Supper* (1494-97) in Santa Maria delle Grazie, the only work of a public character that he ever completed. But Leonardo did not work just as a painter in Milan, but also as a sculptor and architect. In addition, he designed sophisticated war engines, drainage systems for the basin of the Po River, machinery for use in construction and scenery for the theater, as well as carrying out research into optics, geometry, anatomy and botany.

In 1499, with the fall of Ludovico il Moro and the city's occupation by the French, Leonardo left Milan and went first to Mantua and then to Venice, before entering the service of Cesare Borgia as an architect and military engineer. After visiting various cities in Central and Northern Italy, he went back to Florence in 1503, offering his services to Pier Soderini, gonfalonier of the republic. The latter entrusted the artist with the task of frescoing the *Battle of Anghiari* (1503) in the Salone del Gran Consiglio in Palazzo della Signoria, as a companion piece to the *Battle of Cascina* that had been commissioned from Michelangelo. But both artists failed to meet their commitments and departed from Florence, leaving behind the cartoons for the two paintings, which would be admired and studied by young artists for generations. It is generally believed that it was during this second stay in Florence that the artist commenced work on the celebrated portrait of a lady now known as the *Mona Lisa*.

In 1506 Leonardo was back in Milan, in the employment of King Louis XII of France. Following the return of the duchy to Sforza rule, Leonardo left the Lombard city again in 1513, going to work for Pope Leo X's brother Cardinal Giuliano de' Medici in Rome. Finally, on the latter's death, Leonardo moved to France at the invitation of the King Francis I, at whose court he became "premier peintre et ingénieur et architecte du Roi, meschanischien d'estat." The monarch assigned the artist the castle of Cloux, near the royal residence of Amboise, and an extremely generous income. Leonardo died there on May 2, 1519, leaving hundred of drawings accompanied by handwritten notes (in his characteristic left-handed script running from right to left, and therefore only legible in a mirror), which even today testify to the vast range of his interests and experiments.

Annunciation
panel, 98x217 cm
Galleria degli Uffizi, Florence

The celebrated painting was moved from the sacristy of the church of San Bartolomeo at Monteoliveto in the vicinity of Florence to the Uffizi Gallery in 1867. The history of the picture prior to that date is unknown. At the time of its transfer, the *Annunciation* was thought to be the work of Domenico Ghirlandaio, but today it is generally considered one of Leonardo da Vinci's early masterpieces. The recently concluded restoration has freed the painting of darkened layers of varnish and retouches, rendering a

number of important details of the composition visible again, such as the foliage of the trees, the flowers of the meadow, the shadows on the angel's robe and the folds in Mary's, the setting of the bedchamber and the subtle play of light and shade on the walls. The air, steeped in atmospheric light, appears to circulate around the figures and the drapery, over the unkempt and damp vegetation of the meadow, between the pages of the book that slip through the Virgin's hands and then through the landscape to the horizon, where the shapes of mountain peaks dissolve in a whitish mist.
The artist presumably painted the picture in 1470s, while he was still an apprentice

in Andrea del Verrocchio's workshop. Leonardo derived the finely carved marble base of the reading desk from a late classical sarcophagus kept in his master's workshop. As if in a dialectical exchange of impressions and experiences, Verrocchio used the same model for the bronze sepulcher of the tomb of Piero and Giovanni de' Medici in the church of San Lorenzo (1472). It was from Verrocchio's teachings that Leonardo learned the analytical observation of material that allowed him to attain such a vital, vibrant and almost organic representation of form.

Madonna and Child
(*Madonna Benois*)
panel, 48x31 cm
Hermitage, St. Petersburg

In the early years of his career, in
Florence, Leonardo made a thorough
study of the theme of the Madonna and
Child, varying poses, situations and
emotions in a series of drawings and
paintings. The so-called *Madonna Benois*
(named after the owner of the picture
before it entered the Hermitage in 1914)
is a significant example of this genre of
experimentation. Following a scheme that
originated in Flemish painting and
became widespread in the fifteenth
century, the scenes is set in a domestic
interior illuminated by the light entering
through a window. The figures are caught
in a moment of affectionate intimacy as
the Virgin, with girlish features, offers a
flower to the Child seated on her lap. The
latter seizes his mother's hand and tries to
take the flower from her in a naturally
childish gesture, but with an expression of
great concentration on his face as if he
understood its symbolic value: in fact it is
a crucifer flower, alluding to the Passion.

the scene is deepened by the landscape made up of a fantastic tangle of rocks and natural elements silhouetted against the light and forming a sort of secluded refuge for the sacred group, probably symbolic of the Immaculate Conception.

Portrait of Lady with an Ermine
panel, 54x39 cm
Czartoryski Muzeum, Cracow, Poland

The portraits that Leonardo painted in Milan marked a turning point in this genre, especially for Lombard artists. The so-called *Lady with an Ermine* (1488-90) represents the young Cecilia Gallerani, then the mistress of Ludovico il Moro, duke of Milan, for whom the painter was working. The woman is portrayed three-quarters with an ermine in her arms. The animal's name in Greek – γαλη – recalls that of the girl, and at the same time it was a nickname for Ludovico il Moro himself. Leonardo has portrayed the beautiful, intriguing and sophisticated young woman caressing the ermine's soft fur and turning her bust, which emerges from the darkness, to gaze toward a source of light outside the picture.
Cecilia Gallerani was also the model Leonardo used for a study for the angel in the *Virgin of the Rocks* (reproduced below) in a folio now in the Biblioteca Reale of Turin.

Madonna and Child with the Infant Saint John and an Angel (Virgin of the Rocks)
panel, 199x122 cm
Louvre, Paris

On April 25, 1483, the confraternity of the Conception in Milan commissioned Leonardo, along with the brothers Evangelista and Ambrogio de' Predis, to paint a sort of polyptych for the church of Francesco Grande (now destroyed). The central panel of this altarpiece was the so-called *Virgin of the Rocks*, of which two versions have come down to us: the one in the Louvre, considered to be Leonardo's own work, and the one in the National Gallery in London, most of which was executed by the artist's collaborators. The scene is based on an episode recounted in the Apocryphal Gospels, in which the Christ Child and the Infant St. John meet in the rocky desert of the Sinai. From this story Leonardo takes and emphasizes the dialogue between the figures which – arranged in a semicircle according to a pyramidal scheme – are related to one another through the gestures of their hands, their gazes and their attitudes. Even the observer is involved in the scenes, by the angel who looks out of the picture, indicating the Savior. The sense of mystery that pervades

Last Supper
tempera and oil on plaster, 460x880 cm
Refectory, Santa Maria delle Grazie, Milan

In 1494, Duke Ludovico il Moro
commissioned Leonardo to paint the *Last
Supper* in the refectory of the Dominican
monastery of Santa Maria delle Grazie.
The work proceeded very slowly,
prompting complaints from the prior of
the monastery and urgings from the duke
on several occasions. Over the last twenty
years the work, one of the most
celebrated in Italian art, has been
subjected to a restoration, completed in
1999, that was made extremely difficult by
the precarious condition of the surface of
the paint. This problem was largely due to
the technique adopted by Leonardo,
which proved highly susceptible to damp:
in fact the artist utilized temperas with oily
binders, painted on a dry, double layer of
plaster.
In spite of this, the dynamism and drama
of the composition are still clearly
perceptible, revealing the full extent of its
difference from fifteenth-century
representations of the same subject,
particularly common in Tuscan
refectories. In a setting that echoes and
illusionistically amplifies the architecture
of the refectory, the words pronounced by
Christ at the center ("one of you shall
betray me") produce immediate and
spontaneous reactions in the apostles:
arranged in groups of three, they question
one another, show amazement, come
together, draw apart. Thus, on the left,
Judas is the only one who moves back,
feeling himself discovered (the sources
claim that Leonardo gave him the features
of the meddlesome prior who followed
the course of the work with so much
anxiety). In the *Last Supper* each of the
figures displays through his gestures and
attitudes those "movements of the spirit,"
reflections of the psychology of an
individual, that were Leonardo's primary
interest.

LEONARDO DA VINCI

Virgin and Child with Saint Anne
panel, 168x130 cm
Louvre, Paris

A subject to which Leonardo gave
profound thought in his mature years was
the one known in Italian as *Sant'Anna
Metterza*, that is St. Anne represented
together with the Madonna and Child,
who in his turn looks toward the Infant
St. John or a lamb, alluding to the
Baptism and the Passion of Christ
respectively. Before painting the picture
now in the Louvre (1510-13), Leonardo
had experimented with the same subject
on several occasions, ever since the time
the king of France had commissioned a
cartoon of *Saint Anne* from him in 1499
(which some scholars have identified with
the so-called *Burlington House Cartoon*
now in the National Gallery of London).
In the painting in the Louvre the figures
are arranged in a dynamic way that links
them together. The pyramid-shaped
group, organic and compact, stands out
against a landscape with mellow tones
that stretches as far as the eye can see.
The heights and pinnacles of rock, eroded
at the base by water and wrapped in mist
that blurs their outlines, are reminiscent
of the studies into the movement of water
between rocks and in valleys that
Leonardo carried out shortly afterward.
These studies, like the painting, convey
the sense of perennial movement and
imperceptible change that he attributed to
nature, whose spectacle was renewed with
immutable fascination before his eyes.

Portrait of a Woman (*Mona Lisa*)
panel, 77x53 cm
Louvre, Paris

In Florence, around 1505, Leonardo started work on his most famous picture: the portrait of Lisa Gherardini, wife of the Florentine merchant Francesco del Giocondo. It took the artist a long time to paint the portrait and – according to the sources – he found it necessary to entertain his sitter with musicians, singers and clowns. It is likely that Leonardo finished the work in France, where he showed it to Cardinal Louis of Aragon in 1517.

This formula for the portrait of a woman, clipped at the sides and including the hands, had already been adopted by Verrocchio in the *Lady with Primroses* (p. 151). Unlike in this earlier example, however, Leonardo represents the woman at three-quarters and leaning on the arm of a chair. The hands and face – with its intense gaze and bare hint of a smile – are elements of such expressive power that they were immediately taken up by contemporary artists, including Raphael (p. 246). The mystery of that smile, which conceals an elusive and fluid emotion, has the same quality of living impermanence that is conveyed by the landscape in the background, with valleys, winding roads, watercourses and rocky peaks.

Michelangelo Buonarroti

Michelangelo (Caprese, near Arezzo, 1475-Rome 1564) was the second son of Lodovico Buonarroti, the *podestà* of Caprese who moved with his family to Florence a few months later. At first Messer Lodovico had Michelangelo begin a course of classical studies, but then reluctantly agreed to let his son pursue his interest in drawing, apprenticing him to Domenico Ghirlandaio in 1488. Frequenting the garden on Piazza San Marco where young artists went to study the archeological finds in the Medici collection, Michelangelo entered the cultural and artistic circles of Lorenzo the Magnificent.

Following Lorenzo's death (1492) and just a month prior to the expulsion of the Medici from Florence and the entry of King Charles VIII of France into the city (1494), Michelangelo went first to Venice and then to Bologna. Returning to Florence, he left again in 1496 for Rome where, living as a guest of the banker Jacopo Galli, Michelangelo carved the *Bacchus* (Bargello, Florence) for Cardinal Raffaele Riario and the *Pietà* for Cardinal Jean Bilhères (St. Peter's, Vatican).

In 1501, Michelangelo went back to Florence, which by this time had had a republican government for several years. From then on the artist received a series of important public commissions, including the marble statue of *David*, erected in front of the Palazzo della Signoria in 1504, and the fresco of the *Battle of Cascina* (1504), which was to have been executed in the Salone del Maggior Consiglio in the Palazzo Pubblico, alongside Leonardo's *Battle of Anghiari* (p. 208). Both artists, however, soon left Florence and never completed the commission, getting no further than the cartoons. In 1508, in fact, Michelangelo returned to Rome, where Pope Julius II had entrusted the artist with the design of his monumental tomb two years earlier. At the papal court, while Raphael was painting the *Stanze* in the Vatican (pp. 250-3), Michelangelo set about frescoing the ceiling of the Sistine Chapel, which was finished and unveiled in 1512.

On the pontiff's death in 1513, Michelangelo signed a new contract for the tomb, as his heirs wished to reduce its size and cost. This was to be followed by a series of other contracts, until the monument was completed in 1545 and set up with its statues (including that of *Moses*) in San Pietro in Vincoli.

From 1515 to 1534, Michelangelo was living in Florence. For Lorenzo the Magnificent's son, Pope Leo X, and then for his cousin Giulio de' Medici, elected pope in turn in 1523 under the name of Clement VII, the artist undertook various commissions for the complex of San Lorenzo: the design of the façade that was never completed, the New Sacristy intended to house a number of Medici tombs (1519) and the library annexed to the monastery (from 1524). Before finishing the work on the Laurentian complex, however, Michelangelo left Florence forever in 1534, unable to tolerate the despotic rule of Alessandro de' Medici.

At Rome, in 1535, Pope Paul III entrusted the artist with the task of frescoing the *Last Judgment* on the altar wall of the Sistine Chapel and appointed him painter, sculptor and architect of the Vatican Palaces. Once the immense painting was finished (1541), the pope asked the artist to fresco the *Conversion of Saint Paul* and *Crucifixion of Saint Peter* (1542-50) in his private chapel. In the meantime, the artist took on several important architectural and city-planning projects, such as the layout of Piazza del Campidoglio (1538) and the supervision of the construction of St. Peter's (from 1546).

Michelangelo died at his home in the Foro Traiano on February 18, 1564, leaving unfinished his last sculpture, the *Rondanini Pietà* (Castello Sforzesco, Milan). The artist's body was taken to Florence and buried in Santa Croce.

Bacchus
marble, ht. 203 cm
Museo Nazionale del Bargello, Florence

At the age of twenty-one Michelangelo
went to Rome, where he was able to
broaden his knowledge of ancient art by
studying the vast collections of antiquities
possessed by wealthy bankers and
powerful prelates, with whom the artist
quickly established contact. During his
first stay in Rome he was a guest of the
banker Jacopo Galli, and it was with him
that he left the marble *Bacchus* he had
commenced in 1497 to a commission
from Cardinal Raffaele Riario, but which
the latter had probably never taken
delivery of. The work demonstrates the
dialectical and original relationship that
the sculptor established with ancient art.
The youthful god, his features still not
fully formed, teeters drunkenly, barely
maintaining his balance and leaning
backward. His face, turned toward the
antique cup held in his right hand, has the
lost and wavering expression of a
befuddled mind. In his left hand he holds
a lion skin, along with the young faun
behind him who is eating a bunch of
grapes. The perfectly polished surface of
the marble, in the manner of ancient
statuary, heightens the limp sensuality of
the young god.

Pietà
marble, 174x195 cm
St. Peter's, Rome

Not long after the *Bacchus*, Michelangelo carved his first masterpiece, the *Pietà* (1498-99) commissioned by the French cardinal Jean Bilhères de Lagraulas for the church of Santa Petronilla, where the work remained until 1517. Harking back to the dramatic *Lamentations over the Dead Christ* in wood or terracotta of Northern Europe (where they were known as *Vesperbilder*), Michelangelo arrived at a solemn and monumental solution that marked a renewal of the style. The beautiful face of a still youthful Virgin forms the vertex of an imaginary pyramid: her grief is nobly restrained, although her inner turmoil seems to be reflected in the dramatic rise and fall of the almost too abundant drapery. Mary holds the lifeless body of her Son on her lap: perfectly modeled and polished, it is represented in minute anatomical detail (with the right shoulder raised, the head fallen back, the arm hanging straight down, the legs suspended) and conveys an impression of the heaviness and immobility of eternal repose.

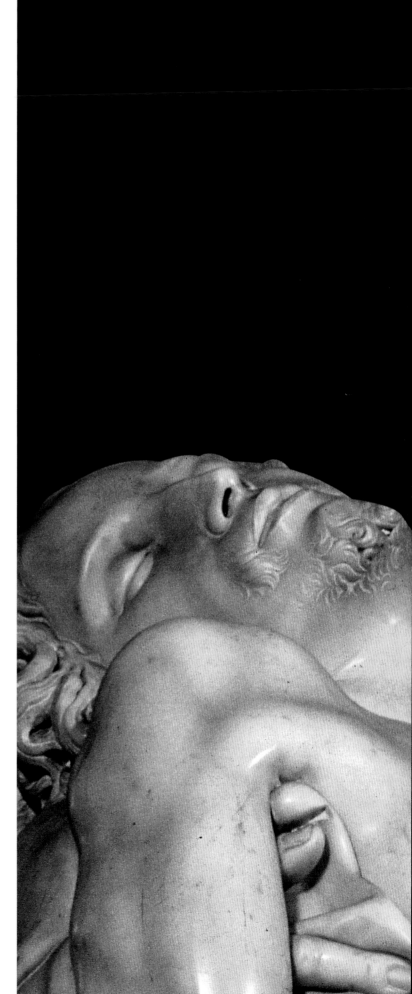

David
marble, ht. 517 cm
Galleria dell'Accademia, Florence

Returning to Florence in 1501, Michelangelo received his first public commission: the Vestry Board of Santa Maria del Fiore asked him to sculpt a gigantic marble figure of *David* for one of the outer buttresses of the cathedral. The artist was assigned a block of marble that other sculptors had already tried to rough-hew without success. Michelangelo, however, proved up to the task and when shown in public, in 1504, the work aroused such admiration that it was felt it should be given a more suitable location. The gonfalonier Pier Soderini set up a

commission of illustrious citizens which decided to erect the statue in front of the Palazzo Pubblico (now Palazzo Vecchio, where it has been replaced by a copy), seat of the republican government that ruled the city at the time.

In contrast to previous versions of *David* by Donatello (pp. 90-1) and Verrocchio, Michelangelo has represented the figure as a formidable hero at the height of his powers, contradicting the description in the Bible itself, where David is said to have been a small and slender youth in contrast to his adversary, the giant Goliath. Here David has not yet won the fight but, with his sling hung over his shoulder, is looking to his left, in the direction of his enemy. His gaze is keen and concentrated, his muscles tensed and ready for action, while his hands are caught in the midst of a slow and careful movement. Thus the work does not celebrate the victorious outcome of the action, but the moment that preceded it. This is the reason why Michelangelo's *David* was seen as a symbol of the proud people of Florence, determined with God's help to stand up to anyone who sought to take away their freedom.

*Holy Family with the Infant
Saint John* (*Doni Tondo*)
panel, diam. 120 cm
Galleria degli Uffizi, Florence

The *Doni Tondo* marks one of the first
chapters in the "grand manner" of the
sixteenth century, as the contemporary
biographer Giorgio Vasari defined it. It is
the only completely finished panel
painting that can be assigned with
certainty to Buonarroti, who also designed
the frame. According to recent studies
(Natali 1985), Michelangelo painted the
large tondo on the occasion of the birth of
Agnolo Doni and Maddalena Strozzi
Doni's first child, Maria (1507). And in
this "divine family of jugglers" (Longhi
1980), her namesake Mary appears to be
the protagonist of the composition, placed
in the foreground while she twists around
in a spiral movement to lift the Child up
with the help of Joseph.
The *Doni Tondo* contains numerous
elements drawn from Hellenistic
sculptures, such as the *Apollo Belvedere*,
Farnese Hercules, *Belvedere Torso*, the
so-called *Dying Alexander* and the group
of the *Laocoön*, discovered in Rome in
1506. It was the encounter with such
works, celebrated by the ancient sources
and rediscovered in the climate of
enthusiasm and wonder that accompanied
a "renaissance," that triggered the
revolution in sixteenth-century art.

Moses
marble, ht. 235 cm
San Pietro in Vincoli, Rome

It was 1505 when Michelangelo went to Rome to receive the commission for an imposing, monumental tomb from Julius II. Enthusiastic about the task entrusted him, the artist set to work straightaway and, following the pope's instructions, conceived a sort of commemorative mausoleum in the ancient manner, three stories and eight meters high and adorned with forty life-size statues. But Julius II's attention was soon diverted toward the rebuilding of St. Peter's and the project for the tomb was shelved. After his complaints were ignored several times, Michelangelo quarreled with the pope and was obliged to flee the city. This marked the beginning of what Buonarroti himself called "the tragedy of the tomb," which led to him revising the original design at least five times over the course of forty years. In fact the heirs of the pope, who died in 1513, renewed the contract for the work several times but made drastic reductions to the project. The undertaking was finally concluded in 1545, when the wall monument, reproduced below, was mounted in San Pietro in Vincoli, where it can still be seen today. The central figure of the tomb is that of *Moses*, carved for the project of 1513: the imposing figure looks like a version in stone of one of the *Prophets* painted on the ceiling of the Sistine Chapel.

View of the Sistine Chapel
Vatican

In 1508 Michelangelo left Florence for Rome, where Pope Julius II Della Rovere asked him to fresco the ceiling of the Sistine Chapel. The chapel had been built some three decades earlier by Sixtus IV, who had summoned the best painters of Central Italy, including Botticelli, Ghirlandaio, Perugino and Signorelli, to fresco the walls with a long series of *Popes* and, below them, with *Scenes from the Lives of Moses and Christ*. The chapel was consecrated on August 15, 1483 and dedicated to Our Lady of the Assumption. The ceiling had been painted a deep blue and dotted with gold to simulate a starry sky, and it was this that was replaced by Michelangelo's powerful and spectacular creation (cf. pp. 232-3). Up until October 31, 1512, Michelangelo worked eagerly on the enterprise, which over the course of time grew increasingly ambitious: in the end it comprised over three hundred figures set in a massive structure of painted architecture. Continuing the theme of the fifteenth-century decoration, Michelangelo's cycle represents stories from the Bible prior to that of Moses, viewed as precedents for the coming of Christ. In the vaulting cells and lunettes around the windows are set the *Ancestors of Christ*; along the sides of the vault appear *Prophets* and *Sibyls*, massive and isolated figures in attitudes that range from the ecstatic to the contemplative; in the middle of the ceiling, finally, nine scenes from *Genesis* are interspersed with youthful *Ignudi* or *Nudes*.

The decoration of the chapel was completed later with the large tapestries depicting the *Acts of the Apostles*, woven in Brussels to cartoons designed by Raphael, and the *Last Judgment* frescoed by Michelangelo himself on the end wall between 1536 and 1541.

The latest chapter in the history of the Sistine Chapel has been the restoration of the frescoes, a challenging task that has produced astonishing results, recently completed in time for the Jubilee of 2000.

Prisoner known as *Atlas*; *Prisoner* known as the *Awakening Slave*
marble, ht. 277; 267 cm
Galleria dell'Accademia, Florence

Prisoner known as the *Dying Slave*
marble, ht. 229 cm
Louvre, Paris

It was under the terms of the second contract for the sepulchral monument of Julius II, drawn up with the Della Rovere family in 1513, that the *Moses* in San Pietro in Vincoli and two of the *Prisoners* now in the Louvre, respectively known as the *Dying Slave* and the *Rebellious Slave*, were carved. According to the new design,

which this time was for a structure set against the wall, the sculptures were to have been placed on the lower level, as allegories of the Liberal Arts enchained and struggling to free the soul from its earthly prison. The *Dying Slave*, bound by ties and bands around the shoulders, the chest and the raised arm, is perhaps Michelangelo's most sublime representation of masculine beauty, with its traits of sensuality and languid suffering.

In 1519, at his studio in Florence, Buonarroti began work on the four *Prisoners* now in the Galleria dell'Accademia, after signing a third contract (1516) for the mausoleum of

Julius II which envisaged a design very similar to the tomb that was actually built. The four gigantic and powerful figures were to have been set on the pilasters of the lower story but in fact were never finished by the artist, too busy with the tasks assigned to him by Pope Leo X. But those incomplete human forms, struggling fiercely to free themselves from the matter in which they are still trapped, clearly reveal Michelangelo's poetic intent: in his view, the sculptor's job was to find within the block of marble the ideal shape that was in his mind, "removing" the superfluous material that imprisoned and concealed it.

New Sacristy
San Lorenzo, Florence

The New Sacristy, so-called to distinguish it from the "Old Sacristy" built a century earlier by Brunelleschi, was commissioned from Buonarroti by Leo X de' Medici in 1520. It was the pope's intention for the chapel to house the remains of his brother Giuliano, duke of Nemours, and his nephew Lorenzo, duke of Urbino (who had died in 1516 and 1519 respectively), along with those of Lorenzo the Magnificent and his brother Giuliano (the former had died in 1492 and the latter in 1478): thus the last representatives of the dynasty, dressed as military "captains" in the old style, would be united with the two "Magnificents" who bore the same names. Michelangelo designed the architectural space in close relation to the sculptures, creating a dialectical and dynamic ensemble that responded to a precise iconological program based on the theme of the Resurrection. Unfortunately, the New Sacristy was still incomplete when the artist left Florence for good in 1534. Buonarroti's marble sculptures were later installed by Giorgio Vasari and Bartolomeo Ammannati (1554-55), artists at the court of Duke Cosimo I de' Medici. The sepulchral monuments of the two dukes are set against the walls of the sacristy, one on each side. They are represented by idealized figures: Duke Giuliano of Nemours, in a determined attitude and dressed as a Roman commander, is situated above a sarcophagus on which are set the reclining allegorical figures of *Night* (cf. pp. 240-1) and *Day*; Duke Lorenzo of Urbino, in a meditative pose (the figure has been nicknamed "the Thoughtful"), appears above his own sarcophagus, with allegories of the *Dusk* and *Dawn* (reproduced on the left). Located in elevated positions, one opposite the other, the dukes are gazing toward the altar, at the group of the *Madonna and Child* which, flanked by *Saints Cosmas and Damian*, is set above the tomb of Lorenzo the Magnificent and Giuliano: thus the Virgin is the spiritual center of the chapel, and it is to her that the effigies of worldly glory (the dukes, personifications of the active and contemplative life respectively) and of time (which consumes earthly life as the parts of the day succeed one another) turn, seeking the peace of a higher spiritual harmony.

Designed at a troubled time in the history of Florence and Italy and in the artist's own life, the New Sacristy is exemplary of the poetics and artistic culture of Mannerism.

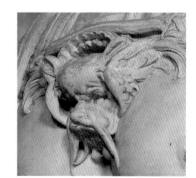

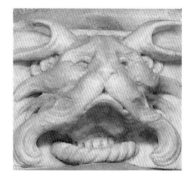

MICHELANGELO BUONARROTI

Last Judgment
fresco, 1370x1220 cm
Sistine Chapel, Vatican

In the imposing scene, executed between 1536 and 1541 under Pope Paul III Farnese, the artist abandoned the architectural framework of the ceiling to represent a host of figures in dramatically animated and varied attitudes, suspended against an abstract blue background, very different from an atmospheric sky. High up and in the middle of the vast composition, bathed in light, appears Christ the Judge, powerful and vengeful. Alongside him is set the shy figure of his Mother and all around terrified and dismayed saints and angels are interceding on behalf of humanity. Adamant, Christ has his arm raised and is condemning the damned, driving them down to the right toward Charon, ferryman of souls destined for Hell. With his other arm he is beckoning the chosen, who rise with difficulty among the clouds. In an incessant whirl of frantic bodies, the composition rotates in a clockwise direction, under the impetus of ineluctable divine justice. Humanity, made up of body and soul, is the exclusive protagonist of the scene, represented totally naked and with exaggerated proportions. This nudity so scandalized his contemporaries that shortly after the artist's death, Daniele da Volterra was ordered to paint "breeches" over the intimate parts of some figures (later alterations were removed during the recent restoration, completed in 1994). Amidst the crowd of tormented and desperate figures we can find the portraits of several of Michelangelo's contemporaries. Minos (at bottom right), for instance, is believed to have been given the features of the pope's master of ceremonies, Biagio da Cesena, who had expressed his disapproval of so much nudity. The artist's self-portrait also appears, perhaps more than once and undoubtedly in the flayed skin St. Bartholomew is holding. This is a mark of Michelangelo's sense of personal involvement in this agonizing theme at a time of spiritual and theological tension that saw deep conflicts within the Church itself and the unbridgeable split between Catholics and Protestants that culminated in the Council of Trent.

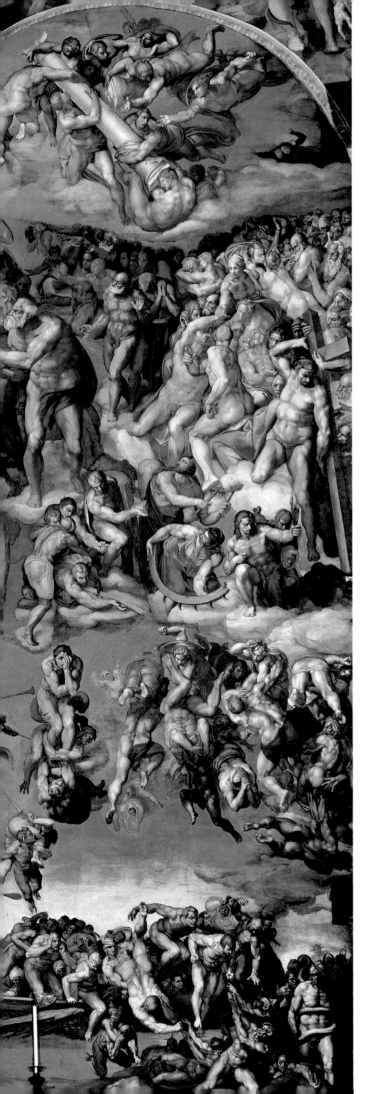

Rondanini Pietà
marble, ht. 195 cm
Civiche Raccolte del Castello Sforzesco,
Milan

Toward the end of his life Michelangelo,
though still engaged in numerous public
commissions at the papal court,
concentrated behind the closed doors of
his studio on the theme of the *Pietà*, a
reflection of his meditations on the
approach of death. In fact Michelangelo
was still working on the *Rondanini Pietà*
(named after Palazzo Rondanini in Rome,
where it used to be located), just a few
days before his death in 1564. The
unfinished sculpture was subjected to
continual revisions and adjustments that
led the artist to fine it down, consuming
more and more of the material. The
result, in spite of its incomplete state, is
intensely moving: Mother and Son have
emaciated bodies, making them both look
fragile, worn-out and disfigured by pain.

Betrothal of the Virgin
(*Lo Sposalizio*)
panel, 170x117 cm
Pinacoteca di Brera, Milan

Painted for the chapel of San Giuseppe in
the church of San Francesco at Città di
Castello, the work is signed and dated in
an inscription on the colonnade of the
temple: "RAPHAEL VRBINAS – MDIIII."

Raphael

Raphael (Raffaello Sanzio, Urbino 1483-Rome 1520) was the son of Giovanni Santi, a painter at the court of Federico da Montefeltro, the duke of Urbino. Brought up in the city's lively culture and initially taught painting by his father, Raphael then entered the workshop of Perugino, with whom he quickly formed a close collaboration.

Becoming a master in his own right, Raphael spent most of the time from 1500 to 1504 at Città di Castello – on the border between Umbria and Tuscany – though he was also in Perugia, Urbino and Venice and may have made journeys for the purpose of study to Florence and Rome (1503 and 1506). From the artist's drawings it can also be deduced that he visited Orvieto, to study the frescoes of Luca Signorelli, and Siena, to collaborate with Pintoricchio on the frescoes of the Piccolomini Library (pp.174-5).

In 1504, he moved to Florence, where he presented himself to Gonfalonier Pier Soderini with a letter of introduction from Giovanna Feltria della Rovere, duchess of Urbino. His work proved highly popular with the upper middle-class families of the Tuscan city (Nasi, Canigiani, Taddei, Doni), for whom he painted devotional pictures and portraits. From 1504 to 1508 Raphael was active in Florence, Perugia and Urbino, and this was a period of profound stylistic maturation.

Leaving the *Dei Altarpiece* for Santo Spirito in Florence incomplete, Raphael set off for Rome at the end of 1508, summoned by Pope Julius II to fresco the Vatican *Stanze*. Named court painter by papal brief, Raphael assembled a large group of collaborators to whom he could assign the innumerable commissions he received, which continued to grow even under Pope Leo X. Among these, Raphael and his team decorated the Vatican Logge with *Scenes from the Old Testament* (1519) and produced the cartoons for the tapestries to be hung in the Sistine Chapel (begun in 1515; now in the Victoria and Albert Museum, London). While continuing the decoration of the *Stanze*, a task increasingly delegated to his assistants, Raphael worked for other distinguished clients, including the banker Agostino Chigi, the nobleman Bindo Altoviti, the writer Baldassarre Castiglione and Cardinal Dovizi Bibbiena.

Engaged in a number of architectural and city-planning projects as well, he was appointed "architect of the Fabric of St. Peter's" in 1514 and produced plans for the new basilica. For this activity, Raphael also carried out a thorough study of Roman antiquities, something that led him to draw up an archeological map of Rome in relief.

He died on April 6, 1520, at the age of only thirty-seven, and was buried in the Pantheon in an ancient sarcophagus for which the man of letters Pietro Bembo wrote the following verses: "This is that Raphael, by whom in life / Our mighty mother Nature feared defeat; / And in whose death did fear herself to die."

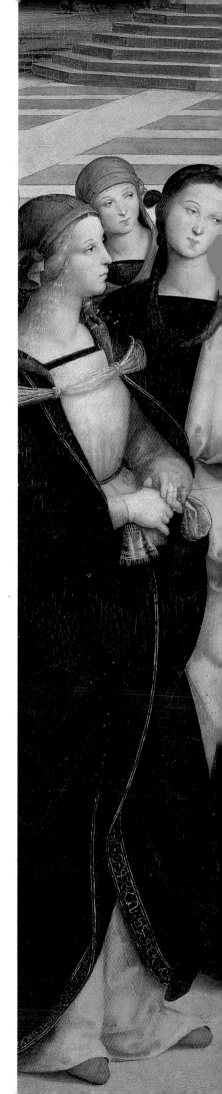

RAPHAEL

Though the composition is based on a scheme already used by Perugino, in contrast to his master Raphael establishes a closer and more organic relationship between the figures and the architectural backdrop, which is used to generate a broad and rational circular space. Raphael's building resembles contemporary designs by the architect Bramante, including the Tempietto of San Pietro in Montorio at Rome, an indication of the common way of thinking of two artists who both received their training in Urbino under the influence of Piero della Francesca.

Portraits of Agnolo Doni and *Maddalena Strozzi Doni*
panel, 65x45·7 cm each
Galleria Palatina, Florence

In Florence around 1506, Raphael painted the portraits of Agnolo Doni, a wealthy Florentine merchant and collector of gems and antiques, and his wife Maddalena Strozzi, whom he had married in 1504. The composition of the two portraits – especially the one of Maddalena – is clearly derived from Leonardo's *Mona Lisa* (p. 221). In contrast to the latter, however, it is not

the subtle and elusive character of the sitter that interests Raphael, but the social status indicated by the clothing and jewelry, sober in compliance with the sumptuary laws in force at the time but made from refined and high-quality materials. Maddalena is wearing a necklace whose symbolism suggests that it was a wedding gift from Agnolo: the unicorn with which the gold setting closes at the top is an emblem of chastity; healing powers were attributed to the emerald; the ruby was considered to bring wealth; the sapphire was a symbol of purity; finally, the pearl pendant alluded to virginity.

RAPHAEL

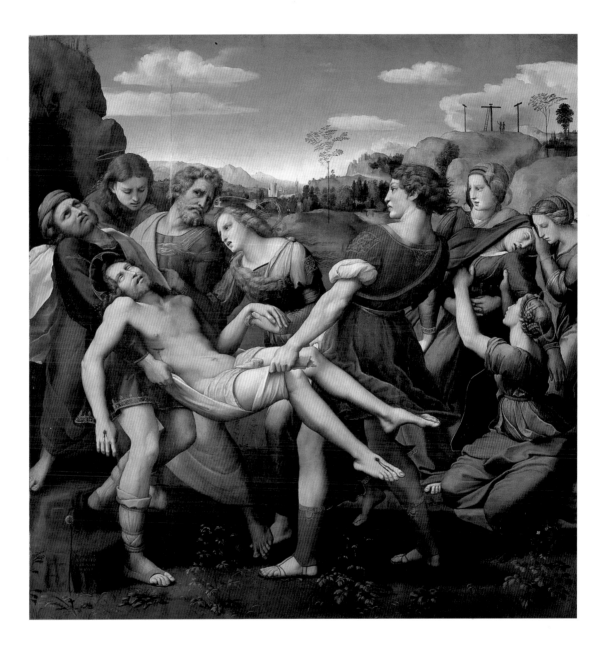

Transport of Christ
(*Borghese Deposition*)
panel, 184x176 cm
Galleria Borghese, Rome

Signed and dated 1507, the picture was painted by Raphael for the church of San Francesco al Prato in Perugia. The client was Atalanta Baglioni, who wanted it to commemorate the death of her son Grifonetto, killed in the city's internecine struggles for power.

In the long elaboration of the subject – for which we have evidence in the form of sixteen drawings now in various European public collections – Raphael passed from a representation of the *Lamentation over the Dead Christ* to the theme of the transport of Christ's body to the tomb. In the figure of the Virgin swooning with grief, the artist may have wanted to suggest Atalanta Baglioni's sorrow over the death of her son.
The dynamism of the scene, the force and

the plasticity of the figures and the brilliant colors show the extent to which Raphael was influenced by Michelangelo. He even included a number of direct citations from his works, such as the body of Christ with his arm hanging loose and head drooping onto his shoulders, from the *Pietà* in St. Peter's (pp. 226-7), and the woman seated on the ground, who is twisting round to support the Virgin, from the Madonna in the *Doni Tondo* (pp. 230-1).

thoughtful and solitary figure with a beard in the foreground, is Michelangelo. Finally, Raphael himself is represented on the far right wearing a black cap.

On the other two walls of the room are depicted the *Parnassus* and the *Theological and Cardinal Virtues*. In the *Parnassus*, poets and men of letters from every age (including Dante at top left, the blind Homer and Virgil) are gathered in the presence of Apollo, who is playing the lyre surrounded by the Muses.

The Mass at Bolsena
fresco, base 660 cm
Stanza di Eliodoro, Vatican

From 1511 to 1514 Raphael frescoed the second room, called the Stanza di Eliodoro after the subject of one of the frescoes, representing the *Expulsion of Heliodorus from the Temple*. The paintings in this room have a different tone: they are narrative and dramatic in character and go in for bold foreshortenings, spectacular actions and marked contrasts, losing the serene and poised harmony of the symbolic images in the previous room. The *Mass at Bolsena* records a miraculous

event that took place at Bolsena in 1263, when a Bohemian priest with doubts about the eucharistic mystery of transubstantiation saw blood flow from the consecrated Host on the altar. The miracle is witnessed by Pope Julius II, kneeling and accompanied by cardinals, Swiss Guards and bearers of the gestatorial chair; the latter, in the foreground, are among the most intense portraits in early sixteenth-century Italian art. The series of four Vatican Stanze is completed by the Stanza dell'Incendio di Borgo (1514-17), frescoed mostly by Raphael's collaborators, and the Stanza di Costantino, completed after the artist's death (1520) by his followers.

pp. 250-1 *School of Athens*
fresco, base 770 cm
Stanza della Segnatura, Vatican

Parnassus
fresco, base 670 cm
Stanza della Segnatura, Vatican

In 1508 Raphael left Florence to settle in Rome, where he had been summoned by Pope Julius II to participate in the pictorial decoration of several rooms in his private apartment. The pontiff was so impressed by the work he did there that he entrusted the whole undertaking to Raphael, dismissing the other artists and having the paintings they had already done erased.

From 1508 to 1511 – while Michelangelo was working on the Sistine Chapel – Raphael frescoed the so-called Stanza della Segnatura (reproduced at top), formerly the seat of the ecclesiastical court of the Apostolic Signatura and then turned into the pope's private library. The artist painted the ceiling with its compartments and the walls with their four large lunettes, whose allegorical scenes were intended to exalt the ideas of Truth, Goodness and Beauty and establish a historical continuity between the culture of the ancient world and Christian spirituality. The *Disputation over the Sacrament*, representing the triumph of the Church and the Eucharist, is a reference to Truth, as is the *School of Athens* on the opposite wall, where philosophers and scientists of antiquity, with Plato and Aristotle at the center, meet in a sort of monumental temple in the sixteenth-century style, recalling Bramante's design for the new St. Peter's: the revealed truth of theology is equated with the rational truth of philosophy. Some of the figures in the *School of Athens* are portraits of contemporary artists: Aristotle is a portrait of the architect Bramante; Heraclitus, a

RAPHAEL

Madonna and Child with the Infant Saint John (*Madonna della Seggiola*)
panel, diam. 71 cm
Galleria Palatina, Florence

This is one of Raphael's most celebrated Madonnas, perhaps commissioned by a dignitary at the papal court or by Leo X himself. In fact the seat from which the painting takes its name (*seggiola*) could be a reference to the pope, resembling as it does the papal faldstool. The Virgin's

mode of dress, with her shoulders covered with a shawl of fine colored silk and her hair bound up in a "striped towel" in the Oriental manner, is consonant with an aristocratic setting. Painted around 1513-14, the picture is a sublime and ineffable representation of maternal affection in a harmonious composition of great technical mastery. The colors help to underline the tenderness of the contact between Mother and Son, with the cold tones used at the edges of the picture shading into warmer ones toward the middle.

Portrait of a Woman (*La Velata*)
canvas, 82x60·5 cm
Galleria Palatina, Florence

Aptly described as "the portrait of a sleeve," the picture (*c.* 1515-16) represents an unknown woman, who on the basis of the sixteenth-century sources has often been identified with the painter's longtime lover, the legendary Fornarina who is now thought to have been Margherita, daughter of the Sienese baker

Francesco Luti in the Santa Dorotea quarter of Rome. Women with the same features appear in other pictures painted by the artist in Rome, including the *Madonna della Seggiola*.

Portrait of Leo X with Cardinals Giulio de' Medici and Luigi de' Rossi

panel, 155·2x118·9 cm
Galleria degli Uffizi, Florence

The son of Lorenzo the Magnificent, elected pope in 1513, Leo X sent this portrait to Florence to represent himself at the banquet held in honor of the marriage between his nephew Duke Lorenzo of Urbino and Madeleine de la Tour d'Auvergne (1518). Thus it is a formal portrait, imposing and magnificent in style, in which each element (for instance, the red shades of the fabrics, or the illuminated book and the chased bell in the foreground) is intended to emphasize the culture, taste and nobility of the sitter. The spherical knob of the armchair, in which the window through which light enters the room is reflected, may be an allusion to the "balls" of the Medici coat of arms.

Diagnostic investigations carried out on the occasion of a recent restoration show that in the first version (c. 1517), Raphael had portrayed the pope alone, against the backdrop of a green drape. It was only later that Giulio de' Medici and Luigi de' Rossi, relatives of Leo X and elevated by him to cardinal's rank, were inserted, perhaps by another hand, and the green drape replaced by an architectural setting.

Giorgione

U nfortunately, any reconstruction of Giorgione's life (Castelfranco Veneto *c.* 1477/78-Venice 1510) can only be made on the basis of scanty documentary evidence. And yet his work marked the turning point in Venetian art, the transition from the fifteenth to the sixteenth century, from the lyrical art of Bellini to the magniloquent style of Titian.

The name Giorgione derives from Zorzo or Zorzi, which in the Venetian dialect means "of very humble birth." The only reliable information about the artist's life we have is the date 1506 on the *Portrait of Laura* (Kunsthistorisches Museum, Vienna) and two orders for payment in 1507 and 1508 for a picture – now lost – to be hung in the Doge's Palace. In addition, between March and November of 1508, Giorgione frescoed an outside wall of the Fondaco dei Tedeschi near the Rialto Bridge, a work that his contemporaries considered revolutionary but which has unfortunately only survived in fragments.

Described by the sources as a man fond of women and music, Giorgione frequented Venetian cultural circles where not only music, but also literature, poetry and philosophy were cultivated. It was amongst this select band of Humanists and scholars that Giorgione found the clients for his works, whose subjects are often difficult to interpret, intended as they were for an exclusive public and for such private and refined settings as studies. The most famous of these pictures are *The Tempest* (Gallerie dell'Accademia, Venice) and *The Three Philosophers* (Kunsthistorisches Museum, Vienna). The sources record that Giorgione also painted frescoes on the façades of the palaces of some noble Venetian families, but these have vanished.

In 1510 Giorgione died of the plague in Venice, but his fame soon spread beyond the confines of the republic. In the pages of his dialogue *Il cortegiano* (*The Courtier*), published in 1528, the writer Baldassarre Castiglione described Giorgione as one of the five most important Italian painters.

Madonna and Child with Saints Liberale (Nicasius?) and Francis (Castelfranco Madonna)
panel, 200x152 cm
Cathedral, Castelfranco Veneto

Giorgione's only known altarpiece was painted for the chapel of the Costanzo family in Castelfranco Cathedral: in fact the Costanzo coat of arms is represented in the middle of the first step of the throne. Datable to between 1504 and 1506, the painting sets the sacred group in the landscape on the other side of the balustrade: in this way Giorgione renewed the fifteenth-century scheme of the altarpiece introduced by Giovanni Bellini, who placed the *Sacra Conversazione* inside monumental architectural settings (pp. 196-7).

The Tempest
canvas, 82x73 cm
Gallerie dell'Accademia, Venice

This is Giorgione's most famous painting,
perhaps completed around 1506-08. It
was commissioned by Gabriele
Vendramin, a member of the Venetian
Humanist circles that set great store by
pictures of a cryptic and elusive
significance, comprehensible only to an
elite group of sophisticated intellectuals.
And the fact is that Giorgione's work is
still a puzzle and, notwithstanding the
numerous proposals, has not yet found a
wholly convincing interpretation.
The title, already assigned to the painting
in the sixteenth century, derives from the
stormy sky rent by lightning. For the first
time the landscape is the protagonist of a
pictorial composition, in close relation to
the silent and solitary figures. The poetic
atmosphere of the scene is enhanced by the
technique adopted by Giorgione, who made
no preparatory drawing but worked directly
on the canvas with the paintbrush. In
addition, the colors shade into one another
through gradual shifts in tone, assuming
tints that vary in relation to the light: note
for instance the gentle and blurred
transitions in the foreground from the
brown of the earth to the green of the grass.
Diagnostic investigations have shown that
Giorgione made some major changes over
the course of the work: the most
interesting discovery has been the
presence of the figure of a nude woman at
bottom left, seated and with her legs
dangling in the water, which the artist
then erased and replaced with the
standing male figure in modern dress.

Portrait of an Old Woman
canvas, 68x59 cm
Gallerie dell'Accademia, Venice

Considered a portrait of the artist's
mother ever since the sixteenth century,
the painting has also been interpreted as
an allegorical representation because of
the scroll with the inscription "COL TEMPO"
("In Time") in the woman's hand. Yet its
significance remains uncertain: perhaps
an allegory of Vanity or a warning about
the fleeting nature of beauty, a eulogy of
old age or a representation of the
corrupting effect of time, to cite some of
the proposals put forward.
Influenced by Leonardo's portraits and
caricatures, the painting shows us a face
of great expressiveness and humanity.
Once again, the sole means used for the
naturalistic rendering of the woman's
lined and weary appearance is color.

The Three Philosophers
canvas, 123x144 cm
Kunsthistorisches Museum, Vienna

Three men – of different ages and origins
– are meditating in silence in a landscape
bathed in the clear light of dawn.
Imposing and isolated, though close to
one another, the three figures are dressed
in clothing of diverse style and color and
engaged in different occupations: the
young man seated on the ground is
tracing geometric figures with a setsquare
and compass, the man in the turban is
reflecting and the old man is unrolling a
parchment with astronomical symbols. In
front of them lies a dark and mysterious
cave, just as the meaning of this
fascinating painting of Giorgione's is once
again mysterious. The three sages are
steeped in the vibrant atmosphere of
nature, in a composition that is

filled with a sense of enchantment.
One of the oldest – and among the most
accredited – hypotheses identifies the
three men as the Magi waiting for the
appearance of the star above Monte
Vittoriale. This interpretation receives
partial support from X-ray analysis
(1932), which has revealed a number of
changes made by the painter: the old man
originally had a crown on his head, the
man in the middle had a darker
complexion and the youth wore a cap.

Sacred Love and Profane Love
canvas, 118x278 cm
Galleria Borghese, Rome

This famous picture of an allegorical
subject was painted by Titian to celebrate
the marriage in May 1514 of Niccolò
Aurelio, Venetian patrician and secretary
of the Council of Ten, to the Paduan Laura

Titian

Arriving in Venice at the age of nine and taught painting by an undistinguished local artist, Sebastiano Zuccato, Titian (Tiziano Vecellio, Pieve di Cadore 1489/1490-
Venice 1576) moved on to the workshops of Giovanni Bellini and then Giorgione.
He collaborated with the latter on the frescoes on the façade of the Fondaco dei Tedeschi at Rialto (1508). In this
early part of his career Titian, showing affinities with Giorgione, painted mostly pictures with Arcadian themes
and complex allegories, such as the *Country Concert* in the Louvre and the *Sacred and Profane Love* (1514)
in the Galleria Borghese, works intended for a select and cultivated public.

Between 1516 and 1518, Titian painted the *Assumption* for Santa Maria dei Frari. This was a new conception
of the altarpiece for Venice, couched in scenographic terms. The work proved such a success that from then on
Titian was considered the official painter of the Serenissima, appreciated for the drama and magnificence of his
images and his original use of color. Giving a precise identity to Venetian art, Titian developed a new approach
to the altarpiece, portrait and mythological painting that drew on central Italian ideas, and in particular
Raphael, Michelangelo and their followers.

Titian established profitable relations with the main courts in Northern Italy, staying with Alfonso I d'Este in
Ferrara (from 1519), Federico II Gonzaga in Mantua (from 1523 and in 1527-28) and Francesco Maria della
Rovere, a condottiere in the pay of the Venetian Republic, in Urbino (from 1532). Even Emperor Charles V
showed an interest in the artist, who first painted his portrait in Bologna at the time of his coronation in 1530
and then again in 1533. The Habsburg ruler bestowed honors and fiefs on Titian, even making him a palatine
count. In the forties, Titian started to abandon the serene equilibrium of his early works and go in instead for
melodramatic compositions and the use of bold foreshortening, emphatic gestures and complex poses.

After a stay in Urbino, Titian was in Rome from 1545 to 1546, where he painted *Paul III and His Grandsons*
(Capodimonte, Naples). The popularity of his work in the papal city earned the artist Roman citizenship, which
he was granted before returning home (1546).

Titian had now become one of the most esteemed artists at the imperial court, especially for his formal portraits.
The Venetian painter went to visit Charles V at Augsburg during the Imperial Diet of 1548 and then again in
1550, when he portrayed the emperor's son Philip. Titian's relations with the two men were long and stormy, as
is borne out by their extensive correspondence (now in the archives at Simancas in Spain): over a period of
twenty years Titian painted numerous devotional and mythological pictures (including *Danaë, Venus and Ado-
nis, Diana and Actaeon* and *Diana and Callisto*) for Philip II, who was a keen collector but reluctant to pay for
the works he commissioned, and was given complete freedom in the choice of subject, interpretation and style.
In the last decades of his life Titian returned to themes he had tackled in the past, such as the *Crowning with
Thorns* (Alte Pinakothek; Munich), which he now
presented in a more dramatic fashion and with
crumbling forms. He died in Venice on August 27,
1576, leaving incomplete the *Pietà* intended for his
own tomb in Santa Maria dei Frari (now in the
Gallerie dell'Accademia, Venice).

Bagarotto. The coat of arms of the Aurelio family is located on the front of the sarcophagus, while that of the Bagarotto is engraved on the bowl.

The title was given to the work in the eighteenth century. In reality the subject is uncertain, as is apparent from the varied interpretations that have been advanced, though it was probably inspired by neoplatonic thought. The composition undoubtedly reflects a theme linked to Love and contrasts two different female figures (perhaps the earthly Venus, clothed, and the celestial Venus, nude). In the middle Cupid is dipping his hand into the water that fills the sarcophagus, which has become the basin of a fountain and therefore been transformed from a symbol of death into one of life.

Assumption
panel, 690x360 cm
Santa Maria Gloriosa dei Frari, Venice

On May 19, 1518, the altarpiece of the *Assumption* was placed on the high altar of the church of the Frari amidst solemn celebrations. The work, which caused a sensation, marked the beginning of Titian's public activity. Reflecting the theological thought of the Conventual Franciscan friars who owned the church, the composition represents the Virgin, immaculate since her conception, ascending in glory to the Eternal Father in the company of a host of angels and bathed in light, while the apostles look on in astonished adoration. The majestic scene, filled with emotional tension, can be compared with the contemporary works of Michelangelo and Raphael:

common to all these paintings is a heroic, spectacular and dramatic style, which in Titian's case is achieved primarily through color and the pictorial values of the image.

Madonna with Saints and Members of the Pesaro Family (*Pesaro Altarpiece*)
canvas, 478x268 cm
Santa Maria Gloriosa dei Frari, Venice

Following the success of his *Assumption*, Titian received the commission for another painting for the same church: the picture for the altar belonging to Jacopo Pesaro, bishop of Paphos. The work, completed in 1526, was to depict the Immaculate Conception (the theme to which the altar was dedicated) and at the same time celebrate the victory over the

Turks at Santa Maura in 1502 by the papal fleet under Pesaro's command. In the painting Jacopo Pesaro is represented on the left with a Turkish prisoner and a soldier bearing the papal standard of the Borgia family. The client is kneeling in front of St. Peter, who is interceding with the Virgin seated near the columns, an allusion to the Marian privilege. On the right are portrayed St. Francis and St. Anthony, accompanied by Jacopo Pesaro's brothers and his nephew Leonardo, the boy who is looking out of the picture.

The composition represents a radical renewal of the traditional scheme of the altarpiece: breaking with the symmetrical layout that was a feature of fifteenth-century paintings, Titian's picture has a diagonal and ascending structure that creates a lively and spectacular effect. It was to have considerable influence on later artists.

Venus of Urbino
canvas, 119x165 cm
Galleria degli Uffizi, Florence

Guidobaldo della Rovere, son of the duke of Urbino, was the client for this painting, one of Titian's most famous and widely imitated. Painted sometime before 1538, the work depicts a nude young woman lying on an unmade bed with her hair down. The woman's soft and vibrant sensuality is emphasized by the domestic setting of the scene: an aristocratic bedchamber where a pair of maidservants are taking clothes out of a chest in the background. Among the various interpretations put forward by art historians, the one that sees the picture as an allegory of conjugal love seems for now to be the most convincing. The hypothesis is supported, in particular, by the roses falling from the young woman's hand onto the bed, alluding to the love of a couple; the dog sleeping at her feet, a symbol of marital fidelity; the myrtle on the windowsill, a plant sacred to Venus; and the wedding chest over which the maid is bent.

TITIAN

Paul III and His Grandsons Ottavio and Cardinal Alessandro Farnese
canvas, 210x174 cm
Gallerie Nazionali di Capodimonte, Naples

Titian was one of the first European artists to practice the genre of the state portrait, proposing a formula that reconciled a glorification of the social and political status of the sitter with a characterization of the individual's physical and psychological traits.
A clear example of this is the portrait of Paul III painted by Titian in Rome in 1546. It was the pope's intention for the picture to be a celebration of the fame of the Farnese family, just as Raphael's *Portrait of Leo X with Cardinals Giulio de' Medici and Luigi de' Rossi* (pp. 256-7) had glorified the Medici dynasty. But for Titian the portrait of the pope and his grandsons provided the opportunity for a subtle and penetrating investigation of the three individuals. Seated at the center of a cursory setting, the pontiff – now elderly but still strong-willed and alert – is turned toward his obsequious and devious grandson Ottavio, while his other grandson Alessandro looks on from behind with deliberate detachment.

Charles V on Horseback
canvas, 332x279 cm
Museo del Prado, Madrid

Paying a visit to the imperial court at Augsburg in 1548, Titian was received with particular informality and favor by Charles V, who considered him *pintor primero* and entrusted him among other things with the task of painting portraits of members of the Habsburg court. On this occasion the Venetian artist painted the picture in the Prado representing Charles V himself on horseback, wearing a gleaming suit of armor and with a proud and determined bearing, ready for battle. He is depicted from a low point of view against the background of a deserted landscape and a sky shot through with glimmers of light.
The painting was intended as an indirect celebration of the victory obtained by Charles V against Protestant forces at Mühlberg just a year previously. In Titian's portrait, the emperor is presented as an imposing and motionless figure, fulfilling his role in history in an image that identifies him with the very idea of power.

Portrait of a Gentleman
(*The Young Englishman* or *The Man with Blue-Green Eyes*)
canvas, 111x96·8 cm
Galleria Palatina, Florence

Recently restored, this beautiful painting can be dated to around 1545. The identity of the sitter and the provenance of the work remain unknown. In a symphony of grays and blacks, the man is set in a self-assured pose and with a "heroic" mien against a neutral ground on which his shadow is cast. From this dark silhouette, constructed with great pictorial skill, the white lace of the shirt that peeps out at the collar and cuffs stands out, underlining the passage from the clothing to the flesh tones. The man's intense and noble expression conveys a rigorous and subtle psychology, which already looks modern to our eyes.

Danaë
canvas, 120x172 cm
Gallerie Nazionali di Capodimonte, Naples

Danaë
canvas, 129x180 cm
Museo del Prado, Madrid

While in Rome working for the Farnese family, Titian painted the *Danaë* now in Capodimonte, representing a mythological subject taken from Ovid: Danaë, the daughter of King Acrisius of Argos, is seduced by Zeus who transforms himself into a shower of gold in order to enter the bronze tower in which the girl has been imprisoned by her father. Using color with an extraordinary freedom that totally excluded the use of line (X-ray photographs have demonstrated the absence of any drawing), Titian has produced an image charged with sensuality in a scene in which the myth is transformed into poetic enchantment. Giorgio Vasari (1568) related how, having gone one day to find Titian in his studio in Rome with Michelangelo, the latter, seeing the *Danaë*, praised it for its color but lamented the absence of drawing, something that was characteristic of Venetian painters. With these words, in fact, Vasari highlighted the cultural and aesthetic contrast between Venetian painting, dominated by color, and Roman and Florentine painting, based on line. Titian returned to the subject and composition of the picture he painted for the Farnese around 1553 in one of the first paintings on a mythological-literary theme, known as "poems," that he produced for Prince Philip, the son of Charles V. The chief difference in this picture – now in the Prado – is the insertion of the old nurse who catches the golden rain in her apron and who is also present in Ovid's tale. Toward the end of his life, Titian used forms that were more and more devoid of any plastic consistency, dissolved and softened into a vibrant pattern of light and shade.

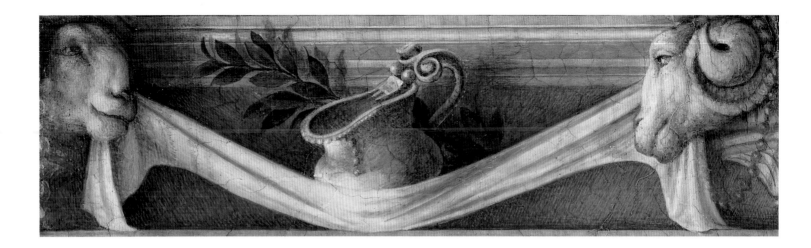

Correggio

Antonio Allegri's byname derives from Correggio, the provincial city near Reggio Emilia where the artist was born and spent his youth (Correggio 1489-1534). Receiving his initial training from his paternal uncle Lorenzo and other modest local painters, the young Antonio looked with interest to the work of Mantegna and the culture promoted by the Mantuan court. Leonardo, Giorgione and Raphael were later to have a powerful impact on the artist and his style, characterized by blurred forms, delicate shades of color and the gracious poses of the figures. Digesting these influences and operating in the towns and cities of Emilia, Correggio developed one of the most original styles in early sixteenth-century art.

In 1519, the painter was entrusted with the task of frescoing the parlor of the abbess Giovanna de Piacenza in the convent of San Paolo at Parma. This was followed by enterprises on a monumental scale that were to serve as significant models for subsequent baroque decoration: between 1520 and 1523 Correggio frescoed the dome of San Giovanni Evangelista with the *Vision of Saint John on Patmos* and, from 1526 to 1530, the dome of Parma Cathedral with the *Assumption of the Virgin*. In the meantime the artist painted some important altarpieces in which he intensified the emotional relationship between the observer and the sacred image through audacious foreshortening and the gazes of the figures (e.g. the altarpiece known as *Night* for San Prospero in Reggio Emilia, commissioned in 1522).

Returning to his hometown, Correggio painted several pictures for the dukes of Mantua: the *Allegories of Vice and Virtue* (c. 1529-30; Louvre, Paris) for the study of Isabella d'Este and a series of canvases representing the *Loves of Jupiter* (1531-34) for Duke Federico II, who gave some of them to the emperor Charles V (*Io* and *Ganymede*, Kunsthistorisches Museum, Vienna).

View of the Abbess's Parlor
convent of San Paolo, Parma

In 1519 Correggio frescoed a room in the private apartment of Giovanna Piacenza, the young and cultured abbess of the Benedictine nunnery in Parma. The cycle painted by the artist is dedicated to Diana the huntress, represented on the cowl of the fireplace with the crescent moon on her head, a symbol that also appears in the abbess's coat of arms in the middle of the ceiling. The decoration is adapted to the architectural structure of the vaulting cells: in fact the artist has conceived a pergola of greenery and flowers with garlands, ribbons and compositions of fruit, supported by reeds woven into an umbrella shape. At the base of each vaulting cell the vegetation opens up to form an oculus through which nude putti can be seen against the background of a luminous sky, holding bows, arrows, horns, dogs and stag's heads, all elements connected with hunting. The sixteen cells terminate in the same number of niches in chiaroscuro, which appear to be illuminated naturally from below, by the light entering through the windows of the room. In each of the niches is set a *trompe l'œil* marble sculpture of a mythological figure drawn from ancient coins and medals. Finally, at the base of the whole decoration, a sort of long white tablecloth links together pairs of ram's heads and supports dishes and crockery that recall the room's use as a dining room.

Here Correggio's style has attained the height of its expressiveness, blending ancient and modern artistic and iconographic sources in a language that exalts the soft vitality and joyful naturalness of the material, the space and the light.

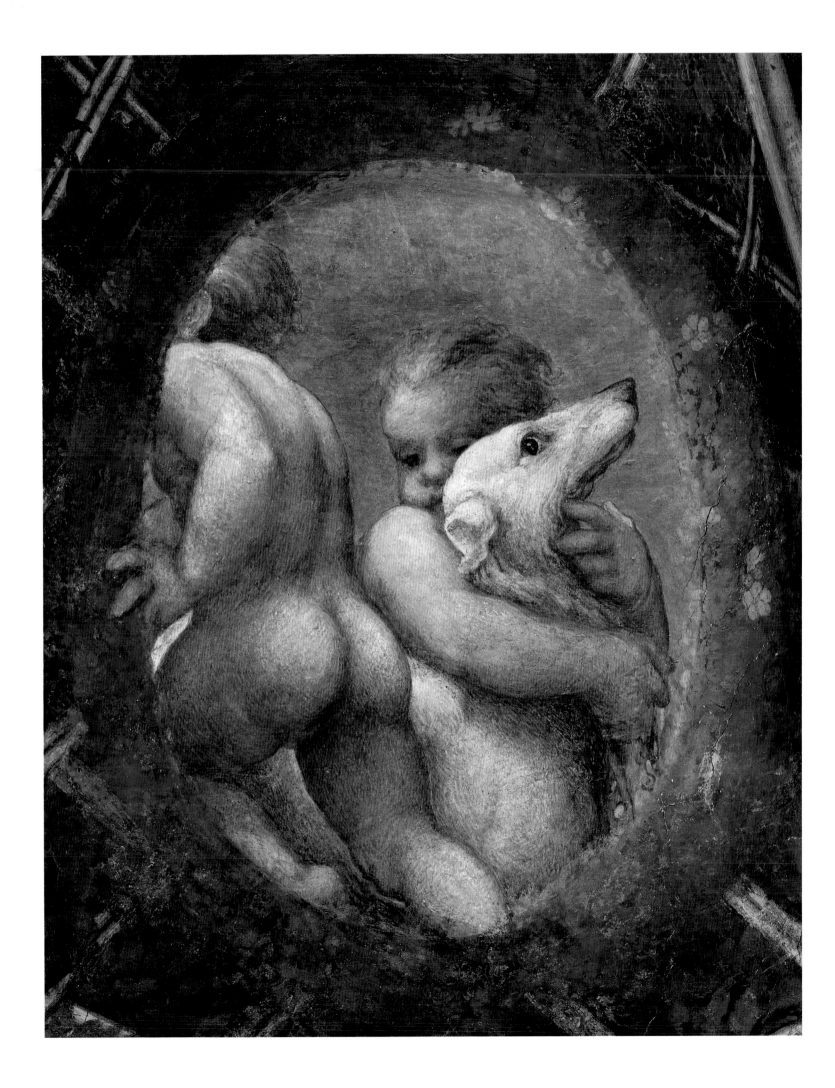

Assumption of the Virgin
fresco, 1093x1195 cm
dome of the cathedral, Parma

Frescoed by Correggio between 1526 and 1530, the dome of Parma Cathedral is dedicated to Our Lady of the Assumption. The artist's masterpiece, its illusionistic, spectacular and emotive handling of space was to have a significant influence on subsequent baroque art.

Correggio has presented the scene of the *Assumption* as a miracle taking place before our eyes, depicted in a daring *sotto in sù* perspective. Gazing up at the scene from the nave, we are caught up in a sense of turmoil, ecstasy and jubilation. The work is conceived on the basis of a dialectical relationship between the painted space and the real space, the painted architecture and the real architecture of the church. The Virgin is represented at the base of the spiral of clouds that leads up to the heights of heaven, situated on the side of the dome that faces onto the nave. The Assumption is witnessed by a host of festive and disheveled angels, their legs kicking wildly, along with saints, the blessed and

figures from the Old Testament. The ascent begins with Adam and Eve, to the left and right respectively, the latter holding the fruit of original sin. At the center of the dome, at the highest and most luminous point of the celestial vision, Christ appears, coming through the joyful riot of bodies, clouds and sky to meet his Mother. To the earthly sphere belong a number of ephebes burning incense on tripods and the apostles, who are watching the scene in rapture, alongside a balustrade in which the eight oculi of the drum are set. Finally, the patron saints of the city are represented inside conches set in the four pendentives at the bottom: John the Baptist, Hilary, Thomas and Bernard.

The fresco was so revolutionary that at first it was not well received by the canons of the cathedral (one of whom described it as a "hash of frog's legs"). It appears that it only avoided destruction because of the words of Titian who, passing through Parma in the retinue of Charles V, exclaimed in admiration: "turn it upside down, fill it with gold, and you will still not have paid enough for it."

Andrea del Sarto

S on of the tailor (*sarto* in Italian) Agnolo di Francesco, Andrea (Florence 1486–1530) frequented the workshop of the painter Piero di Cosimo along with his friend Franciabigio, with whom he formed an independent studio in 1508. After the partnership with Franciabigio was dissolved, Andrea frescoed the *Journey of the Magi* (1511) and the *Nativity of Mary* (1514) on the walls of the cloister of the Vows in the church of Santissima Annunziata, as part of a cycle of paintings to which Pontormo and Rosso also contributed (p. 286 and p. 294) and which marked the beginning of Florentine Mannerism.

Andrea worked for important religious orders, such as the Vallombrosians (monastery of San Salvi, the Celle hermitage at Vallombrosa and the abbey of San Fedele at Poppi) and the Augustinians (church of San Gallo). In 1517 he signed the *Madonna of the Harpies*, a celebrated altarpiece with a complex doctrinal and theological significance intended for the church of the Franciscan Tertiaries near the basilica of Santa Croce. Appreciated by clients of humble extraction as well as by members of wealthy and illustrious families (like Bartolomeo Panciatichi and Cardinal Silvio Passerini), Andrea took part in the production of paintings for the furnishings of domestic settings – such as the Borgherini Chamber and the Benintendi Antechamber – whose wooden structure was made by the sculptor, architect and woodcarver Baccio d'Agnolo.

With the end of the republic and the return of the Medici to Florence (1512), Andrea collaborated on the preparation of decorations for civic festivals and ceremonies and participated in the frescoing of the salon of the Villa Medici at Poggio a Caiano, painting the *Tribute of Caesar* (1520-21). In 1518 he married Lucrezia del Fede, the woman who had served as a model for many of the sacred and profane female figures painted by the artist. In the same year Andrea left for France, where he remained for about a year in the service of King Francis I, much appreciated and esteemed.

Andrea's work, with its elevated, measured and thoughtful style capable of reconciling the principal aspirations of the early 1500s (Vasari described him as a "flawless" painter), was an important point of reference for Florentine artists in the sixteenth and seventeenth centuries, commencing with Pontormo and Rosso.

Annunciation
panel, 185x174·5 cm
Galleria Palatina, Florence

Painted by Andrea around 1512 for the Augustinian church of San Gallo in Florence (now destroyed), the altarpiece was accompanied by a predella painted by Jacopo Pontormo and Rosso Fiorentino, unfortunately lost in the flood of 1557. The work was executed shortly after the visit the three artists paid to Rome in 1511, where firsthand study of the city's celebrated ancient marbles prompted them to introduce greater dynamism into their style.

According to a recently proposed interpretation (Natali 1987) along the lines of Augustinian doctrine, the male nude seated in the background represents Adam, a prefiguration of Christ who is about to be incarnated in Mary's womb.

Scenes from the Life of Joseph the Patriarch: Joseph Explaining the Pharaoh's Dreams; Joseph Telling His Father His Dreams
panel, 98x135 cm each
Galleria Palatina, Florence

The two panels are part of a series of paintings representing episodes from the story of Joseph, the patriarch of the Old Testament who is considered a prefiguration of Christ. The fourteen panels – four of them painted by Jacopo Pontormo – used to form the decoration of the wedding chamber of Pierfrancesco Borgherini and Margherita Acciaioli, who were married in 1515.
Scenes from the life of Joseph were a familiar subject in Florentine artistic culture and had already been represented by Lorenzo Ghiberti around the middle of the fifteenth century on the Gates of Paradise of the Florence Baptistery (pp. 96-100).

In the first of Andrea del Sarto's panels, from left to right, Joseph (the youth in a yellow robe) is telling his dreams to his father Jacob; he is persuaded by Jacob and his mother Rachel to join his brothers; in the background, his envious brothers lower him into a well and, after staining his clothes with the blood of a slaughtered kid, tell their father that the young man is dead. In the second panel the scene is introduced by an allegory of the Nile in the foreground: on the right Joseph explains to the pharaoh the meaning of the dreams that are represented here – that of the seven lean and the seven fat kine and that of the seven thin and the seven full ears of corn. The narration is limpid and vivid, couched in a fluent and colloquial language. In the individual episodes the small and brightly colored figures are presented in lively and natural attitudes in a unified setting created by the rigorous use of geometric perspective.

Last Supper
fresco, 462x872 cm
Museo del Cenacolo di San Salvi, Florence

On June 15, 1511, the Vallombrosian
monk Don Ilario Panichi commissioned
Andrea to paint a fresco in the refectory of
the monastery of San Salvi. At first the
artist painted only the underside of the
arch, with the *Holy Trinity* in the middle
and *Saints Benedict, John Gualberto,
Salvi and Bernard degli Uberti* at the
sides; after a long interruption due to
problems within the order, Andrea
resumed work, painting the *Last Supper*
around 1526-27.
Completed in sixty-four *giornate*, the
fresco was preceded by a long and
thoughtful preparation, attested to by
drawings studying the poses of the nude
figures, the gestures of the hands, the
position of the feet and the faces, based
on portraits painted from life.
Demonstrating his familiarity with a wide
range of contemporary art, Andrea drew
inspiration from illustrious models such
as Leonardo (*Last Supper*, pp. 216-9),
Raphael and Dürer, but blended and fused
the citations into an original, coherent
and sweeping composition. In the clarity
of line that shapes the composition, the
iridescent colors are used to accentuate
the dynamic and emotional attitudes of
the figures.

Pontormo

The son of a modest provincial painter, Jacopo Carucci – known as Pontormo after his birthplace (Pontorme, near Empoli, Florence, 1494-Florence 1557) – came to Florence at the age of thirteen and served his apprenticeship with Leonardo da Vinci, Piero di Cosimo and Mariotto Albertinelli. Trained in the years of the republic (1494-1512), Pontormo was one of the exponents of the Mannerism formulated in Florence in the early decades of the sixteenth century, during a period of great artistic ferment following the return of the Medici to the city (1512) and the election of Pope Leo X Medici, son of Lorenzo the Magnificent.

In 1512, he worked with Rosso on the predella of the *Annunciation* painted by Andrea del Sarto for the church of San Gallo. Like Andrea, Franciabigio and Rosso, Pontormo contributed to the frescoes in the cloister of the Vows at Santissima Annunziata, painting the *Visitation* (1516). In 1518 he signed the altarpiece commissioned by Francesco Pucci for the church of San Michele in Visdomini, a dramatic and restless *Sacra Conversazione*: the work marked a break with the classical and harmonious style based on carefully constructed perspective typical of the Renaissance. Jacopo also took part in joint artistic enterprises, of a public and private character, including the decoration of the Villa Medici at Poggio a Caiano, where the artist painted the lunette with *Vertumnus and Pomona* (1520-21). To escape the outbreak of plague in 1523, Pontormo left the city with his pupil Bronzino and took refuge in the Charterhouse of Galluzzo, where he executed the frescoes with *Scenes from the Passion*, based in part on engravings by the German artist Albrecht Dürer. Again with Bronzino's help (p. 300), he decorated the Capponi Chapel in the church of Santa Felicita (1525-28) with the large panel representing the *Deposition*, regarded as his masterpiece.

In 1529 Jacopo bought a plot of land on Via Laura, near the Santissima Annunziata. A man of melancholic, solitary and cantankerous disposition, the artist designed his house to be a sort of refuge with a loft: he used to stay up there for days at a time, pulling up the ladder so that no one could disturb him.

In spite of the troubled political situation in which Florence found itself in the early decades of the sixteenth century, Jacopo never left the city and from 1535 on worked for the Medici, who had become dukes of Tuscany. His last undertaking was painting the frescoes in the chancel of the church of San Lorenzo (destroyed during the restoration of the church in the eighteenth century), which took both their stylistic and doctrinal inspiration from Michelangelo's *Last Judgment*. It was left to Bronzino to finish the cycle, after Pontormo's death in 1557.

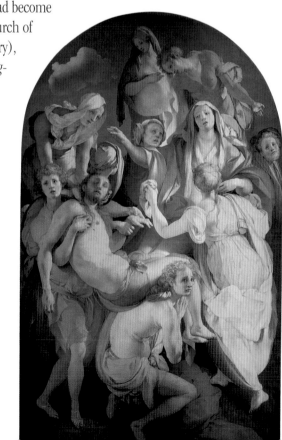

Pietà
panel, 313x192 cm
Capponi Chapel, Santa Felicita, Florence

In 1525 Lodovico Capponi, an influential merchant and banker to the Apostolic Camera, commissioned Pontormo to decorate the chapel he had recently acquired in Santa Felicita, built a century earlier to a design by Filippo Brunelleschi. For the chapel, intended to house the tombs of Capponi and his family, Pontormo conceived an organic set of paintings, including the altarpiece with the *Pietà* (the theme to which the chapel was dedicated).
The scene – in which Mary is led away from the body of her Son before its transport to the sepulcher – is devoid of any setting: the figures, arranged in a cluster, look almost as if they are dancing, suspended in a space that no longer possesses the rational "measure" of geometric perspective but is distorted in a dreamlike vision. The pale and sharp colors, a common feature of Pontormo's palette, appear abstract and unreal. The artist has drawn on recent representations of the same subject, such as those of Botticelli and Michelangelo's *Pietà* in St. Peter's (p. 226), but used them to produce an original solution of great formal refinement. The stunned bewilderment shown by the figures is shared by the artist himself, who is portrayed in the background on the far right.

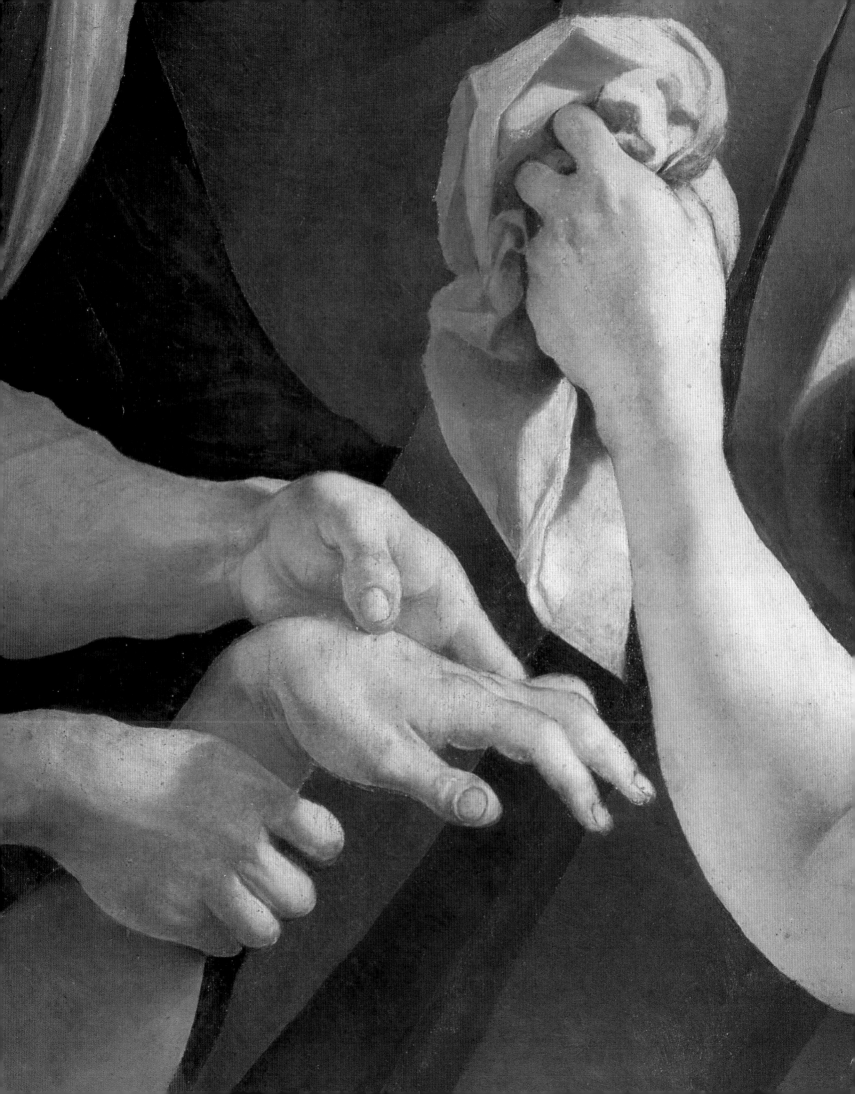

Vertumnus and Pomona
fresco, 461x990 cm
Medici villa, Poggio a Caiano

In 1520 Pope Leo X de' Medici commissioned Pontormo to fresco the lunettes in the stateroom of the villa of Poggio a Caiano, while Andrea del Sarto and Franciabigio were entrusted with the execution of the narrative scenes on the walls. When the pope died the following year, work on the decoration was halted: at that date Pontormo had finished only one lunette representing the myth of Vertumnus and Pomona.

Jacopo's scene is not narrative in character but a learned allegory in which the two personages taken from the classical myth handed down by Ovid are inserted. Vertumnus, "god of the seasons" (perhaps of Etruscan origin), turns himself into an old woman to gain entry to the forbidden garden of his beloved Pomona, goddess of fruit and orchards. Having achieved his aim, Vertumnus assumes the appearance of a handsome young man to seduce the goddess. According to a recently proposed interpretation of the fresco (Falciani 1996), Vertumnus and Pomona are the

young couple on the highest step supporting the branches of laurel: from their union the earth will give forth its fruits, which will be collected by the men and women in the foreground. The laurel is a heraldic device of the Medici: it sprouts luxuriantly from the tree trunk, while the youths suspended on the branches ask the gods to protect those shoots. Thus the composition – devised by the scholar Paolo Giovio – was intended as a good augury for the Medici family and to ward off the adversities of time and fortune.

Pontormo made a long series of pencil studies with figures in various poses for the painting, such as the drawing reproduced here and now in the Gabinetto Disegni e Stampe degli Uffizi.

Visitation
panel, 202x156 cm
San Michele, Carmignano

Coming from the Villa Pinadori at Carmignano, the painting is neither documented nor mentioned in the contemporary sources. Yet it is one of Pontormo's most powerful works, executed around 1530.
The *Visitation* was a popular theme among Florentine artists and traditionally symbolized the passage between the Old and New Testaments. Based on Dürer's engraving of the *Four Witches*,

Pontormo's composition represents Mary and Elizabeth in profile in the foreground, meeting in an embrace. Two more female figures, motionless and viewed from the front, look on from behind: their features are similar to those of the protagonists. The figures are imposing and monumental, dressed in clothing in shades of pink and green that appears to balloon in the wind: the dominant features of the painting are the large and swollen bellies of Mary and Elizabeth that approach and brush against each other, containing the newly conceived lives of Christ and St. John the Baptist.

Deposition from the Cross
panel, 341x201 cm
Pinacoteca Civica, Volterra

Signed and dated 1521, the picture was
painted by Rosso for the chapel of the
Compagnia della Croce adjacent to the
church of San Francesco in Volterra. It is
the artist's most famous painting, long

Rosso Fiorentino

We know nothing of the early training received by Giovan Battista di Jacopo (Florence 1494-Fontainebleau 1540), who was nicknamed Rosso for the red color of his hair. The same age as Pontormo, Rosso had a quite different character: a lively and eloquent speaker, and a good-looking man, he was a lover of philosophy and music. Like Pontormo, Rosso was one of the originators of Florentine Mannerism, along with other painters who had learned their art by studying Michelangelo and Leonardo's cartoons for the two *Battles* in Palazzo della Signoria.

According to tradition, Rosso collaborated with Pontormo in 1512 on the predella (lost) for the *Annunciation* in the church of San Gallo (now in the Galleria Palatina, Florence) painted by Andrea del Sarto. After 1512, following in Andrea's footsteps like Pontormo and Franciabigio, Rosso worked for the Servites of the Santissima Annunziata and frescoed the *Assumption of the Virgin* (1513-14) in the cloister of the Vows. After finishing an altarpiece for the church of Ognissanti which failed to satisfy the client Leonardo Buonafede (1518; now in the Uffizi, Florence), Rosso left Florence for three years, visiting the Appiano court at Piombino and Volterra among other places. Returning to Florence in 1521-22, he painted imposing altarpieces for two important churches: the Dei Chapel in Santo Spirito (1522) and the Ginori Chapel in San Lorenzo (1523).

After the election of Pope Clement VII Medici (1523), Rosso set off for Rome in the hope of receiving prestigious commissions. The following year he decorated the Cesi Chapel in Santa Maria della Pace with paintings and stuccoes. During the Sack of Rome (1527), the artist was taken prisoner and fled the city as soon as he was freed, going first to Perugia and then to various other small cities and towns in eastern Tuscany (Sansepolcro, Arezzo, Città di Castello, Pieve Santo Stefano). It seems that in these years the restless artist was appreciated more by provincial confraternities than by clients of high rank in Florence or Rome. This may have been what induced Rosso to leave Tuscany in 1530, passing through Pesaro and Venice on his way to France, where he presented himself to King Francis I. Appreciated by the monarch and his court, he began to draw up plans for the decoration of the gallery of the royal palace of Fontainebleau in 1532, supervising the work from 1536 on. But his sudden and unexpected death in 1540 (it has even been suggested that he was poisoned), interrupted the venture.

Portrait of a Young Man
panel, 120x86 cm
Gallerie Nazionali di Capodimonte, Naples

Probably executed during or immediately
after his stay in Rome, the picture is one
of the artist's finest portraits, original and
refined in its conception.
The young man – his identity is unknown
– is in an interior filled with furniture and
objects that are indicative of a refined
taste and high level of culture. However,
the room remains in semidarkness, while
the light dramatically picks out the figure,
whose lean and elongated frame emerges
slowly from the gloom, with intense black
eyes set in a melancholic face and noble
tapering hands. It is a portrait of a highly
introspective character, in which the
youth's inner being shines through
mysteriously like a momentary gleam.

esteemed for its expressive and dramatic
intensity.
Against the blue ground of a flat and
abstract sky, the scene fills the
foreground, constructed out of broken
lines around the cross and the ladders.
The agitated figures are characterized by
elongated and spiky forms, distorted and
acrobatic poses and grotesque
expressions frantic with grief and dismay.
The colors are brilliant, iridescent and
complementary: shades of red and yellow
predominate, rendered incandescent by
the intensity of an unreal light.

Marriage of the Virgin
panel, 325x250 cm
San Lorenzo, Florence

Signed and dated 1523, the picture was
commissioned by Carlo Ginori for the
altar of his own chapel in San Lorenzo,
dedicated to Joseph and Mary. In the
painting appear other saints dear to the
client: St. Anne and St. Apollonia are
seated on the steps at the bottom, while
the Dominican St. Vincent Ferrer on the
right is indicating the scene of the
marriage to the observer.
After the violent passions of his youth had
calmed, Rosso developed a style imbued

with a fanciful and refined grace. The
figures crowded around the bride and
groom are characterized by a
sophisticated elegance and elaborate
eccentricity, which were to become the
dominant features of European
Mannerism over the following decades.
The scene is set in an interior, too small
for the throng of figures that have invaded
it, in a darkness that is lit up by gleams of
unreal light and iridescent colors: the
clear and orderly arrangement of
fifteenth-century *Sacre Conversazioni* has
been abandoned in favor of a dreamlike
vision, in which refined artifice prevails
over precise and realistic description.

Bronzino

A gnolo di Cosimo Tori, called Bronzino (Florence 1503-1572), entered Pontormo's workshop around 1518 (p. 286) and went on to collaborate with him on the frescoes in the Charterhouse of Galluzzo (1523-25) and those of the Capponi Chapel in Santa Felicita (1525-28).

In 1530 he was summoned by the Montefeltro, duke and duchess of Urbino, to decorate the Villa Imperiale at Pesaro along with other artists (Girolamo Genga, Raffaellino del Colle, the Dossi brothers). During his stay in the duchy of Urbino, he painted the *Portrait of Guidobaldo della Rovere* (Galleria Palatina, Florence), inaugurating a scheme that he was later to return to many times and develop further: idealized forms and features, minute description of precious details (fabrics, jewelry, weapons), poses and expressions frozen in courtly and majestic attitudes, colors as intense and pure as those of precious stones. Going back to Florence in 1532, he started to collaborate with Pontormo again on frescoes (now lost) in the Medici villas, but at the same time embarked on a successful career painting portraits, for which he was much in demand by the Florentine aristocracy. Thus he was drawn into the refined cultural climate of those circles and in 1538 even published some poetry.

The following year he helped to create the decorations for the wedding of Cosimo I de' Medici to Eleonora of Toledo. From that time on he worked chiefly in the service of the Medici duke, who commissioned from him the decoration of his consort Eleonora's chapel in Palazzo della Signoria (then the Ducal Palace). In the forties, while carrying out this enterprise (which occupied him up until 1552), he painted some of the most celebrated portraits of the Medici family. In 1546 he started to work for the ducal tapestry factory as well, supplying cartoons with *Scenes from the Life of Joseph* and other, profane subjects.

Returning from a brief stay in Rome (1548), Bronzino also received prestigious commissions for devotional paintings (altarpieces and frescoes) for the churches of the Santissima Annunziata, Santa Croce, Santa Maria Novella, Santo Spirito and San Lorenzo. In these paintings it is possible to discern references to complex theological themes suggested by the now widespread ideas of the Counter Reformation.

Scenes from the Life of Moses:
Moses Striking Water from
the Rock and the Fall of Manna
fresco, 320x490 cm
Eleonora's Chapel, Palazzo Vecchio,
Florence

The scene is frescoed on the entrance
wall of the private chapel of Eleonora of
Toledo, consort of Duke Cosimo I de'
Medici. The painting is part of the pictorial
decoration of the chapel executed by
Bronzino between 1540 and 1545.

Scenes from the Life of Moses:
Crossing of the Red Sea
fresco, 320x490 cm
Eleonora's Chapel, Palazzo Vecchio,
Florence

Shortly after his marriage to Eleonora of
Toledo, daughter of the viceroy of Naples,
celebrated in the summer of 1539, Duke
Cosimo I de' Medici asked Bronzino to
decorate the chapel (photograph above)
of his wife's private apartment in the
building that, after serving as the
republican seat of government, had been
turned into a ducal palace.
On the ceiling Bronzino painted Duchess
Eleonora's favorite saints *Michael the
Archangel, Francis, Jerome and John the
Evangelist*; the walls are decorated with
scenes of a religious character and there
is a *Pietà* on the altar. Among the scenes
on the wall are several episodes from the
story of Moses leading the people of Israel
to "salvation" (the *Crossing of the Red
Sea, Moses Striking Water from the
Rock*, the *Fall of Manna* and the *Worship
of the Brazen Serpent*). The figure of
Moses, heroic leader of his people, is
indirectly compared with Cosimo I who,
having assumed ducal authority, will lead
the people of Florence to "salvation."
Bronzino's style is characterized by a
clear and incisive line that sculpts the
forms, rendered precious by cold and
gleaming colors typical of materials of
incorruptible beauty, such as pearls, ivory,
crystals and semiprecious stones. This icy
and abstract, elegant and intellectual
language was the figurative expression
most in tune with the culture of the
Medicean court around the middle of the
century.

Portraits of Bartolomeo and *Lucrezia Panciatichi*
panel, 104x85; 102x85 cm
Galleria degli Uffizi, Florence

Portrait of Bia di Cosimo de' Medici
panel, 59x45 cm
Galleria degli Uffizi, Florence

Bronzino's reputation rests chiefly on his portraits, which share common and highly distinctive characteristics. Through a slow and controlled process of idealization of reality, the artist purified his images of any contingent element, making them look eternal and incorruptible in their abstract beauty. Among the highest examples of this are the portraits of the Panciatichi husband and wife: the figures betray no trace of emotion or thought, but are captured in the paintings in their ideal and perfect essence; the faces, hands, jewelry, costumes and architecture of the setting are all treated in the same way, as a precious, rare and immutable substance, with the emphasis on its formal and chromatic purity. Even the portrait of a little girl – in this case Bia, the illegitimate daughter of Cosimo I who died in 1542 – becomes an image frozen for eternity, unchanging in time, like a cameo carved in a gemstone.

BRONZINO

Benvenuto Cellini

The son of Giovanni d'Andrea, a piper first for Lorenzo the Magnificent and later under the republic, Benvenuto (Florence 1500-1571) resisted his father's efforts to train him as a musician and chose instead to learn the goldsmith's art. His restless life and rebellious and strong-willed temperament took him to various parts of Italy, from Venice to Naples, before he arrived in Rome at the age of twenty-eight and became the favorite artist of Clement VII. In the pontiff's service he worked as a goldsmith, minter of coins and engraver of medals and seals. During the Sack of Rome in 1527 Cellini helped to defend the city and saved the pope's life by killing the lansquenet who was threatening him. Protected by his successor Paul III, Cellini was granted absolution from the charge of murdering a rival goldsmith.

In 1540 he left Rome for France, where he remained until 1545, in the service of King Francis I, who had already been the patron of Leonardo, Andrea del Sarto and Rosso Fiorentino. It was for Francis that Cellini made the famous gold and enamel salt cellar (Kunsthistorisches Museum, Vienna) and his first large-scale sculpture, the bronze *Nymph* for the royal palace of Fontainebleau (now in the Louvre, Paris).

Back in Florence, he was commissioned by Duke Cosimo I in 1545 to execute the statue of *Perseus* for the Loggia in Piazza della Signoria, where it was erected and unveiled in 1554. The work was greatly admired, not just in Florence but in the rest of Europe as well. Yet the envy he aroused and his troubled relationship with Cosimo I prevented Cellini from receiving any more prestigious public commissions, which the duke preferred to give to others. In 1562 the artist completed the white marble *Crucifix* for Cosimo I's son Francesco, who donated it to Philip II of Spain in 1576 (it is now in the Escorial). In the last years of his life, Cellini devoted himself to writing two treatises on sculpture and the goldsmith's art (published in 1568) and an autobiography (*The Life of Benvenuto Cellini Written by Himself*, finished by 1566 but not published until 1728). This remains a fundamental source of information about the artist, his life, his wanderings and the trials he went through during the execution of the *Perseus*, as well as offering a fascinating picture of the cultural climate of Mannerism.

Dying in 1571, Cellini left all his sculptures, "finished or unfinished," to Francesco I, who had in the meantime become the second grand duke of Tuscany.

Salt Cellar of Francis I
gold and enamel, 26x33·5 cm
Kunsthistorisches Museum, Vienna

Introduced at the French royal court by Cardinal Ippolito d'Este, Benvenuto Cellini made the famous salt cellar in gold and enamel (1540-43) for King Francis I. The work is emblematic of European Mannerism in its most precious and refined form, consonant with the cultural

climate at the court of Fontainebleau. On an oval base, personifications of Water and Earth recline on blue drapes adorned with golden lilies (the heraldic device of the house of Anjou), one in front of the other with their legs entwined: the figure of Water, with a trident like that of the god Neptune, is surrounded by fantastic sea creatures and shells near a boat-shaped recipient for the salt; Earth is seated on a promontory covered with fruit and land

animals, alongside a sort of little temple in the form of a triumphal arch, used to hold the pepper. Day and Night, Dawn and Dusk are represented in relief on the side of the ebony base, alternating with four figures that symbolize the principal winds. The allegories of the parts of the day are direct citations of Michelangelo's sculptures in the New Sacristy (cf. pp. 238-41): a tribute paid by Cellini to the great master.

BENVENUTO CELLINI

Perseus

bronze on marble base, ht. 519 cm
Loggia dei Lanzi, Florence

Returning to Florence in 1545, Cellini offered his services as a goldsmith and sculptor to Duke Cosimo I de' Medici. He received the commission for a bronze statue of *Perseus*, the Greek hero and son of Danaë and Jupiter who – according to the myth related by Ovid – was able with the help of the gods to behead Medusa, the Gorgon who turned to stone anyone who met her gaze. The artist set to work at once, making a wax model, but it took him another nine years to finish the sculpture: on April 27, 1554, it was erected under an arch of the Loggia dei Lanzi in Piazza della Signoria, in open competition with Donatello's *Judith* and with Michelangelo's *David* (now replaced by copies). The undertaking – made complicated by the difficult relations between the artist and the client, inadequate funding and the inevitable technical problems associated with casting a statue over three meters in height – proved a success, arousing the admiration of ordinary people as well as writers and poets and the envy of other artists at the court.

The restoration of Cellini's masterpiece,

begun in 1997 and just completed, has revealed traces of the gilding applied by the artist to some details of the statue. In addition, it has been possible to show that the alloy of bronze is not the same in every part of the sculpture, at least partially confirming the account of the casting described in such adventurous tones in Cellini's autobiography: in the final stage, the artist claimed to have added tin plates and crockery to render the metal more fluid. Finally, while it was already known that once the casting was complete the artist spent a long time on the finishing of the details, the restoration has demonstrated that he placed the work on a brazier to soften the surface before polishing certain parts.

Now that the conservation work has been completed, the sculpture has been put back in its original location under the Loggia dei Lanzi. However, the marble pedestal, too fragile to resist atmospheric agents any longer, has been replaced by a copy and moved to the Museo del Bargello, where the originals of the bronze statuettes in its niches (*Jupiter*, *Danaë with Her Son Perseus*, *Minerva* and *Mercury*) and of the relief of the *Freeing of Andromeda* had been transferred several years ago.

The Freeing of Andromeda
bronze, 82x90 cm
Museo Nazionale del Bargello, Florence

The bronze plaque used to be situated under the pedestal of the *Perseus*, set in the balustrade of the Loggia dei Lanzi, where it has now been replaced by a copy. The relief represents another of the Greek hero's adventures: Perseus, wearing the winged sandals and helmet given him by Mercury and carrying Minerva's sword and shield, launches himself from the sky to kill the dragon that is about to devour the beautiful Andromeda, daughter of Cepheus, king of Ethiopia. Cellini has portrayed himself among the bystanders, off to one side.

In the public setting of Piazza della Signoria, in front of the Palazzo Pubblico, the figure of the hero whose victorious deeds brought order where previously chaos had reigned had a precise political significance: Perseus was identified with Cosimo I, client of the work, who thereby issued a warning to anyone attempting to subvert ducal authority and threaten the Medici dynasty.

Bust of Cosimo I
bronze, ht. 110 cm
Museo Nazionale del Bargello, Florence

Finished in 1548, the bronze bust was installed above the entrance to the fortress of Portoferraio on the island of Elba nine years later. In Cellini's portrait, Cosimo I is presented as a military commander in the "old style," imposing and imperturbable, ready for action and dressed in a rich suit of armor adorned with precious ornamental details suited to a military garb.

RVM SORS HVC ACTEONA DVXIT · A

Parmigianino

Francesco Mazzola, called Parmigianino (Parma 1503-Casalmaggiore, near Cremona, 1540), was orphaned at the age of only two. He soon displayed a talent for art, while frequenting the workshop of his paternal uncles, Michele and Pier Ilario Mazzola, provincial painters of modest ability. The biggest influence on the artistic development of the young Francesco was his study of the pictures that Correggio was painting in Parma at that time (pp. 274-9).

Highly precocious and operating on his own from as early as 1519, Parmigianino received several important commissions in 1522, including the frescoes for chapels in San Giovanni Evangelista where Correggio was also at work. Around 1523, Count Galeazzo Sanvitale entrusted Francesco with the task of frescoing a small private room in his fortress at Fontanellato that was used as a boudoir by his wife Paola Gonzaga. Taking his inspiration from Correggio's Camera di San Paolo, Parmigianino represented the *Legend of Diana and Actaeon* set in a sort of refined green bower.

After finishing this decoration, Parmigianino went to Rome in 1524, where he was able to see the works of Raphael and Michelangelo. Celebrated on his arrival as the new Raphael, Francesco came into direct contact with the artists working for Pope Clement VII (including Rosso Fiorentino) and the cultural circles connected with the papal court. To demonstrate his own capacities and his sophisticated and bold style, Parmigianino had brought with him the *Self-Portrait in a Convex Mirror* (Kunsthistorisches Museum, Vienna) and gave it along with other pictures to Clement VII. Of the few works that the painter executed in the papal city, the most important was the *Vision of Saint Jerome* (National Gallery, London), commissioned by Maria Bufalina from Città di Castello.

Fleeing from Sack of Rome (1527) like the majority of the artists resident in the city, Francesco went first to Bologna and then back to Parma in 1531, where he was given the job of frescoing the church of the Steccata. Starting work in 1535, the artist proceeded very slowly, increasingly distracted – according to his biographers – by his alchemical experiments. In 1539 he left the work incomplete and then had to deal with the Board of Trustees, who had him imprisoned. When he was released, Francesco chose to go into exile, settling at Casalmaggiore where he died at the age of just thirty-seven.

Legend of Diana and Actaeon:
Hunters Pursuing a Nymph
Rocca Sanvitale, Fontanellato (Parma)

P A R M I G I A N I N O

Legend of Diana and Actaeon:
Actaeon Turned into a Stag and Diana
frescoes
Rocca Sanvitale, Fontanellato (Parma)

Around 1523, prior to his departure for
Rome, Parmigianino frescoed a private
chamber in the fortress of Count Galeazzo
Sanvitale at Fontanellato. It was a
secluded room, a sort of boudoir for the
toilette of Sanvitale's wife Paola Gonzaga.
The artist adapted his decoration to the
structure of the chamber, which consisted
of a depressed vault supported at the
sides by small domical vaults standing on
lunettes. Parmigianino adopted the same
scheme as was used by Correggio in the
Abbess's Parlor of the convent of San
Paolo (pp. 274-7), accessible to the
public up until 1524. Using this as his
model, he laid out the pictorial
decoration on three levels: the myth itself
in the lunettes at the bottom, a series of
twelve putti set against a pergola of
flowers in the middle section and the
open blue sky on the ceiling above, with a
tondo at the center inscribed with the
words RESPICE FINEM, "observe the
end," i.e. the sad fate of Actaeon.
According to the legend, Actaeon caught
sight of Diana bathing naked at a spring
while out hunting: the angry goddess
turned him into a stag and he was then
torn to pieces by his own hounds. At
Fontanellato the myth is depicted in
thirteen lunettes, while the fourteenth –
above the window – contains a portrait of
Paola Gonzaga in the allegorical guise of
Plenty.
In contrast to the naturalism with which
Correggio interpreted the light, space and
narration, Parmigianino has chosen a
precious and meticulous style, in which
each element is painstakingly modeled to
achieve an exaggerated elegance of form.

TRADITVR ESCA SV

S NON NISI MORTALES ALIQV

Madonna with the Long Neck
panel, 216x132 cm
Galleria degli Uffizi, Florence

Begun after 1534, the work was left
unfinished at the time of the painter's
death in 1542 and was hung in the chapel
of Elena Baiardi in Santa Maria de' Servi
at Parma. It is Parmigianino's most
famous and emblematic painting.
The composition, sophisticated in its style
and content, is based on the mystery of
the Immaculate Conception. Both the
columns and, through a play on words,
the Virgin's long neck (*collum - columna*),
refer to the Marian privilege. The group of
angels, crammed into the narrow space
on the left, is carrying a slender amphora:
a symbolic image that alludes to Mary as
the mystical vessel in which Christ was
made flesh. The Child draped in sleep over
his Mother's legs prefigures the death of
Christ. The right-hand side of the painting
is incomplete: the male figure unrolling a
papyrus is St. Jerome and the artist
intended to place St. Francis by his side,
but all he had time to paint was one foot.
The elongated figures, in elegant and
rhythmic poses, seem to be frozen into
unreal and perfect forms like the columns
in the background, represented in a
contrived and impossible perspective.
Parmigianino has dreamed up an ideal
and remote world, in which an icy and
cerebral beauty holds sway.

Portrait of Galeazzo Sanvitale
panel, 109x81 cm
Gallerie Nazionali di Capodimonte, Naples

The portrait, signed and dated 1524, was
painted by Parmigianino shortly after the
frescoes at Fontanellato, commissioned by
the sitter, Count Sanvitale, a powerful
military leader and elegant nobleman.
In the painting the material and
ornamental qualities of each element are
emphasized: not just the clothes, armor
and jewelry, but also the man's beard,
complexion and tapering hand look
precious and refined. The unflappable
count, seated on a chair, is turned to one
side in an elegant pose to show the
observer a coin engraved with the
numbers seven and two. Interpreted in
alchemical terms (Fagiolo Dell'Arco
1970), the numbers refer to the Moon
and the planet Jupiter, which are located
in the seventh and second "Hermetic"
circles respectively. The Pillars of
Hercules represented on the medal
pinned to the count's plumed hat are
another reference to the culture of
Hermeticism.

Tintoretto

Jacopo Robusti (Venice 1518-1594) was nicknamed Tintoretto because he was the son of a dyer (*tintore* in Italian). Right from his earliest works, the artist displayed an originality and an independence from the teachings of Titian, who according to some of the old sources had been his master. Influenced by Michelangelo, Tintoretto got involved in the debate that was taking place in the circles of Tusco-Roman Mannerism on the question of the illusion of perspective. In fact the Venetian painter had a liking for pictures with a theatrical and scenographic setting in which dramatic actions and emotions are represented with strong contrasts of light. For the same reason, the artist showed a predilection for subjects linked to unforeseen, miraculous and transcendental events.

In 1545, after he had become an independent painter, he decorated two ceilings in the house of the writer Pietro Aretino, who thanked the artist in a letter. Three years later Aretino wrote another letter praising Tintoretto for the *Miracle of Saint Mark* he had painted for the Scuola Grande di San Marco. In 1547 he finished the *Last Supper* for the church of San Marcuola, a work in which the artist showed a marked interest in spectacular and striking solutions. These may have been the consequence of a journey he made to Rome to study the works of Michelangelo's followers. Over the next few decades, Tintoretto continued his quest for theatrical, grandiloquent images with a strong emotional impact in various works for Venetian churches and confraternities (Scuola della Trinità, church of the Madonna dell'Orto, Scuola Grande di San Marco, San Trovaso, San Polo). He was also a skilled and esteemed portraitist, capable of capturing the essential traits of his sitters' inner character. Tintoretto's masterpiece can be said to be the paintings for the Scuola Grande di San Rocco (1564-87), intended for the Sala dell'Albergo, as well as for the upper hall and the one on the ground floor: the painter represented the scenes from the Old Testament and Gospels in evocative tones and with a sense of personal and human involvement, achieving almost visionary accents and a high degree of lyricism in the last paintings in the series (e.g. the *Saint Mary of Egypt*, 1582-87).

An outstanding figure in Venetian painting, he took part in work for the Doge's Palace on several occasions. Here, after finishing the *Battle of Zara* for the Sala dello Scrutinio in 1587 and following the death of Veronese (p. 328), he painted the gigantic picture of *Paradise* that the latter had planned for the rear wall of the Sala of the Maggior Consiglio.

Discovery of the Body of Saint Mark
canvas, 405x405 cm
Pinacoteca di Brera, Milan

This is another *telero* or large canvas for the Scuola Grande di San Marco (1563-66). The scene is set in Alexandria and comprises several episodes: the body of the saint is found in one of the tombs on the right; St. Mark himself is represented standing in front of the body lying on the floor; alongside a man possessed by the devil is held back by a person infected with the plague. In a dramatic and striking effect, the artist has

imparted depth to the composition through the perspective created by the lines of tombs on the walls, arches of the vault and flags of the floor, all converging on the backlit figures at the rear. In addition to the blade of light in the background, light enters from the right to illuminate the main figures in the foreground. The use of two sources of light, common in Tintoretto's work, accentuates the dynamic and spectacular effect of the scene.

Saint Mark Freeing the Slave
canvas, cm 416x544
Gallerie dell'Accademia, Venice

Painted in 1548, it was the first picture executed by Tintoretto for the Scuola Grande di San Marco. The work made a strong impression by the novelty of its conception and style and made the artist's name. What people admired in the work was the painter's capacity to lay out the scene in a spectacular way, with bold foreshortenings and dramatic and frenzied action.

According to the story taken from Jacobus de Voragine's *Golden Legend*, St. Mark was miraculously able to free the slave of a knight from Provence, condemned to various tortures for having venerated the saint's relics.

Tintoretto's style presents the typical characteristics of Mannerist language: abrupt turns, twistings, contrived foreshortenings and a spectacular and dramatic use of light and shade. The figures, characterized by their plastic force and distorted poses, show a debt to the models of Michelangelo. In particular, the warrior in red on the right and the slave lying down with his legs folded are reminiscent of the sculptures of the *Dusk* and *Day* in the New Sacristy (pp. 238-41).

Crucifixion

canvas, 536x1224 cm

Scuola Grande di San Rocco, Venice

The painting, completed in 1565, is on the wall opposite the entrance to the Sala dell'Albergo and is one of the first Tintoretto executed for the Scuola Grande di San Rocco, a task on which the artist was engaged from 1564 up until the last years of the his life.

The *Crucifixion* is a theme the Venetian painter tackled frequently, each time trying out new solutions of great spatial breadth. The San Rocco composition is imposing and is organized horizontally. At the center, in isolation, Christ on the cross above the group of mourning women forms the fulcrum of the scene, from which beams of light radiate outward like spokes. Between them are set the various episodes that extend from the back to the foreground, such as the cross with the thief on the left which is being hoisted with ropes. The figures at the front, plastically constructed with marked outlines and a dynamic chiaroscuro, give way in the background to figures sketched with thin and luminous brushstrokes. Here the dramatic episode from the Gospels takes on the tones of an epic and majestic event.

pp. 324-5
Slaughter of the Innocents, detail
Scuola Grande di San Rocco, Venice

TINTORETTO

Slaughter of the Innocents
canvas, 422x546 cm
Scuola Grande di San Rocco, Venice

Painted in 1582-83, the canvas represents another story from the Gospels that is transformed into an epic event by Tintoretto, a brilliant choreographer of sweeping scenes filled with dynamic and spectacular inventions. The tragedy, depicted in a series of episodes, reaches its climax in the tangle of bodies in the foreground on the left that loom above the observer. Each figure, each pose, each view is carefully studied and blended into the overall perspective, in a composition that drew its inspiration from such recent illustrious examples as Raphael's *Fire in the Borgo* in the Vatican Stanze and Michelangelo's *Last Judgment* (p. 242).

Last Supper
canvas, 365x568 cm
San Giorgio Maggiore, Venice

This was one of the last pictures painted by Tintoretto before he died (1592-94), for the presbytery of the church of San Giorgio Maggiore. The artist had tackled the theme of the *Last Supper* several times over the course of his career. However, this final version is pervaded by a particularly intense and profound spirituality. The composition is organized around the oblique angle of the laid table: this use of perspective, with an extremely elevated point of view, creates a very imposing effect. The setting, objects and figures are picked out from the darkness by the glow of the light: it is a spiritual and marvelous light that issues from the haloes of Christ and the apostles, as well as from the lantern hanging from the ceiling, out of which emerge figures of angels as evanescent as phantoms.
In its representation of the episode from the Gospels, the painting places the emphasis on its significance: according to the dictates of the Counter Reformation, the communion of the apostles stands for the moment of the solemn institution of the sacrament of the Eucharist.

Paolo Veronese

The son of a stonecutter, Paolo Caliari (Verona 1528-Venice 1588) was called Veronese after the city of his birth. His training and early activity were influenced by the Mannerist schools of Mantua and Parma, in particular the work of Correggio and Parmigianino.

In the early fifties the painter left Verona to work in the surrounding region and for the Gonzaga in Mantua. In 1553 he was summoned to Venice to paint in the Doge's Palace. This was the first in a series of public commissions in the lagoon area, in which the artist adopted a solemn and decorative style accompanied by a pale and luminous palette of cool shades, quite different from the tonal painting of Titian and the luministic effects and chiaroscuro of Tintoretto.

In 1556 he took part in the decoration of the ceiling of St. Mark's Library, for which he was awarded a gold chain that was given to him personally by Titian. He spent the rest of his life in Venice, though he did carry out commissions elsewhere (Padua, Verona, Vicenza). In 1566 he married Elena, daughter of the Veronese painter Antonio Badile to whom he had been apprenticed.

In the sixties Veronese became the decorator most in demand by the Venetian aristocracy for the villas and church buildings constructed to designs by Andrea Palladio, such as Villa Barbaro at Maser (*c.*1560-61) and the refectory of San Giorgio Maggiore in Venice (1562-63). Veronese's favorite subject was the banquet, which he represented in pictures like the *Supper at Emmaus*, the *Feast in the House of Simon* and the *Marriage at Cana*. This gave the artist the opportunity to depict sumptuous and spectacular settings that he used to link the painting with the architecture of the building in which it was located.

After the fires that destroyed the rooms and decorations of the Doge's Palace (1574 and 1577), Veronese was the artist who personally took charge of the work of reconstruction (1575-77, 1578-82), drawing up plans and designs and leaving the execution to his workshop. It was during the second phase of this undertaking that Veronese designed the *Paradise* for the main wall of the Sala del Maggior Consiglio which, after the artist's death, was painted by Tintoretto.

Frescoes in Villa Barbaro
Maser (Treviso)

Between 1560 and 1561 Paolo Veronese frescoed several rooms in the villa built by Andrea Palladio for the brothers Marcantonio and Daniele Barbaro, located in the Veneto countryside near Asolo.

The two clients were Venetian patricians: Daniele was a Humanist and enthusiast for astronomy, music and architecture, Marcantonio a diplomat, lover of

literature and amateur sculptor.
At Villa Barbaro Veronese carried out the most celebrated enterprise of his career, the decoration of the rooms in the central block – a cross-shaped hall with windows opening onto the garden – and the adjoining rooms. The cycle of paintings is in perfect keeping with the architecture of the Palladian villa, entering into relationship with the surrounding scenery. Veronese conceived a coherent mock architectural structure in which he then inserted figures and landscapes, in a

succession of surprising and fanciful illusionistic scenes and *trompe-l'œil* expansions of space. Life-sized figures appear at the doors and balconies; portraits of the villa's inhabitants (the *Man with a Dog* shown on p. 328 may be the artist's self-portrait) are placed alongside mythological personages in the same context; the windows and porticoes open onto views of imaginary landscapes with classical ruins or contemporary buildings in a natural setting similar to the one surrounding the villa and visible through its real windows. Veronese's style is vivid and serene, but at the same time skillfully managed so as to maintain the subtle and cerebral interplay between fiction and reality.

The dominant theme of the frescoes in Villa Barbaro is perhaps that of Celestial and Universal Harmony, conjured up in the cross-shaped hall, reproduced on these pages, by the eight *Muses* depicted in the arches above cameos in the antique manner. Harmony is the leitmotif of the entire set of frescoes, touching on every aspect of the lives of the two clients: order, law, landscape, conjugal love, fertility, music, culture and prosperity.

Feast in the House of Levi
canvas, 555x1310 cm
Gallerie dell'Accademia, Venice

In 1573 Veronese painted the huge canvas for the refectory of the Dominican monastery of Santi Giovanni e Paolo (otherwise known as San Zanipolo), to replace a picture by Titian that had been destroyed in the fire of 1571. Sumptuous, solemn and spectacular *Feasts* were a recurrent theme in Veronese's art, especially in the 1560s and 1570s. Against an architectural backdrop that recalls the sets used in theaters of the time, the laid table extends horizontally underneath elegant arches and between flights of steps. The scene is crowded with figures: noble guests, footmen, servants, soldiers, buffoons, children and pets. As was pointed out almost four centuries ago (Ridolfi 1648), in no other picture has Veronese better captured "the joy, made more magnificent the beauty, rendered more festive the cheer."

The friars had commissioned a painting of the *Last Supper*, and so were nonplussed when they saw that the artist had treated the subject as a lavish and crowded banquet of a profane character held in the house of a rich Venetian

patrician. The painter was even
summoned to defend his work before the
Inquisition's tribunal of the Holy Office,
which ordered him to modify the
composition at his own expense within
three months. But, as X-rays of the
picture have demonstrated, Veronese
made no significant changes apart from
inserting an inscription on the cornice of
the pillars that gave the painting a
different title: the *Feast in the House of
the Publican Levi*, an episode
described in the Gospel according to
Luke (V, 27-32).

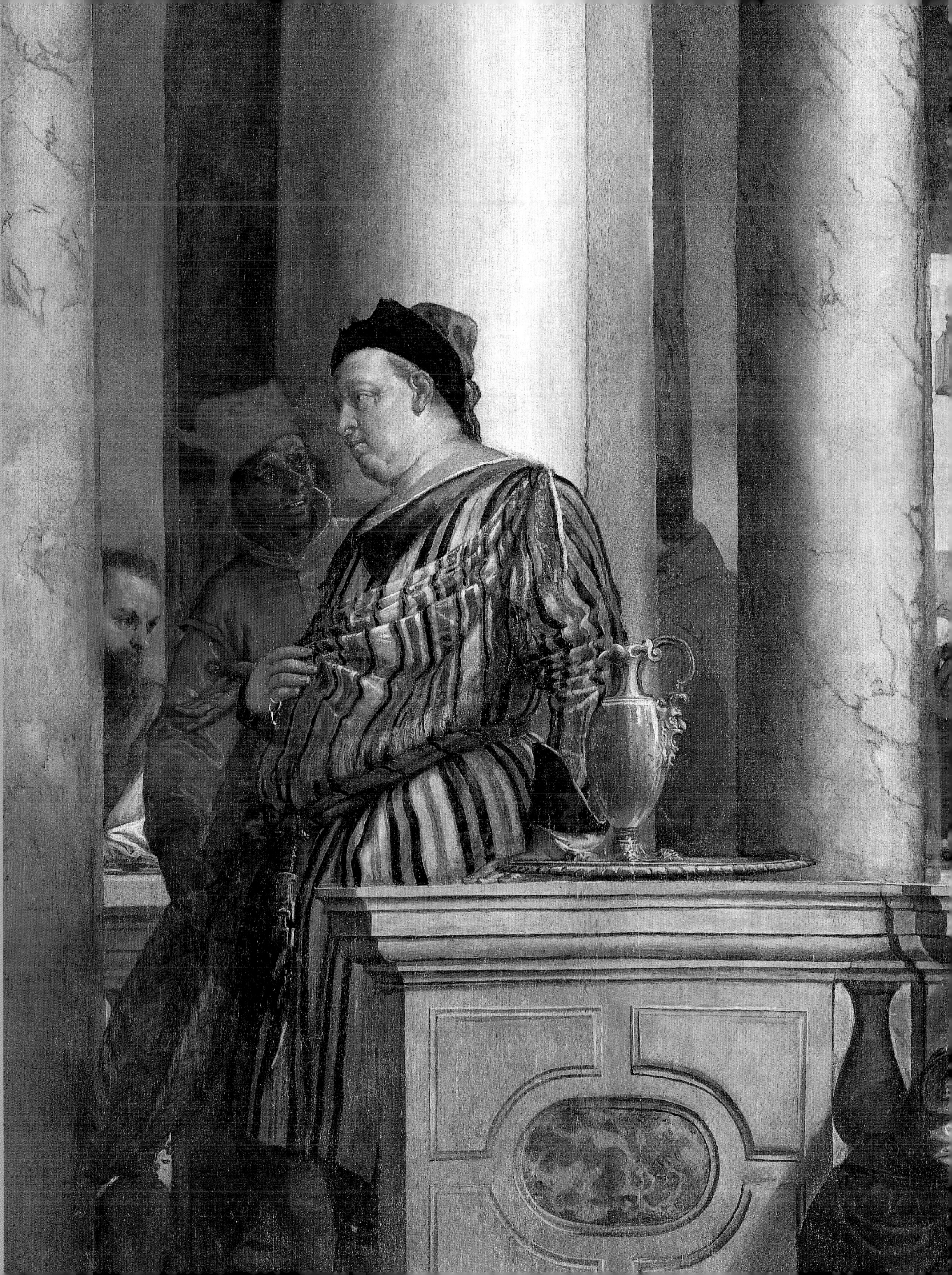

17TH CENTURY

Annibale Carracci

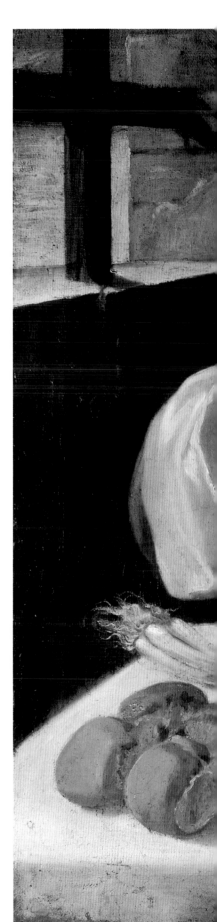

At Bologna, in the closing decades of the sixteenth century, the brothers Agostino and Annibale Carracci (Bologna 1560-Rome 1609) and their cousin Ludovico promoted a "reform" of painting that was intended to break with the stilted and over-intellectual style of Mannerism. With their works, in fact, the Carracci introduced a naturalistic and didactic style that was based on clarity of narrative and immediacy of expression and inspired by the great masters of the sixteenth century (Raphael, Michelangelo, Titian, Correggio), in which the exercise of drawing from life played an important part. In the Emilian city the Carracci founded what was first known as the Accademia de' Desiderosi (1582) and then the Accademia degli Incamminati (1590), a school with a systematic program of teaching where students could learn and practice the art of painting and drawing from life and at the same time receive a broad literary and scientific education. Having built up extensive experience in his hometown and on journeys for the purpose of study to Parma, Tuscany and Venice, Annibale went to Rome in 1595, called there by Odoardo Farnese to decorate his family palace. His masterpiece in this enterprise was the ceiling of the gallery, finished in 1601, where he took his ideas from Michelangelo's frescoes on the ceiling of the Sistine Chapel and Raphael's in the Loggia of Psyche at the Farnesina and developed them in an original manner.

After finishing the ceiling of the gallery and tired of the difficulties encountered in his relationship with Odoardo Farnese during the work, Annibale accepted various commissions from the Aldobrandini, a powerful Roman family (to which Pope Clement VIII belonged) and rivals of the Farnese. Between 1603 and 1604 Cardinal Pietro Aldobrandini gave Annibale the job of painting six lunettes with *Scenes from the Life of the Virgin* set in striking landscapes to adorn the chapel in his palace on the Corso. The series of lunettes – especially the *Flight into Egypt* – presented a new conception of the landscape that was to have a great influence on painting of classical inspiration in the seventeenth century (Domenichino, Poussin). Always a hypochondriac, Annibale's health deteriorated from 1605 onward, forcing him to delegate more and more of his commissions to pupils and collaborators. When Annibale died he was buried in the Pantheon in accordance with his own wishes.

The Eater of Beans
canvas, 57x68 cm
Galleria Colonna, Rome

An early work by Annibale Carracci, the picture shows a man of humble origin, perhaps a peasant, seated at a table laid with a rustic and frugal meal: eating hungrily from a bowl of beans, he is peering at the observer. The subject is derived from Flemish painting, which had spread the taste for genre scenes representing butcher's shops, kitchens, fishmongers, markets and taverns throughout Europe. The vogue for such pictures had caught on in Northern Italy around 1580, together with pastoral themes and landscape scenes inspired by Giorgione. Annibale's painting, which makes no attempt at irony or caricature, reveals the artist's interest in objective and natural reality, in the aspects of everyday life, distancing himself from the refined, complex and contrived forms of Mannerism.

Ceiling of the Galleria Farnese:
Venus and Anchises
fresco
Palazzo Farnese, Rome

In Palazzo Farnese Annibale frescoed the
tunnel vault of the long gallery, located on
the second floor and used to house the
noble Roman family's collection. The
decoration, commenced in 1597 and
finished by 1601, marks one of the most
important chapters in the history of Italian
art and served as a fundamental point of
reference for the baroque art that
emerged over the following decades.
At the outset Cardinal Odoardo Farnese,
who commissioned the work, had asked
for the ceiling to be frescoed with scenes
commemorating his father Alessandro, an
able military commander who was killed
in Flanders in 1592. But then, after a long
period of preparation from which
numerous drawings have survived, the
project took a different turn and became
a joyful celebration of scenes from
mythology in framed panels set in an
architectural and decorative framework
painted in *trompe-l'œil*. The frieze
comprises four scenes of lovers from
classical mythology, including *Venus and
Anchises*, out of whose union was born
Aeneas, founder of the Roman race. So
the narrative compositions painted by
Carracci celebrate profane love and, with
it, the natural beauty and idyllic happiness
of a poetic pagan world as handed down
and ennobled by classical literature.

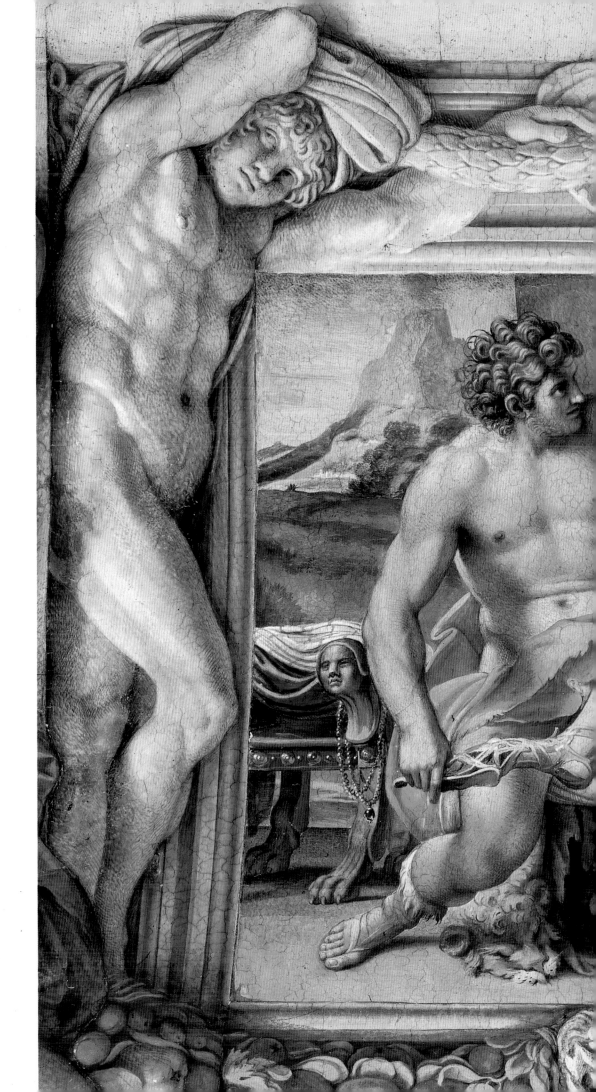

GENVS·VNDE
LATINVM

Ceiling of the Galleria Farnese
fresco
Palazzo Farnese, Rome

The decoration of the vault of the Farnese Gallery consists of nine mythological scenes, represented as if they were pictures with gilded wooden frames hung from the ceiling, in a *trompe-l'œil* structure (*quadri riportati*, as they were called in Italy in the seventeenth century). The scene set in the middle of the ceiling, larger in size than the others and depicting the *Triumph of Bacchus and Ariadne*, exalts the sensual love and beauty of the two protagonists,

surrounded by all the pageantry and excitement of the festive procession. In the frieze painted at the base of the vault, narrative scenes alternate with other painted elements that "imitate" bronze medallions, stone moldings, stuccoes, nude figures of youths and putti.
It was the artist's intention to create the illusion of a collection of pictures hung in an ornamental setting of magnificent and monumental architecture: this effort to "trick" the observer's eye, creating a sense of wonder, was to become an essential component of baroque figurative culture.

Landscape with the Flight into Egypt
canvas, 122x230 cm
Galleria Doria Pamphilj, Rome

The picture is one of the most intense and significant examples of landscape painting in Europe. The lunette is part of a series of six canvases with landscapes painted by Annibale and his collaborators to a commission from Cardinal Pietro Aldobrandini between 1603 and 1604 for the chapel of his palace on the Corso in Rome. Only two of the six lunettes can be ascribed to Carracci himself: the *Landscape with the Flight into Egypt* and the *Landscape with the Deposition*, both

of them in the Galleria Doria Pamphilj. In these paintings the narrative scene is subordinate to the landscape, to the point where it appears to be no more than a pretext for the composition. The figures are set in harmonious and idealized natural surroundings, pervaded by a sense of gentle melancholy – of literary and poetic origin – intensified by the warm light of an autumnal dawn. The Aldobrandini lunettes, with their lyrical and skillfully controlled tone, had a powerful influence on those artists in Rome (both Italian and foreign) who tried their hand at this genre of painting, interpreted by Annibale in such a classical and ideal manner.

Caravaggio

ichelangelo Merisi's byname derives from the small town of Caravaggio near Bergamo, where his family came from. The painter was born in Milan on September 29 (Milan 1571-Porto Ercole, Grosseto, 1610), the feast day of St. Michael Archangel. He received his training in Lombardy and in 1592 set off for Rome. Here, a few years later, he met Cardinal Francesco Maria Bourbon del Monte, ambassador of the Medici to the papal curia, who became the artist's patron, commissioning many paintings from him (*Bacchus*, Uffizi, Florence) and letting him stay as a guest in his own residence (now Palazzo Madama) for several years. Through the good offices of del Monte, Caravaggio also received orders for pictures from a select circle of art lovers: Cardinals Federico Borromeo and Massimo Massimi, the banker Ottavio Costa and the noblemen Vincenzo Giustiniani and Ciriaco Mattei.

Between 1599 and 1600 Merisi produced his first public works, the *Calling of Saint Matthew* and the *Martyrdom of Saint Matthew*, two canvases for the side walls of the Contarelli Chapel in San Luigi dei Francesi. These were followed in 1602 by the altarpiece for the same chapel with *Saint Matthew and the Angel*, of which he painted two versions (one still *in situ*, the other formerly in the Kaiser Friedrich Museum, Berlin, but now destroyed). After these came numerous paintings for other important Roman churches: the Cerasi Chapel in Santa Maria del Popolo (1601), Sant'Agostino (1603-06), the Chiesa Nuova (1604), Santa Maria della Scala (1605) and St. Peter's (1605-06). The naturalism of Caravaggio's pictures shocked and dismayed his clients, who sometimes demanded that he replace them with new versions (as in the case of the *Saint Matthew with the Angel* for San Luigi dei Francesi) or even rejected them altogether (as with the *Death of the Virgin* in Santa Maria della Scala and the *Madonna dei Palafrenieri* for a chapel in St. Peter's).

A man of restless and turbulent character, Caravaggio frequently got into brawls and trouble with the law. The most serious of these occurred on May 28, 1606, when the painter killed one Ranuccio Tommasoni over a game of tennis. Merisi was placed under a "capital ban" (i.e. the death penalty could be inflicted on him by anyone in any place) for the murder and he was forced to flee the city and wander for the rest of his life.

Seeking refuge first in the fiefs of the Colonna family in Lazio, he went to Naples in 1606. He stayed about ten months in the city, turning out large numbers of pictures representing episodes from the Bible or other religious scenes. He made contact with young local painters, exercising a decisive influence on their work and style.

In 1607 Caravaggio went to Malta, where he was granted the honorary title of "Knight of Justice" by the Grand Master of the Order of Malta, Alof de Wignacourt. But Caravaggio was expelled from the order and imprisoned, perhaps because word of his crime had reached the island. On October 6, 1608, he managed to escape and took sail for Sicily. A year later, Merisi returned to Naples, from where set off in 1610 in an attempt to reach Rome by boat, having heard rumors of a papal pardon. But the artist never reached his destination and died on July 18 at Porto Ercole.

Bacchus
canvas, 95x85 cm
Galleria degli Uffizi, Florence

An early work by the artist, datable to the last decade of the sixteenth century, the picture was probably painted by Caravaggio for Cardinal del Monte, his patron in Rome. It represents the god of wine with the features of a youth and wearing a wreath of vine leaves, lying on a triclinium in the manner of the ancient Romans. According to some scholars, the sensual figure of *Bacchus* is actually a self-portrait. In any case it is evident that the figure is painted from life and that the model was chosen and adapted for the occasion. The light defines the human figure, the vegetation and objects with the same clarity, and in fact it was the artist's custom to paint them from their reflections in a mirror.

The young man dressed up as the god of wine is holding a glass goblet of disproportionate size and filled with wine, which he seems to be offering to the observer. On the table in the foreground stand the bottle and a bowl full of fruit, elements painted from life – like the figure – but placed in a symbolic context. Thus the fruit which is beginning to rot and the withering leaves may be an allusion to *vanitas*, i.e. to the impermanence of earthly things, while the wine offered by Bacchus may be a reference to the eucharistic wine and therefore to the incarnation of Christ.

Basket of Fruit
canvas, 31x47 cm
Pinacoteca Ambrosiana, Milan

Painted for Cardinal Federico Borromeo,
perhaps before the end of the sixteenth
century, the picture is Caravaggio's only
still life, and the first in the history of
Italian art (though the genre was already
common in Flemish art). Starting out
from an actual object, depicted with great
precision, the composition is carefully
thought-out and constructed: its meaning
goes beyond a mere transcription of
reality. In fact, just like in the *Bacchus* in
the Uffizi, the withered leaves and worm-
eaten fruit allude to the corruptibility of
nature, the *vanitas* of earthly things and
the transience of beauty and youth. By
choosing to make the basket of fruit the
sole subject of the picture and assigning it
a precise symbolic meaning, the artist was
challenging the canons of traditional and
academic art, which relegated painting
from "life" to the status of a minor genre.
Whereas, in Caravaggio's view, an artist
ought to be able to demonstrate just as
much ability and dedication painting "a
good picture of flowers, as one of
figures."

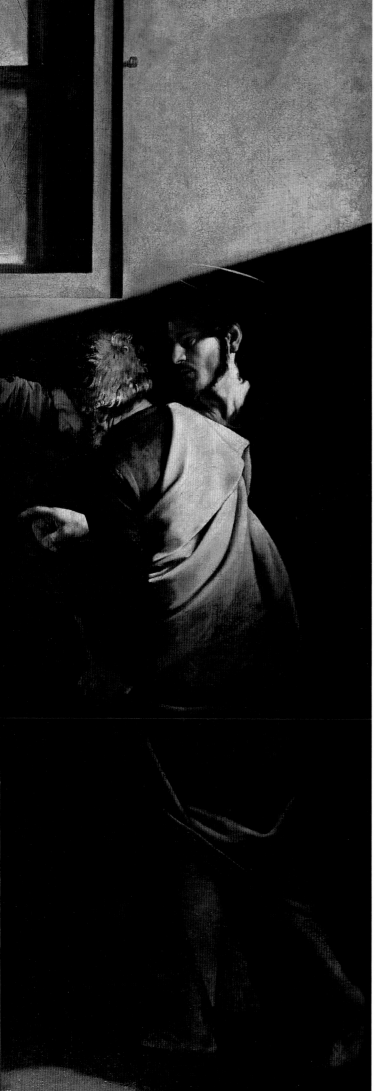

Calling of Saint Matthew;
Martyrdom of Saint Matthew
canvas, 322x340; 323x343 cm
Contarelli Chapel, San Luigi dei Francesi,
Rome

In 1599 Caravaggio obtained his first public commission, for paintings to be hung on the walls of the chapel owned by the Frenchman Matthieu Cointrel, known as Matteo Contarelli in Italian, datary of Pope Gregory XIII and later cardinal, who died in 1585. The executors of the high prelate's will were the Crescenzi family, friends of Cardinal del Monte, who acted as a go-between for the commission from Merisi.

On the instructions of the Crescenzi, the artist painted two canvases with the most important episodes from the life of St. Matthew, Contarelli's namesake and titular of the chapel: his *Calling* and *Martyrdom* (1599-1600). Following the success of these works, Caravaggio was asked to paint the altarpiece as well, an image of *Saint Matthew and the Angel.*

The cycle represented a crucial moment in Merisi's career, finally allowing him to try his hand at sacred subjects. The painter abandoned the brightly-colored manner of his early works in favor of a style with heavy chiaroscuro, producing dramatic pictures with luministic effects of great expressive force and symbolic value. The scene of the *Calling of Saint Matthew* shows Jesus and his disciples in the office of the tax collector Levi son of Alphaeus – later to be called Matthew – who is seated in front of the money that has just been collected, counted

avariciously by his assistants. The darkness of the room is rent by a beam of light that enters from the right – where we see Christ and Peter – and skims the wall and window before falling on the faces of the tax collectors, and Matthew in particular, who displays incredulity at the summons. The figures around the table are wearing contemporary clothing and are undoubtedly portrayed from life. The setting is reminiscent of a tavern of the period: thus the sacred story has been transported into the dimension of the artist's own life. The light plays a very important role: it brings out the material qualities of the fabrics, the details of the costumes and the features of the figures, but also takes on a symbolic meaning, representing the light of God that pierces the darkness and shows the way to salvation.

The scene of the *Martyrdom of Saint Matthew* is more dramatic and agitated. Radiographic analysis of the painting has shown that Caravaggio had initially conceived a different composition from the one we see today. Once again the light plays a primary role: a bright and unexpected shaft of light breaks in from the left, picking out the executioner who is about to finish off the saint, fallen to the ground in the struggle to defend himself. The other figures draw back in terror: one of the most memorable – and frequently imitated by later artists – is the child screaming and running away on the right. On the other side, in the background, the man with a beard, shocked by the brutal murder, is a self-portrait of the painter.

Sacrifice of Isaac
canvas, 104x135 cm
Galleria degli Uffizi, Florence

Caravaggio painted the *Sacrifice of Isaac* in 1603 for Cardinal Maffeo Barberini, later to become Pope Urban VIII. The scene focuses on the figures in the foreground, represented at three-quarter length: the climax of the drama is captured by Isaac's desperate cry, uttered against the backdrop of a landscape that appears by contrast tranquil and serene, with characteristics typical of Venetian painting.

This picture has also been subjected to X-ray analysis, revealing the procedure followed by the artist. He made no drawing prior to painting, but did cut a few rapid lines into the primed canvas as essential points of reference around which to construct the figures painted directly from life, with posed models. In particular, it is possible to make out the lines marking the position of the heads, arms and, in Isaac's face, eyes and screaming mouth. The profile of the angel is especially interesting: once the outline of the head had been engraved, the artist spread a dark ground, on which he painted the face from life (perhaps using the same model who had posed for Isaac) and then altered it to make the features more regular and idealized (Gregori 1991). Such a method shows that he had made a careful study of the works Leonardo had left in Lombardy, which exercised a decisive influence on Caravaggio's formation.

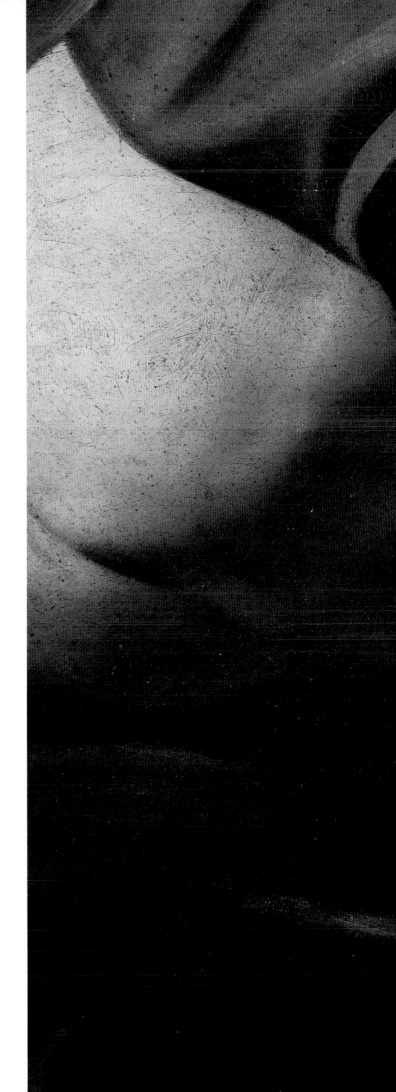

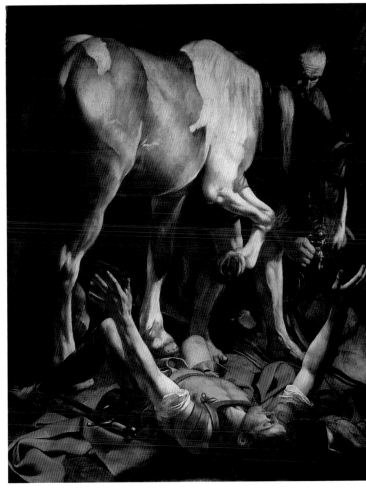

Crucifixion of Saint Peter;
Conversion of Saint Paul
canvas, cm 230x175 each
Cerasi Chapel, Santa Maria del Popolo,
Rome

After he had finished the canvases for the
Contarelli Chapel in San Luigi dei
Francesi, Caravaggio received a
commission from Monsignor Tiberio
Cerasi on September 24, 1600, to paint
two pictures for the side walls of his own
chapel in Santa Maria del Popolo,
representing the *Crucifixion of Saint
Peter* and the *Conversion of Saint Paul*.

The artist completed the paintings in a
year, after the first versions had been
rejected by the client. In the meantime,
again to a commission from Monsignor
Cerasi, Annibale Carracci painted the
altarpiece with the *Assumption of the
Virgin*.
Both of Caravaggio's compositions are
arranged diagonally and focus on life-size
figures set against an impenetrable dark
background. In the *Crucifixion* the
dramatic scene is presented in a natural
and everyday setting: the light picks out
the wrinkled and suffering features of
Peter, the shabby clothing of the hooded

executioners who are weighed down by
their onerous task and the dirty feet of the
kneeling man. Yet once again it is the
redeeming light of God, which comforts
Peter by promising him salvation after his
martyrdom. The same effect is to be found
in the *Conversion of Saint Paul* who,
according to the *Acts of the Apostles*, fell
from his horse after being dazzled by a
brilliant light while a voice called on him
to believe. The scene has a theatrical
quality, with the horse standing over the
fallen rider, blinded by the sudden flash of
light, so that the two figures form
intersecting diagonals.

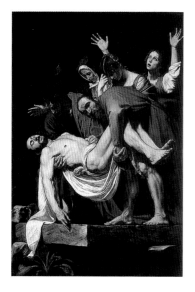

Deposition in the Tomb
canvas, 300x203 cm
Pinacoteca, Vatican

Caravaggio painted the *Deposition* in the Vatican some time before 1604 for Pietro Vittrice's chapel in the Roman Chiesa Nuova (Santa Maria in Vallicella). The imposing body of Christ hangs from the arms of the compact group of mourners as they lower him into the tomb. The figures in the Gospel scene are humble personages, dressed in simple clothing, their faces lined and their feet and limbs worn out by their labors. Yet they assume the solemn poses of an ancient tragedy and the scene takes on a majestic tone, whose significance goes beyond a simple account of the event and alludes symbolically to the Resurrection. The artist was able to achieve such a majestic and balanced composition through his study of such illustrious sixteenth-century models as Michelangelo's *Pietà* in St. Peter's (p. 226) and Raphael's *Deposition* (p. 248) in the Galleria Borghese.

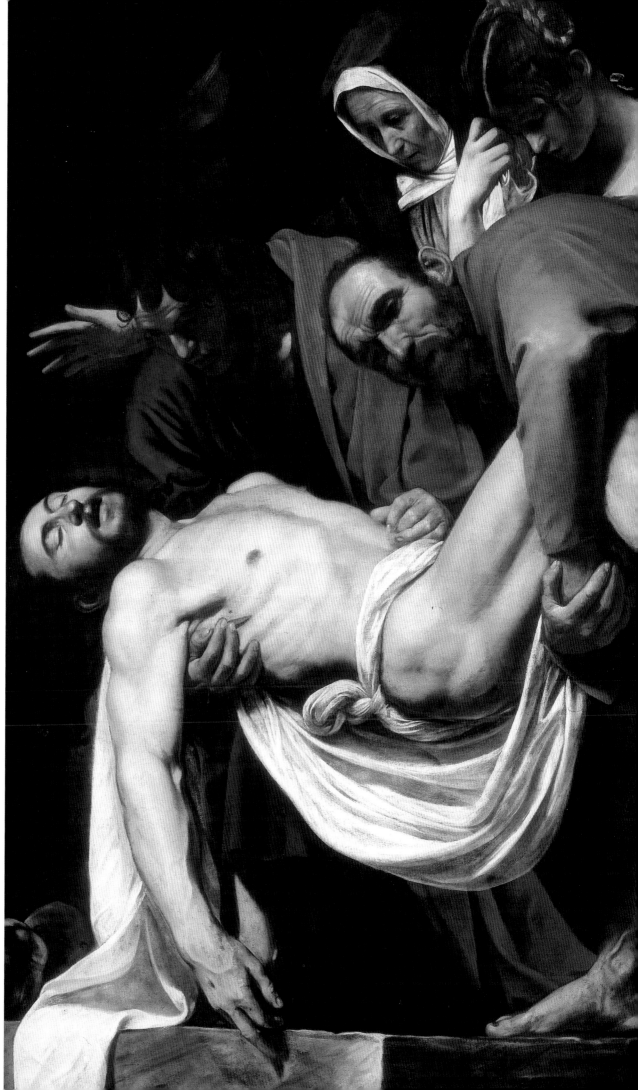

CARAVAGGIO

Supper at Emmaus
canvas, 145x195 cm
Pinacoteca di Brera, Milan

The *Supper at Emmaus*, painted by
Caravaggio in 1606 at the end of his stay
in Rome, is set in a bare and dark
interior. The rude simplicity and poverty
of the figures, with their tired and lined
faces, recalls the denizens of a humble
tavern. Entering from the left, the light
picks out Christ's face at the center and
his hand raised in blessing, to which the
amazed gesture of the apostle behind him
and the stiffening of the man seated

alongside him at the table are responses.
And the light also plays over the loaf of
bread in the piece of still life laid out on
the crude table. The figures and objects
take on sculptural forms as they emerge
from the darkness, which grows more
and more oppressive and impenetrable in
Caravaggio's late works.

**Beheading of Saint John
the Baptist**
canvas, 361x520 cm
St. John's Co-Cathedral, Malta

On Malta around 1608, Caravaggio
painted pictures of imposing size and
dramatic and heart-rending effect, using a
rapid, summary and vigorous technique,
almost in monochrome, which appears to
reflect the life led by the artist over the
last few years. The figures are no longer
placed in the foreground and life-sized,
but on a smaller scale, seen in the
distance against dismal and shabby

buildings, with high and rough walls. The
Beheading of Saint John the Baptist
takes place outside the prison, observed
by two convicts from behind the bars. At
the imperious command of the man in the
middle, the executioner sets about cutting
off the Baptist's head, to be placed on the
tray held by a serving maid under the
horrified eyes of an elderly woman, the
only person to display any emotion. It is
Caravaggio's only signed picture, and may
be a reflection of his personal experience:
in fact the signature is grimly traced by
the trickle of blood flowing from the
Baptist's neck.

Gian Lorenzo Bernini

Gian Lorenzo Bernini (Naples 1598-Rome 1680) was taught sculpture by his father Pietro, of Florentine origin, who moved with the family from Naples to Rome in 1606. Here Gian Lorenzo continued his artistic education in late Mannerist circles, while making an enthusiastic study of the great protagonists of sixteenth-century art and of ancient sculpture, especially that of the Hellenistic era.

In his first portrait busts and the sculptural groups he executed from 1618 for Cardinal Scipione Borghese, Bernini already displayed the great mastery of technique that he was to retain throughout his life. But the artist's triumph came with the election of Maffeo Barberini as Pope Urban VIII, who was already a friend of the artist. In fact the pope assigned Bernini the most prestigious commissions of his pontificate (1623-44), giving him the opportunity to work not just as a sculptor, but also as an architect, a designer of theatrical scenery and decorations for festivities, a playwright and a painter, imposing a new style on the papal city through the force of his inexhaustible imagination. Between 1624 and 1633 Bernini made the baldachin located at the center of the new basilica of St. Peter. From then on, the artist – appointed architect of St. Peter's in 1629 – undertook a series of works for the basilica that were to keep him occupied for the rest of his life.

During the pontificate of Urban VIII the Roman artistic scene was dominated by Bernini, on whose good offices the other artists of the papal court were dependent for their commissions. After an initial falling out with his successor Innocent X, Bernini regained his position of prestige. This was confirmed under Alexander VII, who made the artist his personal architect and commissioned the design of St. Peter's Square from him (begun in 1657). In addition to this work in the Vatican, the most important architectural projects carried out by Bernini in these years were the church of Sant'Andrea al Quirinale (1658) and Palazzo Montecitorio (1650-55). Bernini was the most brilliant interpreter of baroque spirituality, with its emphatic gestures and transports of joy, through the scenic use of light and materials with a strong emotional impact. Examples of this can be found in the *Ecstasy of Saint Teresa* in Santa Maria della Vittoria (1644-52) and in the *Blessed Ludovica Albertoni* in San Francesco a Ripa (1671-74), or in the new scheme for the sepulchral monument he adopted for the tombs of Urban VIII (1628-47) and Alexander VII (1671-78).

In 1665 Bernini was summoned to Paris by King Louis XIV, who asked the artist to draw up plans for the reconstruction of the Louvre, but they were never put into effect.

Rape of Proserpine
marble, ht. 225 cm
Galleria Borghese, Rome

This is one of the marble sculptures executed by Gian Lorenzo Bernini between 1619 and 1625 for his patron, Cardinal Scipione Borghese. In these works, whose subjects are based on narrative themes drawn from literary texts, the artist set out to emulate the principal points of reference in his training: the sculpture of ancient Greece and Rome, that of sixteenth-century Mannerism and the art of Michelangelo. The *Rape of Proserpine* takes its inspiration from Ovid's *Metamorphoses*: Proserpine, the daughter of Gaea (the Earth), strives to break free from the powerful grip of Pluto, king of the Underworld, who wants to make her his wife; alongside the couple stands the three-headed dog Cerberus. The group is dynamic in appearance, with the spiraling

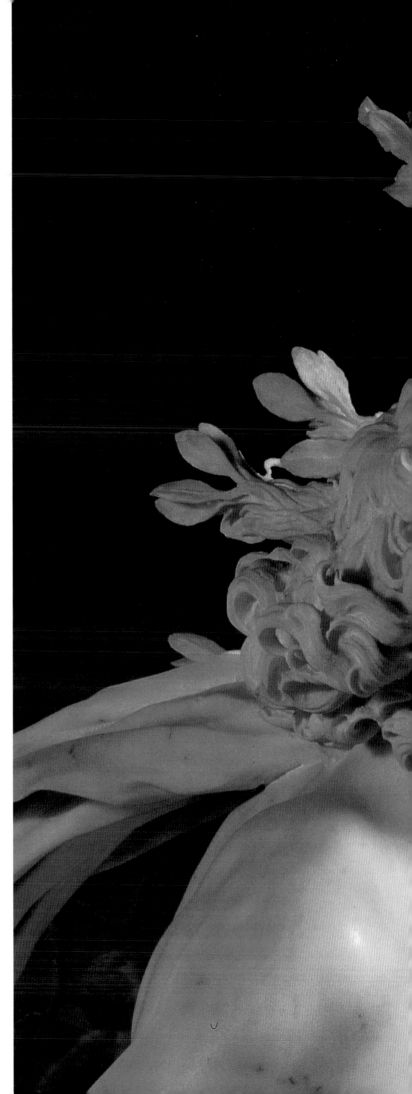

GIAN LORENZO BERNINI

and opposing motion of the two bodies, one pushing away and the other holding back. The work reproduces the action as it takes place: viewed from the left, the group shows Pluto seizing the girl, suspended in the air; from the front, the god seems to be displaying triumph at the capture of his prey; from the right, we see Proserpine looking desperately toward the sky, tears running down her face, while the monstrous dog barks below. The sculpture is theatrical, even melodramatic in conception, placing the emphasis on pathos and the palpable illusion of the material: in fact the massive structure of Pluto's body is stressed, along with the soft skin of Proserpine, into which the god of Hades sinks his fingers, gripping her with force.

Apollo and Daphne
marble, ht. 243 cm
Galleria Borghese, Rome

Of all the works carved by Bernini for Cardinal Scipione Borghese, the group with *Apollo and Daphne* (1622-25) is undoubtedly the most famous. It represents another theme drawn from Ovid's *Metamorphoses*: the nymph Daphne fleeing from Apollo and turning into a laurel tree as soon as the infatuated god catches up with her and touches her. The artist has chosen to represent the most moving part of the myth: the instant – momentary and fleeting – in which the god's hand grazes the nymph's body and she begins to change her appearance. The sense of movement, the pathetic and emphatic emotion and the illusory quality of the material – features typical of baroque art in general – are once again the characteristic elements of the sculpture. Through a masterly and virtuoso handling of the surface, Bernini is able to create the illusion that the inanimate material of the marble takes on life, throbbing and moving in the space perceived by the observer. The sense of strength and impetus conveyed by the *Rape of Proserpine* gives way in the *Apollo and Daphne* to grace, to the sensitive naturalism of the materials (the clothing, the hair, the bark, the leaves) and to the intense expression of the figures.

Scipione Borghese
marble, ht. cm 100
Galleria Borghese, Rome

Cardinal Scipione Borghese was Bernini's first important client. The favorite nephew of Pope Paul V, he was patron of the greatest artistic talents in Rome during the sixteenth century and a keen and quite ruthless collector, to the point of arranging the theft of Raphael's *Deposition* from the church of San Francesco in Perugia (p. 248). The ancient and modern works collected by the high prelate were used to adorn the rooms of the Villa Borghese, outside Porta Pinciana, which Scipione had had built in the setting of a florid garden and decorated inside in a sumptuous antique style that shaped the taste of a whole era. Fascinated by Bernini's personality, Scipione was gratified and filled with admiration when the artist presented him with two versions of his portrait bust (1632). In fact the sculptor had carved the first bust out of marble from a drawing on paper (Pierpont Morgan Library, New York), but had then realized that a vein in the marble resulted in a split in the forehead. So, within a short space

of time, he executed a second version with a few but significant variations, demonstrating his technical virtuosity (both the busts are now in the Galleria Borghese). A lively caricature of the cardinal sketched by Bernini (Biblioteca Apostolica, Vatican) testifies to the relaxed and friendly relationship between the artist and his patron.

Costanza Bonarelli
marble, ht. 72 cm
Museo Nazionale del Bargello, Florence

Carved in 1635, it is Bernini's only private portrait. Costanza Bonarelli, the artist's young lover, is presented with sensual, haughty and strong-willed features. The hastily arranged hairstyle and housecoat open at the breast accentuate the familiar and intimate character of the portrait. The woman does not appear posed, but in the act of suddenly turning to one side, with a gesture of surprise and a spontaneous and natural expression on her face.

Ecstasy of Saint Teresa
marble
Cornaro Chapel, Santa Maria della Vittoria, Rome

In 1644 Cardinal Federico Cornaro asked Bernini to renovate the left transept of the Carmelite church of Santa Maria della Vittoria, transforming the space into a mortuary chapel for his family dedicated to St. Teresa of Avila, founder of the Carmelite Order. The chapel designed by Bernini is the fruit of a happy marriage between architecture, sculpture and painting, in a riot of light, color and a variety of materials that reflects the unitary and visual conception of the arts displayed by the artist on more than one occasion. The theatrical layout of the whole is also the result of Bernini's experience as a designer of scenery for the Teatro Barberini and of temporary decorations for public celebrations, both religious and secular.
In the Cornaro Chapel the observer is caught in the mesh of visual and emotional relationships established between the various parts of the decoration, and is drawn into the space of the work. From the balconies on the side

walls of the chapel peer out seven cardinals of the Cornaro family, including Federico and his father, the Venetian doge Giovanni Cornaro: talking animatedly among themselves, they are witnesses to the *Ecstasy of Saint Teresa*, which is set in a niche above the altar and represents the fulcrum of the entire decorative complex.
The saint appears to have swooned, with her lips parted, her head tilted back and her arms hanging loose, in an attitude that conveys an impression of sensuality rather than of suffering and suggests a physical and mental transport. Illuminated by the natural light that enters through a concealed window, the nun is shown in a transcendental state, suspended among the clouds while a smiling angel prepares to pierce her with an arrow, symbol of the love of God. From above descend the golden rays of divine grace. Along with the members of the Cornaro family, we appear to be present at a spectacular tableau vivant, where through the art of "persuasion" – typical of seventeenth-century culture – the observer is made to share emotionally in the scenic illusion and in the exaltation of the senses born out of a powerful religious experience that is renewed in the present.

Pietro da Cortona

Pietro Berrettini (Cortona, near Arezzo 1596-Rome 1669) served his artistic apprenticeship in the city of his birth, Cortona, under the Florentine painter Andrea Commodi whom he followed to Rome in 1612. In the papal see he was introduced into the cultivated circles of antiquarians and noble dilettanti with a passion for both ancient and modern art. It was here that he met Cassiano del Pozzo and Marcello Sacchetti, who became Pietro's first patrons and friends.

Berrettini was appreciated above all for his decorations on a grand scale, where he was able to devise majestic and spectacular settings, transforming any kind of space in a unitary and imaginative fashion. The favor he won with the Barberini earned the artist a series of important commissions. In 1631 Pietro began the frescoes in the palace of the powerful family: his ceiling fresco representing the *Allegory of Divine Providence* (1632-39) was to have a particularly strong influence throughout the century, serving as a model for subsequent baroque decoration.

Pietro da Cortona temporarily interrupted the work on Palazzo Barberini in 1637 to make a journey to Northern Italy that lasted for several months. On the way, the artist also stopped in Florence, where Grand Duke Ferdinando II de' Medici asked him to fresco the Saletta della Stufa in the grand ducal residence of Palazzo Pitti with *The Four Ages of Man*. In 1640 the Medici summoned Berrettini back to Florence to design and execute the decoration of the seven reception rooms in the grand ducal apartments.

Returning to Rome in 1647, Pietro executed a series of important frescoes in Santa Maria della Vallicella for the Oratorian fathers, in the dome (finished by 1651), tribune (1655) and nave (1665), in what was his most demanding work of sacred painting. In the meantime, he completed the frescoes in the gallery built by Francesco Borromini in Palazzo Pamphilj on Piazza Navona: commissioned from him by Pope Innocent X Pamphjli, they represented *Scenes from the Legend of Aeneas* (1654).

Over the course of his career Berrettini drew on his talent for the creation of spectacular scenery to work as an architect as well, among other things designing the villa at Pigneto for the Sacchetti (by 1630), now destroyed, the new church of Santi Luca e Martina (from 1634) and the façade and interior decoration of Santa Maria della Pace (1656-57).

The Golden Age
fresco
Galleria Palatina, Palazzo Pitti, Florence

In 1637 Pietro da Cortona temporarily interrupted work on the frescoes in Palazzo Barberini in Rome (p. 366) to go to Florence, where the grand duke of Tuscany, Ferdinando II de' Medici, asked him to fresco the Saletta della Stufa adjoining his own bedchamber, on the *piano nobile* of Palazzo Pitti. Here the artist painted the walls with *The Four Ages of Man*, the mythical history of human civilization as handed down by various classical authors, including Ovid in the *Metamorphoses*. The series of four scenes begins with the

Golden Age, a primitive era of peace in which human beings lived without knowing the fatigue of labor, in perfect harmony with a luxuriant and tranquil nature (note the child playing with the tame lion, lying down next to a hare). The scene is idyllic, painted in a luminous and pale palette, with colors that are usually identified with spring: greens, blues, pinks and whites.
It is followed by the *Silver Age*, in which humanity is still engaged in serene activities but needs agriculture and stock rearing to sustain itself, the *Bronze Age*, when war is born together with art and culture, and finally the *Iron Age*, dominated by the greed, avarice and brutality of human beings who wage unjust and devastating wars.

of the pope: *Peace Enthroned and Wrath Enchained*; *Minerva Driving Out the Giants*; *Religion and Wisdom*; *Hercules Putting the Harpies to Flight*.

From below, the frescoes on the ceiling of Palazzo Barberini have the appearance of a violent and unstable composition over which the eye roams in search of a fixed and certain point of reference. With great freedom of invention, the episodes succeed one another at a relentless pace and the artist's mastery of perspective illusionism allows him to make the figures look as if they are looming above the observer, almost threatening to fall. The real space seems to expand outward into the landscapes on the walls and the clear sky on the ceiling.

Venus Seeking to Hold Back Mars
fresco
Galleria Palatina, Palazzo Pitti, Florence

In 1640, after completing the decoration of Palazzo Barberini in Rome, Pietro da Cortona returned to Florence, where he remained until 1647, designing and in part executing the fresco and stucco decoration of the grand duke's reception rooms. These were known as the "planetary" rooms as they were dedicated to the planets Venus, Mars, Jupiter and Saturn. The artist from Cortona conceived a different scheme for each of them, devoted to one of the corresponding deities who presided over a period in the education and life of the virtuoso ruler, influencing his qualities and attributes. In fact the ceiling of the first room, dedicated to Venus, is painted with a scene in which the prince, still a youth, is taken from the arms of Venus, goddess of love, by Minerva, goddess of wisdom, and handed over to Hercules, recognizable by his club and lion skin. The latter will be his traveling companion, teaching him Virtue and Fortitude. The main figures hover in the open sky, devoid of shadows, while the others seem to be balanced on the edge of the frame at the side.

The lunettes underneath, surrounded by stuccoes, are decorated with legendary episodes providing examples of the victory of the virtues over the passions.

Allegory of Divine Providence
fresco
Palazzo Barberini, Rome

Between 1632 and 1639 Pietro da Cortona frescoed the ceiling of the main hall of Palazzo Barberini, built to a design by Gian Lorenzo Bernini. The decoration was commissioned by Pope Urban VIII, the most important member of the Barberini family, who wished to celebrate

its glories in a triumphal manner. The bees inside a laurel wreath in the middle of the ceiling are a reference to the heraldic device of the Barberini, while the papal insignia allude to Urban VIII himself and the crown of stars to his immortality. The program for the decoration was drawn up by the scholar Francesco Bracciolini. The immense series of frescoes – covering around 600 square meters – is dominated at the center by

papal heraldic emblems and, below, by the *Allegory of Divine Providence* in a halo of golden light, ringed by the three Fates, Time and the Virtues. The central scene, consisting of a daring *sotto in sù* perspective against a luminous blue sky, is surrounded by a painted architectural frame adorned with medallions and mock stuccoes. Outside the frame are set four more mythological scenes – one for each wall of the room – alluding to the virtues

18TH CENTURY

Giambattista Tiepolo

R ight from the days of his training, the primary influence on Giambattista Tiepolo (Venice 1696-Madrid 1770) was the painting of Paolo Veronese. The artist also displayed a great gift for drawing, which he always used as the basis for the magnificent decorations he carried out throughout his career, for churches and palaces not just in Venice but all over Europe.

In 1726 Tiepolo received his first major commission: in the service of Dionisio Dolfin, patriarch of Aquileia, he frescoed the archbishop's palace and cathedral in Udine. The artist's palette gradually took on lighter tones and his fanciful style created transparent and airy figures bathed in light. Commissions outside the borders of the Venetian Republic started to come in thick and fast: Tiepolo was at Milan in 1731 and again in 1740, at Bergamo in 1732 and at Vicenza in 1734.

In his decorations – ever more sumptuous and daring in their conception – Tiepolo was often assisted by Girolamo Mengozzi, called Colonna, an expert in *quadratura*, i.e. the painted architecture that created the illusion of being an extension of the room's real architecture: this was the framework within which Tiepolo would then organize the narrative scene. With Mengozzi's help, Tiepolo frescoed the walls of the reception room in Palazzo Labia with *Scenes from the Story of Antony and Cleopatra* (*c.* 1745-50).

In 1750 Tiepolo, together with his sons Giandomenico and Lorenzo, was summoned to Würzburg by Prince-Bishop Karl Philipp von Greiffenklau, where the artist stayed for three years frescoing the Kaisersaal in the Residenz with mythological, historical and allegorical themes: this decoration on a gigantic scale represents one of the highest peaks attained by European rococo.

Returning to Venice in 1758 with an enhanced reputation, Tiepolo painted various cycles of frescoes and altarpieces, for which he received an unceasing flow of commissions: the church of the Pietà (1754-55), the decorations in Villa Valmarana at Vicenza (1757), the ceilings of two rooms in Ca' Rezzonico at Venice (1758), the oratory of the Purità at Udine and Villa Pisani at Stra (1761-62).

In 1762 Tiepolo left the republic again and went to the court of Charles III of Bourbon in Spain. He spent the rest of his life in the service of the Spanish monarch, painting frescoes in the royal palace at Madrid (the *Apotheosis of Spain* in the Throne Room; 1762-66).

Rachel Hiding the Idols
fresco
Palazzo Patriarcale, Udine

Starting in 1726, Tiepolo spent several years frescoing the palace of the patriarch of Aquileia at Udine, carrying out the most important undertaking of his early career and his first on the mainland. It was in the gallery that the artist did his best work, earning himself the description of a "celebrated and lucid painter" in the documents of the Udine archives. In this setting, where he painted several scenes linked to the stories of Biblical patriarchs

like Abraham and Jacob, Tiepolo put aside the rhetorical hyperbole and emphasis on decoration typical of the late baroque in favor of a realistic and incisive narration, combined with a technique based on brilliant and festive color, steeped in light. In the fresco of *Rachel Hiding the Idols*, the artist takes a monumental approach, finding space for Arcadian episodes (note the pastoral scene on the left) and elements of great naturalness (the women and children on the right). The forms stand out strongly from the ground, painted in solid and crystal-clear colors, in an unfading luminous atmosphere.

The Meeting of Antony and Cleopatra; The Banquet of Antony and Cleopatra
fresco, 650x300 cm each
Palazzo Labia, Venice

The decoration of Palazzo Labia (*c.* 1745-50) marks one of the highpoints in Tiepolo's career as a painter of cycles of profane pictures. The ballroom is frescoed on the great circular ceiling with *Bellerophon Flying on Pegasus into Glory and Eternity* and on the walls with two episodes from the story of Antony and Cleopatra: the *Meeting* and the *Banquet*. The magnificence and splendor of the scenes and their settings, as well as of the costumes worn by the protagonists and their retinue, were intended to reflect the worldly and aristocratic pomp that surrounded the Labia family, a wealthy member of the new Venetian nobility. In the *Banquet* Cleopatra is shown dipping her pearls in a glass of wine, a solemn gesture that may have been intended as a reminder of another celebrated banquet held in that very palace, at which the Labia had invited their guests to throw the gold cutlery of the luxurious service into the Grand Canal (where it was promptly fished out again by the servants, who had placed nets under the water).

The two scenes are set in architectural spaces that appear to extend beyond the walls, offering *trompe-l'œil* views through the two adjoining arches. The imposing perspective scenery was painted by Girolamo Mengozzi Colonna, an excellent *quadraturista* who often assisted Tiepolo in his pictorial decorations.

Rinaldo Abandoning Armida;
Aeneas Presenting Cupid to Dido
Disguised as Ascanius;
The Sacrifice of Iphigenia
(pp. 378-9)
fresco, 220x310; 230x240; 350x700 cm
Villa Valmarana, Vicenza

In 1757 Giustino Valmarana summoned
Tiepolo to Vicenza to decorate the main
house and guest quarters of the so-called
Villa of the Dwarfs, located to the south of
the city on the hill of San Bastian.
Giambattista devoted his attention to the
frescoes in the main house, leaving the
decoration of the guest quarters to his son
Giandomenico, now thirty years old.
The narrative scenes painted by
Giambattista Tiepolo in the small

seventeenth-century rooms of the main
house are based on celebrated poems of
classical antiquity and the Renaissance,
such as Homer's *Iliad*, Virgil's *Aeneid*,
Ludovico Ariosto's *Orlando Furioso* and
Torquato Tasso's *Jerusalem Delivered*.
They were probably chosen by Giustino
Valmarana himself, a cultured man and a
lover of literature and the theater. And it
may well have been Valmarana who
suggested the sentimental and slightly
melodramatic tone that characterizes the
paintings, where the heroes and heroines
adopt eloquent and theatrical attitudes in
a setting that is fairly intimate and simple,
with architectural backdrops (or
quadrature) once again entrusted to the
skillful hands of Girolamo Mengozzi
Colonna (as in the *Sacrifice of*
Iphigenia).

Canaletto

Giovanni Antonio Canal, called Canaletto (Venice 1697-1768), was the son of Bernardo Canal, a painter of theatrical scenery. After a visit to Rome in 1719, Canaletto started to paint views of urban settings from life. The artist showed a preference for this genre throughout his career, though in his early years he had also been interested in "caprices," i.e. imaginary landscapes with ancient ruins. In fact Canaletto's first dated and documented work is a *Caprice* painted in 1723 (now in a private collection).

Canaletto's *vedute* of the Grand Canal, the squares of Venice (the so-called "campi") and the city's hinterland proved extremely popular with collectors. Appreciated not just by the Venetians, but also by foreign and in particular British travelers, Canaletto formed a partnership with Joseph Smith, a British collector and businessman resident in Venice. For a long time Smith was the main buyer of Canaletto's works, as well as a sort of agent for the artist, promoting the sale of his friend's paintings and their reproductions. Between 1729 and 1734 he painted twelve small views of the Grand Canal for Smith and engravings of these by Antonio Visentini were then published in the volume *Prospectus Magni Canalis Venetiarum* (1735).

Around 1740, Canaletto made a journey up the Brenta River looking for new subjects for his paintings, drawings and engravings, accompanied by his nephew Bernardo Bellotto who was himself to become a famous *vedutista*. In these years Canaletto worked almost exclusively for Joseph Smith, who had in the meantime been appointed British consul in Venice (1744). The artist dedicated a series of etchings to him entitled *Other Invented Views Taken from Other Places* (1744), in which the "invented views" were imaginary scenes that included buildings from different urban settings.

With Smith's backing, Canaletto set off in 1746 for England, where there was already a flourishing market for his paintings. With good contacts among the London aristocracy, he painted various views of the Thames, showing Westminster Bridge at different stages in its construction. Meanwhile, the demand for Canaletto's pictures was spreading to other parts of Europe and some of his paintings were put on show in Paris in 1755. Canaletto returned to Venice after about ten years, sometime around 1760, but his style grew increasingly stiff and he started to paint views that were often repetitive or simple replicas of his earlier works.

View of the Grand Canal from Palazzo Balbi Looking Toward the Rialto
canvas, 144x207 cm
Ca' Rezzonico, Venice

The first views Canaletto painted of Venice are four large pictures now in the Thyssen Collection in Madrid and the museum of Ca' Rezzonico in Venice. In the *View of the Grand Canal from Palazzo Balbi Looking Toward the Rialto*, executed before 1723, the artist adopted a technique drawn from theatrical scene painting: he has placed two sources of light in the foreground, coming from different directions. This allows the shadows of both Palazzo Balbi on the left and the Mocenigo houses on the right to be cast onto the water, giving the view a greater sense of depth. This device and the complex perspective construction are the fruit of his training and early activity alongside his father Bernardo Canal, a scene painter.

*Reception of the Ambassador
in the Doge's Palace*
canvas, 184x265 cm
Private collection

This is one of the earliest of Canaletto's paintings of public ceremonies. The picture represents the rite that accompanied the installation in office of the imperial ambassador to the Republic of Venice, Count Giuseppe Bolagnos, on May 29, 1729. The work was commissioned by Bolagnos himself. The scene is depicted in a limpid and luminous style: the view is bathed in clear sunlight, bringing the buildings into sharp focus, while the figures are enlivened by bright colors.

Canaletto's compositions stand out from other *vedute* painted at the time for their precise reflection of the reality of the places represented. To achieve this, the artist relied in part on the aid of the camera obscura, a mechanical device that was an indirect forerunner of today's photographic camera. In the Museo Correr in Venice there is an example of a portable model that, according to an old but undocumented tradition, was once owned by Canaletto. It is a sort of box painted black on the inside, with a hole and a system of mirrors and lenses (similar to those of a reflex camera) that projected an image of the chosen view onto a pane of ground glass, allowing the artist to make a summary tracing of the essential lines and colors on a sheet of paper.

Fonteghetto della Farina
canvas, 66x112 cm
Private collection, Venice

The picture, probably painted in 1740 for the man of letters and bibliophile Giovan Battista Recanati, shows a popular and rundown quarter of "minor" Venice (just a short walk from the celebrated St. Mark's Square), represented with immediacy in an image of affectionate and tranquil contemplation. The view focuses on the warehouse on the right, which was to house the Academy of Painting and Sculpture from 1750 onward. The work is also an important record of an evocative corner of the city that has changed a great deal over the years. In the early nineteenth century an elegant coffee house was installed in the building and the bridge in the picture demolished. More recently a road (*fondamenta*) has been constructed outside the ancient building, along with a new bridge, now used by tourists on their way to St. Mark's Square from the ferry. The old Fonteghetto della Farina ("Flour Warehouse") painted by Canaletto is now the Harbor Office.

pp. 386-7
View of the Basin of St. Mark
canvas, 125x204 cm
Museum of Fine Arts, Boston

This view, along with several other masterpieces by Canaletto, arrived at Castle Howard in England, the magnificent stately home that the earl of Carlisle had decorated with paintings by Venetian artists.

In this picture, dating from around 1738, Canaletto has presented an exceptionally broad panorama, blending several images viewed from different angles and from a raised position (the Punta della Dogana at the mouth of the Grand Canal) into a unified and consistent whole. The binding element is the intense, almost magical light, effectively re-creating the effect of the reflections on the surface of the water on a warm and sunny day at the beginning of fall. The buildings that face onto the basin of St. Mark and form the horizon are depicted with painstaking precision and scrupulous fidelity to reality. Among them it is possible to recognize the domes and campanile of St. Mark's, the Doge's Palace and the so-called "Bridge of Sighs" on the left, while the façade of San Giorgio Maggiore on the island of the same name can be seen on the right. The various types of craft are depicted in equal detail: fishing boats, gondolas and sailing vessels of various sizes. The craft are bustling with the activity of tiny figures, Venetians and foreign tourists, fishermen and gondoliers dressed in caps and red breeches.

Francesco Guardi

Born to a family of artists from Trent, Francesco Guardi (Venice 1712-93) often collaborated in his early years with his brother Giannantonio (1699-1760) on narrative and devotional paintings. Together, the two artists painted the seven canvases depicting the *Scenes from the Story of Tobias and Tobit* in the church of the Arcangelo Raffaele at Venice, a cycle of paintings that represents one of the finest examples of Venetian rococo.

After Giannantonio's death (1760), Francesco began to work independently, establishing a reputation as a painter of *vedute* for Venetian and foreign clients but without ever achieving the international fame of Canaletto. Along with airy views of the city and of ceremonies held indoors at important moments in Venetian public life, Guardi painted his so-called *Caprices*, fanciful representations of landscapes peopled with tiny figures, boatmen with their simple craft and ancient ruins. Introverted and shy, Guardi never left Venice, which provided the sole source of inspiration for his views. Though his work was initially derived from that of Canaletto, Guardi preferred images veined with lyricism and melancholy to the older painter's limpid vision.

The shift away from Canaletto's style was complete in the cycle of the *Twelve Dogal Festivals* (1770-75), painted by Guardi for Doge Alvise IV Mocenigo. These were followed by a series of representations of official events staged in Venice in those years. In 1782, in fact, the artist was commissioned to paint a set of pictures of the celebrations for Pope Pius VI's visit to Venice and others of the festivities held to mark the visit of the "Counts of the North," Archduke Paul and Archduchess Maria Feodorowna of Russia. In the *Ascent of the Montgolfier* Guardi recorded the flight of a hot-air balloon over the lagoon on April 15, 1784. On several occasions, Guardi represented the sumptuous and spectacular Venetian regattas: the *Regatta on the Grand Canal*, now in the Mondiano collection in Bologna, was the last *veduta* painted by the artist, sometime around 1791.

Venetian Courtyard
canvas
Pushkin Museum, Moscow

*The Coronation of the Doge
on the Scala dei Giganti
of the Doge's Palace*
canvas, 66x101 cm
Louvre, Paris

The Doge at the Basilica della Salute
canvas, 68x100 cm
Louvre, Paris

Where Canaletto preferred to steep his limpid and tranquil views in a clear and warm light that picked out the details with an almost "photographic" accuracy, Francesco Guardi chose to paint his pictures under dark skies, often immersed in a misty atmosphere. His figures and buildings are abbreviated and imprecise forms, sketched with rapid and restless brushstrokes and in rarefied tints. Guardi's *vedute* present a poetically transfigured Venice, shot through with subtle strains of disquiet and veined with gentle melancholy. Views of the lagoon, pervaded by a diffuse and vibrant luminosity, corners of solitary and silent little squares, lavish ceremonies staged amidst teeming crowds and shimmering lights: all seem to reflect – in spite of the diversity of the subjects – the crisis and the moods of an era in decline. The collapse of faith in an objective vision of reality left more and more room for the emergence of spiritual feelings.

Antonio Canova

Antonio Canova (Possagno, near Treviso 1757-Venice 1822) was one of the greatest exponents of neoclassical art and perhaps the last great Italian artist of international renown. Over his brilliant career, Canova's principal aim was to free art from its subjection to those in power and their authoritarian meddling, despite having lived through the dramatic events that overtook Europe between the end of the eighteenth century and the first few decades of the nineteenth.

In 1768 Antonio came to Venice with his master, the sculptor Giuseppe Bernardi. Trained by his grandfather Pasino, a stonemason, Canova attended the academy of nude drawing in the city and studied the casts of ancient works in the gallery of Palazzo Farsetti. Setting up his own studio, he made a journey to Rome in 1779, passing through Bologna and Florence. The following year he went to Naples as well and visited Salerno, Paestum, Pompeii and Caserta. Granted a three-year pension by the Venetian senate, he spent the whole time in Rome, executing among other things the *Monument to Pope Clement XIV* in Santi Apostoli (1787) and the *Monument to Clement XIII* in St. Peter's (1792). On the proclamation of the Roman Republic and the exile of Pope Pius VI, he returned home to Possagno in 1798.

Canova soon became one of the most highly esteemed and famous artists in the Napoleonic empire. He carved numerous portraits of Napoleon and his relatives and allies, including *Napoleon as Mars the Peacemaker* (1803-06; Wellington Museum, London) and the *Portrait of Pauline Borghese Bonaparte as Venus Victrix* (1804-08; Galleria Borghese, Rome). At the same time, however, his innate diplomatic skills permitted the artist to complete the *Monument to Archduchess Maria Christina* at Vienna in 1805.

In 1811 Canova, who had gone to Paris to execute a portrait of the empress Marie-Louise, submitted a petition to Napoleon asking him to return the works of art that had been looted from various Italian cities. In 1815 Pope Pius VII made Canova head of the delegation of the Holy See to the Congress of Vienna, where the artist finally succeeded in negotiating the restitution of the works of art. The same year he went to London too, where he was greatly impressed by the marbles from the Parthenon.

Canova's fame even spread across the Atlantic and in 1817 the government of the state of North Carolina asked the artist to execute a monument to George Washington, which he finished in 1821.

Cupid and Psyche
marble, 155x168 cm
Louvre, Paris

As Canova himself explained (1801), the sculpture represents "Cupid and Psyche embracing: a moment of action taken from Apuleius's fable of the *Golden Ass*." The artist has chosen the most moving moment from the story, which Voltaire considered the finest of all Greek myths: Cupid bends down to restore Psyche to her senses with a kiss after she has opened the vase of Hades in spite of Venus's prohibition. The tender embrace of the young couple is only hinted at and their hands just skim over each other's bodies as if in a dance, with no sign of passion: grace and the supreme control of form are the dominant notes in what is one of the artist's most famous works. The group is designed to be seen from multiple points of view, all of equal significance, in a harmonious and perfectly balanced composition. The work required long and careful preparation: first drawings, then terracotta maquettes on a small scale and in simplified form and finally the rough hewing of the marble. Canova usually delegated the latter phase to his assistants, intervening afterward to smooth the surface of the sculpture, working long and tirelessly with rasps under both natural and artificial light so that any imperfections would be revealed. The artist's aim was to achieve the image of ideal beauty, born out of the happy union of reason and sentiment, that lay at the base of neoclassical culture. The sculpture, now in the Louvre, was commissioned by Colonel John Campbell in 1787, while Canova was in Naples. The artist carved a replica of the statue in 1794 for Prince Yusupov (now in the Hermitage, St. Petersburg).

ANTONIO CANOVA

Italic Venus
marble, ht. 172 cm
Galleria Palatina, Palazzo Pitti, Florence

Canova carved the sculpture for the king
of Etruria, Louis I of Bourbon, who
wanted a prestigious copy to replace one
of the most valuable ancient statues on
display in the Galleria degli Uffizi: the
Medici Venus, a work from the second
century AD that had been removed by the
French authorities from the Tribuna of the
museum (where it can now be seen
again) in 1802 and sent to Paris.
Reluctant to accept the commission at
first, the sculptor gave in to pressure from
Baron Giovanni degli Alessandri,
president of the Florentine Academy of
Fine Arts, who told him that making up
the gallery's "painful loss" would be a
significant patriotic gesture. Canova asked
to be supplied with a block of "excellent"
marble, of a quality and purity worthy of
the original classical sculpture. Once he
had commenced the work, it turned
into a sort of personal challenge in
which he set out to rival the sculptor of
the ancient statue. So he put aside the
copy he had started and carved instead
an original version of the same subject.
It was delivered in 1812 to the Tuscan
queen Elisa Bonaparte Baciocchi, who
persuaded her brother Napoleon, now
emperor, to pay the artist 25,000 francs.
To emphasize the originality of his
creation, Canova made it a condition
that his sculpture should not be set on
the pedestal of the *Medici Venus*.
The work was much appreciated in
Florence and praised by critics and
writers. Among the latter, Ugo Foscolo –
in a letter written in 1812 – noted the
individual and earthy grace of Canova's
figure, in contrast to the abstract beauty
and austere idealization of the ancient
statue: if the *Medici Venus* was "a
beautiful goddess, this [...] is a beautiful
woman."

Pauline Bonaparte Borghese as Venus Victrix
marble, l. 200 cm
Galleria Borghese, Rome

Pauline Bonaparte, Napoleon's sister and wife of the Roman prince Camillo Borghese, was portrayed by Canova as "Venus Victrix" between 1804 and 1808. The representation of a living woman in the nude and posed as an ancient goddess was something wholly exceptional for the time. Portrayed semi-naked and lying on a Roman triclinium, the young woman is holding the apple that according to myth Paris awarded to Venus, preferring her over Juno and Minerva: in doing so the Trojan prince chose love rather than power or wisdom. The work is one of the peaks of the neoclassical style: it is a marvelous example of the principle of "noble simplicity and quiet grandeur" that for Johann Joachim Winckelmann underpinned the ideal of beauty in classical art.

The triclinium on which the marble sculpture is set is carved out of wood and decorated in the manner of a catafalque. It conceals a mechanism that can be used to make the statue turn around in the middle of the room. The true splendor of the work became apparent at night, when the candlelight was reflected from the white surface of the polished marble (a finish that has been preserved and brought back to light in the recent restoration).

Funerary Stele of Giovanni Falier
marble, 173x117 cm
Santo Stefano, Venice

Canova regarded the man who commissioned his first works, Giovanni Falier, as one of his "benefactors." Though it did not reach Venice until 1823, the stele had been carved around 1808: it remained in the sculptor's Roman studio up until his death. It represents Gratitude weeping over the herm of the deceased. The work echoes the structure of the ancient funerary stele, with a composition that assumes the characteristics of the classical elegy. For Canova (as for Foscolo in literature), the function of cenotaphs and sepulchral monuments was to immortalize the civic virtues of the deceased and to keep their memory alive in the present. Canova's funerary stele started a vogue that was to last throughout the nineteenth century and spread all over Europe.

Bibliography

The bibliographical notes that follow are intended to draw the reader's attention to a number of monographic titles – recently published and easy to get hold of – that can serve as an aid to the understanding of individual artists and set them in the perspective of their time and culture. Consequently this list makes no pretense to be complete but is simply meant as a guide.
I have received invaluable advice on the choice of entries in the bibliography from Andrea Baldinotti, whom I would like to thank here for his generous collaboration.

FOURTEENTH CENTURY

A. Bagnoli, *La Maestà di Simone Martini*, Cinisello Balsamo (Milan) 1999.

L. Bellosi, *Giotto*, Antella (Florence) 1981.

A. Busignani, *Giotto*, Edizioni d'Arte 'Il Fiorino,' Florence 1993.

E . Carli, *Duccio* ('I maestri,' vol. 11), Milan 1999.

E. Carli, *Giovanni Pisano. Il pulpito di Pistoia*, Milan 1986.

E. Carli, *Simone Martini: la Maestà*, Milan 1996.

M.M. Donato and F. Brugnolo, *Ambrogio Lorenzetti. Il Buon Governo*, ed. by E. Castelnuovo, Milan 1995.

C. Jannella, *Duccio di Buoninsegna*, Antella (Florence) 1991.

C. Jannella, *Simone Martini*, Antella (Florence) 1989.

F. Flores d'Arcais, *Giotto*, Milan 1995.

C. Frugoni, *Pietro and Ambrogio Lorenzetti*, Antella (Florence) 1988.

P. Leone De Castris, *Simone Martini. Catalogo completo dei dipinti*, Florence 1989.

E. Lunghi, *The Basilica of St Francis in Assisi*, Antella (Florence) 1996.

A. Martindale, *Simone Martini. Complete Edition*, Oxford 1988.

G. Pampaloni, *Giotto ad Assisi* (Documenti d'Arte), Catalogo Istituto Geografico de' Agostini, Novara 1998.

G. Previtali, *Giotto e la sua bottega*, 3rd edition ed. by A. Conti, Milan 1993.

G. Ragionieri, *Duccio. Catalogo completo dei dipinti*, Florence 1989.

A. Tartuferi (ed.), *Giotto. Bilancio critico di sessant'anni di studi e ricerche*, exhibition catalogue, Florence 2000.

M.L. Testi Cristiani, *Nicola Pisano architetto scultore. Dalle origini al pulpito del Battistero di Pisa*, Pisa 1987.

C. Volpe, *Pietro Lorenzetti*, ed. by M. Lucco, Milan 1989.

B. Zanardi, *Il cantiere di Giotto: le storie di San Francesco ad Assisi*, Milan 1996.

FIFTEENTH CENTURY

C. Acidini Luchinat, *Benozzo Gozzoli*, Antella (Florence) 1994.

C. Acidini Luchinat, *Pintoricchio*, Antella (Florence) 1999.

C. Acidini Luchinat (ed.), *Benozzo Gozzoli. La Cappella dei Magi*, Milan 1993.

P. Adorno, *Il Verrocchio. Nuove proposte nella civiltà artistica del tempo di Lorenzo il Magnifico*, Florence 1991.

L. Arbace, *Antonello da Messina. Catalogo completo dei dipinti*, Florence 1993.

C. Avery, *Donatello. Catalogo completo delle opere*, Florence 1991.

U. Baldini and O. Casazza, *La Cappella Brancacci*, Milan 1990.

G. Barbera, *Antonello da Messina* ('I maestri,' vol. 9), Milan 1998.

E. Battisti, *Piero della Francesca*, new revised and updated edition with scientific coordination by M. Dalai Emiliani, 2 vols., Milan 1992.

L. Berti and R. Foggi, *Masaccio. Catalogo completo dei dipinti*, Florence 1989.

F. and S. Borsi, *Paolo Uccello*, Milan 1992.

Botticelli pittore della Divina Commedia, catalogue of the exhibition in Rome, 2 vols., Milan 2000.

A. Butterfield, *The Sculptures of Andrea del Verrocchio*, New Haven-London 1997.

C. Caneva, *Botticelli. Catalogo completo dei dipinti*, Florence 1990.

M. Cordaro (ed.), *Mantegna. La Camera degli Sposi*, Milan 1992.

A. De Marchi, *Gentile da Fabriano. Un viaggio nella pittura italiana alla fine del gotico*, Milan 1992.

A. De Nicolò Salmazo, *Mantegna* ('I maestri,' vol. 7), Milan 1997.

D. Dini (ed.), *Gli Affreschi di Beato Angelico nel convento di San Marco a Firenze: rilettura di un capolavoro attraverso un memorabile restauro*, Turin 1996.

R. Fremantle, *Masaccio. Catalogo completo*, Florence 1988.

G. Gaeta Bertelà, B. Paolozzi Strozzi and M. Spallanzani (eds.), *Eredità del Magnifico, 1492-1992*, exhibition catalogue, Florence 1992.

V. Garibaldi, *Perugino. Catalogo completo*, Florence 1999.

G. Gentilini, *I Della Robbia. La scultura invetriata nel Rinascimento*, Florence 1992.

G. Gentilini (ed.), *I Della Robbia e l'"arte nuova" della scultura invetriata*, catalogue of the exhibition at Fiesole, Florence 1998.

M. Gregori, A. Paolucci and C. Acidini Luchinat (eds.), *Maestri e botteghe. Pittura a Firenze alla fine del Quattrocento*, catalogue of the exhibition in Florence, Cinisello Balsamo (Milan) 1992.

P. Humfrey, *Carpaccio. Catalogo completo dei dipinti*, Florence 1991.

P. Joannides, *Masaccio and Masolino. A Complete Catalogue*, London 1993.

R.G. Kecks, *Domenico Ghirlandaio und die Malerei der Florentiner Renaissance*, Munich 2000.

R. Krautheimer, *Lorenzo Ghiberti*, Princeton 1983.

La Cappella Nova o di San Brizio nel Duomo di Orvieto, Milan 1996.

R. Lightbown, *Sandro Botticelli*, New York 1989.

R. Lightbown, *Piero della Francesca*, Milan 1992. Pub. in New York-London-Paris, 1997.

A.M. Maetzke, *Introduzione ai capolavori di Piero della Francesca*, Cinisello Balsamo (Milan) 1998.

M.P. Mannini and M. Fagioli, *Filippo Lippi. Catalogo completo*, Florence 1997.

J. Martineau (ed.), *Andrea Mantegna*, exhibition catalogue, London-New York 1992.

F.I. Nucciarelli, *Studi sul Pinturicchio. Dalle prime prove alla Cappella Sistina*, Spoleto 1998.

A. Padoa Rizzo, *Benozzo Gozzoli. Catalogo completo dei dipinti*, Florence 1992.

A. Padoa Rizzo, *Paolo Uccello. Catalogo completo dei dipinti*, Florence 1991.

A. Paolucci, *Luca Signorelli*, Antella (Florence) 1990.

A. Paolucci, *Piero della Francesca. Catalogo completo dei dipinti*, Florence 1990.

Pisanello. Le peintre aux sept vertus, Paris 1996.

N. Pons, *Botticelli. Catalogo completo*, Milan 1989.

N. Pons, *I Pollaiolo. Catalogo completo*, Florence 1994.

J. Pope-Hennessy, *Donatello Sculptor*, New York-London 1993.

L. Puppi (ed.), *Pisanello. Una poetica dell'inatteso*, Cinisello Balsamo (Milan) 1996.

P.L. Rubin and A. Wright (eds.), *Renaissance Florence. The Art of the 1470s*, exhibition catalogue with an essay by N. Penny, London 1999.

P.L. Roberts, *Masolino da Panicale*, Oxford 1993.

A. Rosenauer, *Donatello*, Milan 1993.

J. Ruda, *Fra Filippo Lippi. Life and Work with a Complete Catalogue*, London 1993.

P. Scarpellini, *Perugino*, Milan 1984.

J.T. Spike, *Angelico*, Milan 1997.

C.B. Strehlke, *Angelico*, Milan 1998.

A. Tempestini, *Giovanni Bellini*, Milan 1997.

P. Zampetti and P. Donnini, *Gentile e i pittori di Fabriano*, Fiesole (Florence) 1992.

SIXTEENTH CENTURY

C. Acidini Luchinat, M. Gregori, D. Heikamp and A. Paolucci (eds.), *Magnificenza alla corte dei Medici. Arte a Firenze alla fine del Cinquecento*, catalogue of the exhibition in Florence, Milan 1997.

B. Aikema, B.L. Brown and G. Nepi Sciré (eds.), *Il Rinascimento a Venezia e la pittura del Nord ai tempi di Bellini, Dürer, Tiziano*, catalogue of the exhibition in Venice, Milan 1999.

J. Anderson, *Giorgione. Peintre de la "Brièveté Poétique." Catalogue raisonné*, Paris 1996

D. Arasse, *Léonard de Vinci. Le Rythme du monde*, Paris 1997.

L. Bardeschi Ciulich (ed.), *Michelangelo: grafia e biografia di un genio*, exhibition catalogue, Milan 2000.

P. Brambilla Barcillon and P.C. Marani, *Leonardo. L'Ultima Cena*, Milan 1999.

D.A. Brown, *Leonardo da Vinci. Origini di un genio*, Milan 1999.

A. Cecchi, *Agnolo Bronzino*, Antella (Florence) 1996.

A. Cecchi and A. Natali (eds.), *L'Officina della maniera*, catalogue of the exhibition in Florence, Venice 1996.

B. Cellini, *La Vita*, edition ed. by E. Camesasca, Milan 1999

R.P. Ciardi and A. Mugnaini, *Rosso Fiorentino. Catalogo completo dei dipinti*, Florence 1991.

P. Costamagna, *Pontormo*, Milan 1994.

J. Cox-Rearick, *Bronzino's Chapel of Eleonora in the Palazzo Vecchio*, Berkeley-Los Angeles-Oxford 1993.

P. De Vecchi (ed.), *La Cappella Sistina. La volta restaurata: il trionfo del colore*, Novara 1992.

M. Di Giampaolo, *Parmigianino. Catalogo completo dei dipinti*, Florence 1991.

M. Di Giampaolo and A. Muzzi, *Correggio. Catalogo completo dei dipinti*, Florence 1993.

C. Falciani, *Il Rosso Fiorentino*, Florence 1996.

S. Ferino Padgen and M.A. Zancan,

Raffaello. Catalogo completo dei dipinti, Florence 1989.

A. Forlani Tempesti and A. Giovannetti, *Pontormo. Catalogo completo*, Florence 1994

L. Fornari Schianchi, *Correggio*, Antella (Florence) 1994.

D. Franklin, *Rosso in Italy. The Italian Career of Rosso Fiorentino*, New Haven-London 1994.

R. Goffen, *Titian's Women*, New Haven-London 1997.

C. Gould, *Parmigianino*, New York-London-Paris 1994.

M. Hirst and J. Dunkerton, *Making and Meaning. The Young Michelangelo*, exhibition catalogue, London 1994.

La Cappella Sistina. I primi restauri: la scoperta del colore, Novara 1986.

Le Siècle de Titien. L'age d'or de la peinture à Venise, exhibition catalogue, Paris 1993.

M. Lucco, *Giorgione*, Milan 1995.

P.C. Marani, *Leonardo. Catalogo completo dei dipinti*, Florence 1989.

P.C. Marani, *Leonardo. Una carriera di pittore*, with apparatus ed. by P.C. Marani and E. Villata, Milan 1999.

J. Meyer zur Capellen, *Raphael in Florence*, London 1996.

A. Natali, *Andrea del Sarto. Maestro della "maniera moderna,"* Milan 1998.

T. Nichols, *Tintoretto. Tradition and Identity*, London 1999.

K. Oberhuber, *Raffaello. L'opera pittorica*, Milan 1999.

R. Pallucchini and P. Rossi, *Tintoretto. Le opere sacre e profane. I ritratti*, 3 vols., Milan 1990, reprinted Milan 1994.

A. Paolucci, *Cellini*, Florence 2000.

L. Partridge, F. Mancinelli, G. Colalucci, *La Cappella Sistina. Il Giudizio restaurato*, Novara 1998.

F. Pedrocco, *Titian*, Antella (Florence) 1993.

F. Pedrocco, *Veronese*, Antella (Florence) 1998.

A. Perissa Torrini, *Giorgione. Catalogo completo dei dipinti*, Florence 1993.

T. Pignatti and F. Pedrocco, *Veronese. Catalogo completo*, 2 vols, Milan 1995.

J. Pope-Hennessy, *Cellini*, London 1985.

M. Scalini, *Benvenuto Cellini*, Antella (Florence) 1995.

Tiziano, exhibition catalogue, Venice 1990.

G. Vasari, *Le Vite de' più eccellenti pittori scultori e architettori nelle redazioni del 1550 e del 1568*, edition ed. by R. Bettarini and P. Barocchi, 6 vols., Florence 1966-87.

W. E. Wallace Levin, *Michelangelo: the Complete Sculpture, Painting, Architecture*, Hong Kong 1998.

K. Weil-Garris Brandt, C. Acidini Luchinat, J.D. Draper and N. Penny (eds.), *Giovinezza di Michelangelo*, exhibition catalogue, Florence-Milan 1999.

Le Siècle de Caravage dans les collections françaises, exhibition catalogue, Paris 1988.

A. Lo Bianco (ed.), *Pietro da Cortona, 1597-1669*, catalogue of the exhibition in Rome, Milan 1997.

M. Marini, *Caravaggio. Michelangelo Merisi da Caravaggio, "pictor praestantissimus,"* Rome 1987.

Nell'età del Correggio e dei Carracci, catalogue of the exhibition in Bologna, Washington and New York, Bologna 1986.

R. Wittkower, *Gian Lorenzo Bernini. The Sculptor of the Roman Baroque*, 3rd ed. revised by H. Hibbard, T. Martin and M. Wittkower, Oxford 1981.

SEVENTEENTH CENTURY

A. Angelini, *Bernini*, Milan 1999.

C. Avery, *Bernini. Genius of the Baroque*, London 1997.

M.G. Bernardini and M. Fagiolo Dell'Arco (eds.), *Gian Lorenzo Bernini regista del Barocco*, catalogue of the exhibition in Rome, Milan-Rome 1999.

M. Calvesi, *Le realtà di Caravaggio*, Turin 1990.

Caravaggio, catalogue of the exhibition in Madrid and Bilbao, Madrid 1999.

M.B. Castellotti, *Il paradosso di Caravaggio*, Milan 1998.

A. Chastel, G. Briganti and R. Zapperi, *Gli amori degli dei*, Rome 1987.

M. Cinotti, *Caravaggio: la vita e l'opera*, Bergamo 1991.

C.L. Frommel and S. Schütze (eds.), *Pietro da Cortona. Atti del Convegno Internazionale, Roma-Firenze, 12-15 novembre 1997*, Milan 1998.

M. Gregori (ed.), *Michelangelo Merisi da Caravaggio. Come nascono i capolavori*, catalogue of the exhibition in Florence and Rome, Milan 1991.

Le Carrache et les Décors profanes. Actes du Colloque organisé par l'École française de Rome (Rome, October 2-4, 1986), Rome 1988.

EIGHTEENTH CENTURY

S.O. Androssov, G. Briganti, N.K. Kosareva and G. Romanelli (eds.), *Canova all'Ermitage: le sculture nel museo di San Pietroburgo*, catalogue of the exhibition in Rome, Venice 1992.

K. Batjer and J.G. Links, *Canaletto*, Rome 1996.

M. Gemin and F. Pedrocco, *Giambattista Tiepolo. I dipinti. Opera completa*, Venice 1993.

Giambattista Tiepolo: 1696-1996, catalogue of the exhibition in Venice and New York, New York-Milan 1996.

M. Levey, *Giambattista Tiepolo. His life and art*, 2nd ed. New Haven-London 1994.

S. Loire and J. de Los Llanos (eds.), *Giambattista Tiepolo (1696-1770)*, exhibition catalogue, Paris 1998.

G. Pavanello and G. Romanelli (eds.), *Antonio Canova*, catalogue of the exhibition in Venice and Possagno, Venice 1992.

F. Pedrocco, *Canaletto and the Venetian Vedutisti*, Antella (Florence) 1995.

O. Stefani, *Antonio Canova. La statuaria*, Milan 1999.

D. Succi, *Francesco Guardi: itinerario dell'avventura artistica*, Cinisello Balsamo (Milan) 1993.

The illustrations in this volume have been
supplied by the SCALA PICTURE LIBRARY,
the largest source of color transparencies
and digital images of the visual arts in the
world.

The over 60,000 subjects visible at the site
www.scalarchives.it
can be accessed through computerized
procedures that permit easy and rapid
picture searches of any complexity.

e-mail: archivio@scalagroup.com